Superbrands

AN INSIGHT INTO 50 OF THE WORLD'S SUPERBRANDS
VOLUME II

This book is dedicated to my parents Henry
and Renate Knobil who have shown me the
finest brand of love imaginable

Creative & Commercial Communications

Editor
Marcel Knobil

Deputy Editor
Sheena Mehta

Author
Catherine Stewart

Designer
Paul Carpenter

© 1996 Creative & Commercial
Communications Ltd

Published by Creative & Commercial
Communications Ltd
246/248 Great Portland Street
London W1N 5HF

Tel   0171 388 0357
Fax   0171 388 0370

Printed in Hong Kong

ISBN 0 9528153 1 1

ABBEY NATIONAL
Abbey National PLC
Abbey House
201 Grafton Gate East
Milton Keynes
MK9 1AN

AMERICAN EXPRESS
American Express Europe Limited
Portland House
Stag Place
London
SW1E 5BZ

ANDREX
Kimberly-Clark Limited
Larkfield
Aylesford
Kent
ME20 7PS

BBC
BBC
Henry Wood House
1 Langham Place
London
W1A 1AA

BIRDS EYE WALL'S
Birds Eye Wall's
Station Avenue
Walton on Thames
Surrey
KT12 1NT

BLACK & DECKER
Black & Decker
210 Bath Road
Slough
SL1 3YD

BMW
BMW (GB) Limited
Ellesfield Avenue
Bracknell
Berkshire
RG12 8TA

BOVRIL
CPC (UK) Limited
Claygate House
Littleworth Road
Esher
Surrey
KT10 9PN

BRITISH AIRWAYS
British Airways
2123 Speedbird House
PO Box 10
Heathrow Airport
Hounslow
TW6 2JA

BT
BT
RM A248
BT Centre
81 Newgate Street
London
EC1A 7AJ

CHANEL
Chanel
19-21 Old Bond Street
London
W1X 3DA

CHANNEL 4
Channel Four Television Corporation
124 Horseferry Road
London
SW1P 2TX

CHIVAS REGAL
The Chivas & Glenlivet Group
The Ark
201 Talgarth Road
Hammersmith
London
W6 8BN

CLUB MED
Club Med
106-110 Brompton Road
London
SW3 1JJ

COCA-COLA
Coca-Cola Great Britain & Ireland
1 Queen Caroline Street
London
W6 9HQ

FOSTER'S
Scottish Courage Ltd
Abbey Brewery
111 Hollyrood Road
Edinburgh
EM8 8YS

GILLETTE
Gillette UK Ltd
Syon Lane
Isleworth
Middlesex
TW7 5NP

HOVIS
British Bakeries
King Edward House
King Edward Court
PO Box 527
Windsor
Berkshire
SL4 1TJ

IBM
IBM United Kingdom Limited
PO Box 41
North Harbour
Portsmouth
PO6 3AU

ICI
ICI
9 Millbank
London
SW1P 3JF

INTERFLORA
Interflora (British Unit) Limited
Interflora House
Sleaford
Lincolnshire
NG34 7TB

JOHN SMITH'S BITTER
Scottish Courage Ltd
Abbey Brewery
111 Hollyrood Road
Edinburgh
EM8 8YS

KELLOGG'S CORN FLAKES
Kellogg Company of GB Limited
The Kellogg Building
Talbot Road
Manchester
M16 0PU

LEVI'S
Levi Strauss UK Limited
1A Marlborough Street
London
W1V IHB

MARLBORO
Rothmans (UK) Limited
Oxford Road
Aylesbury
Buckinghamshire
HP21 8SZ

MARMITE
CPC (UK) Limited
Claygate House
Littleworth Road
Esher
Surrey
KT10 9PN

McVITIE'S
McVitie's
The Watermans Business Park
The Causeway
Staines
Middlesex
TW18 3BA

MICHELIN
Michelin Tyre PLC
The Edward Hyde Building
36 Clarendon Street
Watford
Hertfordshire
WD1 1SX

MICROSOFT
Microsoft
Microsoft Place
Winnersh
Wokingham
Berkshire
RG11 5TP

MINI
Rover Group Limited
PO Box 395
Lickey Road
Longbridge
Birmingham
B31 2TL

PERRIER
Perrier Vittel (UK) Limited
Trinity Court
Church Street
Rickmansworth
Herts
WD3 1LD

PERSIL
Lever Bros Limited
3 St James's Road
Kingston-Upon-Thames
Surrey
KT1 2BA

PG TIPS
Van den Bergh Foods
Brooke House
Manor Royal
Crawley
RH10 2RQ

PHILISHAVE
Philips DAP
The Philips Centre
420-430 London Road
Croydon
CR9 3AR

RAY-BAN
Bausch & Lomb UK Limited
106 London Road
Kingston-upon-Thames
Surrey
KT2 6TN

ROYAL DOULTON
Royal Doulton PLC
Minton House
London Road
Stoke-on-Trent
Staffordshire
ST4 7QD

SAINSBURY'S
J Sainsbury plc
4th Floor
Stamford House
Stamford Street
London
SE1 9LL

SAVE THE CHILDREN
The Save the Children Fund
17 Grove Lane
London
SE5 8RD

SELLOTAPE
The Sellotape Company
Sellotape GB Limited
The Woodside Estate
Dunstable
Bedfordshire
LU5 4TP

SONY
Sony Consumer Products Group
The Heights
Brooklands
Weybridge
Surrey
KT13 0XW

ST MICHAEL
Marks & Spencer PLC
Michael House
147-167 Baker Street
London
W1A 1DN

STELLA ARTOIS
Whitbread Beer Company
Porter Tun House
500 Capability Green
Luton
LU1 3LS

TEFAL
Tefal UK Limited
11-49 Station Road
Langley
Slough
SL3 8DR

THE ECONOMIST
The Economist
25 St James's Street
London
SW1A 1HG

VASELINE
Elida Faberge Limited
3 St James's Street
Kingston
Surrey
KT1 2BA

VIRGIN ATLANTIC
Virgin Atlantic Airways Limited
Ashdown House
High Street
Crawley
West Sussex
RH10 1DQ

WALKERS
Walkers Snack Foods Limited
1600 Arlington Business Park
Theale
Reading
RG7 4SA

WH SMITH
WH Smith Limited
Greenbridge
Swindon
Wiltshire
SN3 3LD

WILKINSON SWORD
Wilkinson Sword Limited
Sword House
Totteridge Road
High Wycombe
Buckinghamshire
HP13 6EJ

YELLOW PAGES
BT Yellow Pages
Queens Walk
Reading
RG1 7PT

CONTENTS

FOREWORD MARCEL KNOBIL

Chairperson, Creative & Commercial Communications
Chairperson, Superbrands Council

Great brands have experienced some quirky beginnings.
When Robert Augustus
Chesebrough heard that Pennsylvanian oil workers were smearing
their skin with a residue from drill heads to heal their wounds he
travelled to the oil fields to witness the phenomenon. Chesebrough
refined and purified this residue and named it Vaseline.

Levi Strauss, a peddler, intended
to profit from selling tough canvass to gold-miners for building tents.
When no interest was shown he manufactured the canvass into
overalls instead. They proved an outstanding success and inspired
Strauss to focus upon clothing.

The Kellogg brothers were
developing a nutritious cereal for patients at the Seventh Day
Adventist Battle Creek sanitarium where they worked. A freak
accident exposed cooked wheat to open air for over a day. The
brothers then processed the wheat through rollers - resulting in
wheat flakes. The patients loved this new flaky cereal product and
demanded supplies even after leaving the sanitarium.

Marc Gregoire was a Parisian
aeronautics engineer and fishing enthusiast. In 1952 he developed a
non-stick coating which he applied to his fishing rod, thinking that it
would be easier to reel in fish. However, his wife suggested applying
the coating to pots and pans putting an end to the nightmare job of
scouring dirty dishes. Two years later he set up a company called
Tefal operating out of a garage.

Although some Superbrands may
have enjoyed entertaining and accidental births they have all evolved
into powerful entities which impact upon customers throughout the
world.

The 50 brands featured in this
volume are selected from a list of brands formulated by the
Superbrands Council. The Council is made up of eminent figures
working in advertising, design, market research and PR who together
evaluate hundreds of established brands. Every member obviously
has a deep appreciation of what makes a great brand.

The following definition has been
developed for a Superbrand. "A Superbrand offers consumers
significant emotional and/or physical advantages over its competitors
which (consciously or sub-consciously) consumers want, recognise,
and are willing to pay a premium for."

The Superbrands book explores
the history of these brands, observing how they have developed over
the years and highlighting their marketing, advertising and design
successes.

Whatever their beginnings each
Superbrand has a captivating story to tell.

HOW TO BECOME A SUPERBRAND

ACCORDING TO MEMBERS OF THE SUPERBRANDS COUNCIL

John Ballington
Sales Director
Lever Brothers Limited

Any brand that aspires to Superbrand status must possess certain ingredients. Firstly, there must be a clear proposition that meets the needs of consumers, and then exceeds their expectations by constantly surprising and delighting them in terms of performance. Secondly, the brand must have a distinctive character which consumers come to know and trust, identifying with its 'personality' as they build up a long-term relationship. Thirdly, there must be a passionate commitment to quality so that every aspect of the brand establishes, and clearly communicates, a reputation for consistency and reliability.

Yet there are many brands which combine these ingredients, but have still never acquired that special place in our lives which sets them apart from the rest.

It is hard to define the final touch of magic that transforms a mere brand into a Superbrand. Some succeed through sheer persistence, weaving themselves into the very fabric of our everyday experience. Others burst onto the marketplace with such vigour and creativity that they seem to demand our instant loyalty.

One thing is certain - the world would be a duller and greyer place without them.

Quentin Bell
Chairman
The Quentin Bell Organisation plc
Vice Chairman
Public Relations Consultants Association

I've been a brands man all my life.

*Superbrands - as ably championed by this superb publication - are uniquely wistful, alluring; and **tangible**. We all know that the Filofax is just a diary; that Coca-Cola is just a fizzy drink; and that British Airways is probably just a Boeing. But Superbrands can demonstrate that magical 10% (maybe 1%) performance that makes for an enduring star.*

*But times are still changing. We now have the corporate brand. How do employees view the corporation that makes the famous product (or provides the famous **service**?). How does the community respect it? What do suppliers and distributors think? What values, vision and ethics does the corporation inspire by its actions and its reactions?*

How to manage these corporate stakeholders is the challenge of the future. Overall corporate reputation is the most valuable asset: backdrop to all product brands.

I predict it will be inherent in the Superbrand of the future.

Alison Canning
Chief Executive
Burson-Marsteller

We recently undertook the largest ever world-wide survey into brands - BrandAsset Valuator. It covered 30,000 respondents in 19 countries and examined 6,000 brands, 450 of which were global. The findings showed remarkable similarity across different countries and industry sectors, in terms of how brands are built and how they decline. It showed that brands are built on four, sequential pillars:
*(1) **Differentiation** - how is this different from anything else on the market? (2) **Relevance** - why is this relevant to me? (3) **Esteem** - did the product or service live up to its promise (only evaluated following trial) ? (4) **Familiarity** - is this brand ubiquitous and readily accessible?*

*'Superbrand' status can only be accorded to those brands that meet all of these four criteria and therefore have both **vitality** (differentiation and relevance) and **stature** (esteem and familiarity). The research also showed that brands in decline always lose vitality before they lose stature - in other words, the most difficult pillars to build are also the most resilient in times of trouble.*

Winston Fletcher
Chairman
Delaney Fletcher Bozell
Chairman
Advertising Association

'How do you build a Superbrand?' is as unanswerable as 'How long is a piece of string?' You cannot lie in your bath on a Sunday morning, declare 'Right, I'll build a Superbrand tomorrow', and start first thing Monday.

It can't be done because building Superbrands demands creativity, long-term consistency, resources, luck, and a myriad of factors all combining in often unplannable ways. The notion that Mr. Kellogg, or even Mr Branson, initially set out to build Superbrands is ludicrous. They simply set out to manufacture and market excellent products which would sell and make profits.

History, when written, looks all-too-purposeful. The wisdom of hindsight is a wondrous thing. Once you've arrived it is easy to see how you got there.

Having said which, Messrs. Kellogg and Branson would have been right. Product and marketing excellence, consumer satisfaction and profitability are the keystones of every Superbrand. How difficult it is to achieve them.

Kip Knight
Vice President
Pepsico Restaurants International

An analogy to this issue could be that in order to get great children, be sure to start with great parents! In thinking about how most truly "super" brands get started, they aren't brought into this world by advertising agencies or marketing teams but rather by an individual with a passionate idea or dream that they wanted to come alive. People like Walt Disney, Ray Kroc, Richard Branson or Colonel Sanders are some of the innovative "brand parents" that come to mind.

Once this new brand is created, the other key to success is brand stewardship. There's too great a temptation among many a marketing manager or account executive that they're going to leave their own unique contribution to the brand when in fact they're changing a winning formula. As a former brand manager to Ivory Soap in the U.S. at Procter and Gamble, its "winning formula" of representing purity has stood the test of time for over a century and is still the leading bar soap sold in America.

So, in essence, if you are so lucky as to have a brand that was created by loving and gifted "parents", protect and nurture their creation. As it is when you're a parent, it's the most important job you've got.

Lord Lawson
Chairman
Central Europe Trust Company Ltd.

Even to play the game of becoming a Superbrand, a product must be of high quality and consistency, and must have a certain uniqueness. To win the game, I suspect there have to be two key additional elements in a company's strategy.

First, there must be a commitment to continuous innovation - this means hiring creative people and giving them the resources they need. The innovation could be in the technical side of the product (for example, in a detergent or food) or it could be in understanding the customer better (for example, Club World, or Windows).

As one looks down the list of Superbrands it is hard to avoid the feeling that just when you thought there was nothing new in telephones (or CD players, or jeans, or chocolate bars) the Superbrand-owner surprises you again and again with innovation.

Second, however good a product is, it still has to be sold. This means that there has to be a commitment to maintain the intensity of advertising and promotion at all levels (to the trade and consumers) through the vicissitudes of the economic cycle.

Wally Olins
Chairman
Wolff Olins

A product/service as good as the best there is. A clear positioning in the market. A simple, brilliant, creative idea capable of infinite modulation. Low manufacturing cost, combined with total product consistency. Ubiquitous distribution. Heavy promotion.

Or put another way: brilliant creativity combined with obsessive attention to detail, mind numbing repetition - and a lot of money.

The question is - do you have to do things differently? Only sometimes.

Michael Peters OBE
Chairman & Executive Creative Director
The Identica Partnership

Most of the great Superbrands have achieved their status through the careful nurture of brand values over many years from birth to maturity. But today nothing is more important than change, and speed has replaced longevity as the essential criteria in defining the Superbrand.

In no time at all, historically speaking, Branson has created a huge awareness of Virgin, and Nike has become a household name. These are the new Superbrands created via information technology and instantaneous marketing; they all display guile, ingenuity and creativity in their determination to acquire a global personality: These are the brands that talk the language of the street and that have attained their cult status overnight.

But the speed of Superbrand creation brings new challenges to brand custodians - how will such superstars stay at number one, and how will global synergy be created instantly between all elements of the marketing mix? Welcome Swatch and Manchester United to the cut-throat and challenging world of the Superbrand League.

Chris Powell
Chief Executive
BMP DDB Needham

Spot a fundamental change early on (you generally need to be early to be a leader) and make your brand definitive of the mainstream in the new market - in quality, price and positioning.

The early days will need a tireless driver obsessed in making it the best it can be.

Never stop innovating.

James M Rose
Managing Director
AC Nielsen UK & Ireland

Nielsen recently did some research to determine what marketing strategies result in building successful brands over the long-term. Based on over 300 products from 50 different retail categories, the research revealed that no single type of marketing activity accounted for changes in brand performance.

However, by categorising the brands into different product groups including alcoholic drinks, food, toiletries, household and non-alcoholic beverages, the results suggested very clearly that different strategies work better in these different categories.

Innovation proved to be the major driver. Despite brand size or category, providing more choice to the consumer is key for delivering long-term success. In addition, depending on the category, price competitiveness and promotional activity, including media support, proved to be the other key influencers.

Ultimately, when building a Superbrand, marketers should concentrate on innovation and to ensure continued consumer loyalty, invest in above and below-the-line brand support. One only has to look at Coca-Cola, Nescafé, Walkers Crisps, Ariel and Persil, to see how such strategies have made them Superbrands.

Martin Runnacles
Marketing Manager
BMW (GB) Ltd.

If a brand is a product with a personality then a Superbrand is a product or service with a huge personality. Superbrands invariably develop over a long period of time and when established tend to maintain their unique presence seemingly without effort. My own belief is that this is far from the truth and it is the nurturing of a Superbrand that maintains its pre-eminent position. Obviously, Superbrands have one important ingredient. The product or service offering has been able to demonstrate and maintain a real competitive advantage over other lesser products or services.

I believe that every one of the Superbrands in this book conforms to these basic requirements but, as they say, it must be remembered that genius will not out without persistence.

ABBEY NATIONAL

THE MARKET

There are 540 different banks in the UK, five of which are major clearing banks. These are Abbey National, National Westminster, Midland Bank (now part of HSBC), Lloyds Bank and Barclays.

In 1995, these five banks accrued profits amounting to more than £10 billion.

ACHIEVEMENTS

In 1989 Abbey National became the first building society to convert to banking status. Since then, the company has gone a long way to fulfilling its goal of becoming the outstanding financial services provider in the UK.

Abbey National has already become the fifth largest banking group in the UK and is currently the second largest mortgage lender in the country, helping out over two million people to buy their homes. In fact, Abbey National can claim a relationship with one in three UK households.

But despite its more recent success as a

bank, Abbey National was for many years a building society with a traditionally friendly face. It has enjoyed a long heritage, since its official founding in 1944, as a helping hand to enable UK families to save for their futures and own their own homes.

One of Abbey National's chief achievements has been to combine this quality with its newly-acquired modern banking status.

As Peter G Birch, the chief executive of Abbey National plc, says: "We're not a building society, and we're not a bank; we're Abbey National - a unique hybrid of the best of both".

As a bank, Abbey National has been able to fulfil its potential. It is now a diversified financial business operating a wholesale

banking division and a string of international units, including subsidiary companies in Jersey, Gibraltar, Spain, Italy and France. Mortgages and savings accounts are still of prime importance, but Abbey National also offers a full range of varied financial services to meet all its customers' needs, including pensions, life assurance and general insurance policies, unsecured loans, personal investment planning and of course, an interest-bearing cheque account and credit card.

Abbey National's chairman, Lord Tugendhat, sums up his company's overwhelming achievement in recent years: "We have built on our building society heritage. We've retained the traditional values of a building society, but we have gained the cutting edge and the commercial discipline associated with being a major publicly quoted company".

HISTORY

Abbey National was the fruit of a union forged between the London-based Abbey Road Building Society (founded in 1874) and the National Building Society (established in 1849) in 1944. There was large-scale public demand for housing in post-war Britain - a demand which the newly-formed Abbey National helped to meet by providing mortgages.

At first, Abbey National focused on savings accounts and mortgages, but throughout the 1960s and 1970s, a wider range of financial services was gradually introduced. By 1989, when Abbey National was officially recognised as a bank by the Bank of England following its conversion to become a public limited company, Abbey National had 681 branches dotted throughout the UK - a huge leap from 1960, when the building society had been able to boast just 60.

Abbey National's transition to plc status in 1989 was strongly supported by its members. Up to five million voted their approval of the switch in a private ballot. Almost overnight, the total number of private shareholders in the UK rose from six million to nine and a half million. Today, Abbey National has around two and a half million shareholders, of whom a fair number have held shares since 1989. Abbey's transformation was marked by the formation of its wholesale banking arm, Abbey National Treasury Services plc.

Every leading brand has its legend. And Abbey National is no exception. But in Abbey's case ... it really is a legend, the beloved fictional detective Sherlock Holmes, with whom the bank enjoys a strong association. The company's London headquarters occupy the famous address

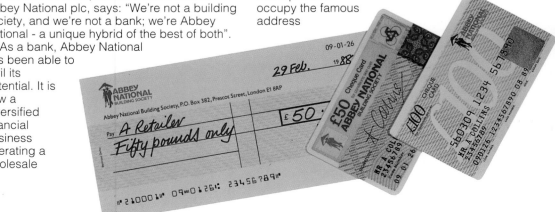

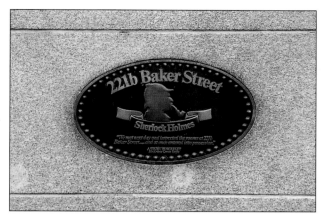

at 221b Baker Street - the home of Sherlock Holmes. Abbey House, as the head office is known, has received thousands of letters over the years from fans all over the world, addressed to Sherlock Holmes, seeking assistance in solving crimes or just fan-mail.

To this day, Abbey National employs a secretary on behalf of the great detective, informing interested parties that Sherlock Holmes has retired from the strains of detective work and now keeps bees in Surrey.

THE PRODUCT

Abbey National offers a whole range of financial services, from banking services and mortgages to insurance and financial planning, ensuring that its customers can come to Abbey National for all their financial needs. Mortgages have always been the backbone of Abbey National's business, and today it holds the position of being the second largest mortgage lender in the UK, helping more than 2 million people buy their homes. It offers an extensive range of mortgages, from the pension-plan mortgage, which is particularly popular with self-employed or people not eligible for a company pension, to the investment-linked mortgage, which allows you to link the mortgage to an investment of your choice, such as a PEP, bond or unit trust. Helping people to become homeowners has always been, and will continue to be, one of Abbey National's prime objectives. Mortgages also feature as part of Abbey National's Financial Planning Service. Here, advice is available from one of their Financial Planning Advisors to guide customers through a lifetime of personal needs and financial goals. Whether it is protection for the family, a mortgage or investments and savings, Abbey National can offer the tailored advice to suit every individual's needs and constraints.

It acquired Scottish Mutual in 1992, and though it continues to operate independently, it has helped Abbey National set up its own-brand life assurance operation, Abbey National Life plc, which provides protection products, mortgage related products, savings and investments and pension plans through the Abbey National branch network.

Abbey National also offers a full range of Banking services, including a bank account, credit card, savings accounts and a variety of loans to reflect different needs. Abbey National's bank account is one of the most user-friendly, paying out interest on accounts with balances of as little as £1.00. The account also comes with an overdraft facility, an ideal way to bridge a gap or cover unexpected expenses. Other features include a 24-hour telephone banking service and AbbeyLink Automatic Teller Machines (ATMs), linked to the largest network in the country.

There is also a range of savings accounts for people with anything from £1 to £2 million to invest. These accounts range from the Action Saver, for savers aged 15 or under, with preferential rates on amounts up to £500, to the High Yield Bond, for savers with more than £10,000 to invest, who do not need access to their savings for at least a year. At the other end of the scale Abbey National also offers personal loans, to enable customers to borrow the money they need for key purchases.

RECENT DEVELOPMENTS

The last few years have seen Abbey National use its banking status to develop its business still further.

In 1992 the acquisition of Glasgow-based Scottish Mutual led to the formation of Scottish Mutual Assurance plc, followed by the setting-up of Abbey National Life plc in 1993.

1994 saw two further acquisitions, that of the UK residential mortgage operation of the Canadian Imperial Bank of Commerce, renamed Abbey National Mortgage Finance, and HMC Group plc, an independent centralised lending company.

The acquisition in February 1995 of UK health insurance provider, Pegasus Assurance Group Ltd, took Scottish Mutual into the growth markets of health care and critical illness insurance. In July 1995 a joint venture with Commercial Union created Abbey National General Insurance, the company's insurance wing. In August, Abbey National acquired the UK's largest finance house for consumer credit, First National Finance Corporation, strengthening its share of the personal loan market.

In the same year, Abbey National agreed to merge with another popular UK financial institution, the National and Provincial Building Society.

PROMOTION

Driving Abbey National's marketing thrust has been the 'Abbeyness' concept. Abbeyness has taken a grip of the company's advertising through a wide range of media, including TV advertising, radio, magazines, posters, newspapers, and can be summed up by the caring approach Abbey National strives to engender in its efforts with customers. Abbeyness stresses the security enjoyed by the bank's customers.

All advertising is rigorously evaluated pre-launch, to ensure the campaign conjures positive, memorable images.

To ensure this is carried through into real-life operations, Abbey National operates 'CRM', its Customer Relationship Management discipline, a sustained analysis of all its product/customer relationships.

In 1990, Abbey National set up the Abbey National Charitable Trust to offer support to organisations and projects focused on housing issues, family life, equal opportunities and disabled members of the community.

Abbey National has also been an active campaigner for the children's telephone helpline service ChildLine, raffling 675 teddy bears at Abbey National branches throughout the country in 1993 and 1994 and amassing a gift of £173,000 to offer the charity.

BRAND VALUES

Abbey's unique positioning in the banking marketplace is typified by its mission statement which reflects the company's desire to blend the old with the new. Abbey National's vision is to prove to be the outstanding financial services company in the UK. Its purpose is summed thus: "To achieve above average growth in shareholder value over the long term, which can only be achieved if we meet the needs of our customers, our staff, and all the other stakeholders in the business."

This approach, combined with its history of helping the British public into long-term financial security, is key to Abbey National's 'Abbeyness'.

Things you didn't know about Abbey National

○ About one in seven home loans in Britain are provided by Abbey National, making it the second largest mortgage lender in the UK.

○ At peak times, the Abbey National network averages forty-five transactions per second and its ATM network handles sixteen transactions per second.

○ Branch staff carry out around 250 million transactions for customers every year.

○ Abbey National owns several channel tunnel trains and a cruise liner through its Treasury subsidiary.

○ In November 1984, Abbey National became the first building society to offer a £100 cheque guarantee card.

○ In 1989, Abbey National became the first UK company to sell mortgages over the telephone.

○ During the 1989 ballot to decide Abbey's conversion to plc status, there were three flights a day to Germany to pick up ballot boxes billeted at the British army bases.

○ An artesian well, extending 600 ft below Abbey House, the Baker Street head office, supplies fresh water to the building.

THE MARKET

Plastic money is fast replacing hard cash as a means of payment. Credit cards and charge cards are increasingly viewed as a convenient and easy way to pay.

In the UK, the credit and charge cards is buoyant. According to the Euromonitor International Market Survey on credit and charge cards, turnover rose by 11% in 1994 to £37.3 billion. In 1994 around 40.32 million credit and charge cards were in circulation.

ACHIEVEMENTS

Since its founding almost 150 years ago American Express has played an important part in facilitating global travel and instigating a world-wide system of financial services. It is also the world's largest travel organisation.

American Express is a 'blue chip' organisation with an enormous global presence, employing 71,000 people across the world. Its 'Blue Box' logo is one of the most widely recognised corporate symbols. The classic green American Express Card, first launched in 1958 and introduced into Britain in 1963, is the most famous charge card in the world. It is accepted in about 160 countries, in around 4 million establishments. There are

currently over 37.8 million cards in use world-wide. In 1995 alone, about $162 billion was spent on American Express cards.

American Express offers a wide range of benefits to its members which ensures its popularity remains undimmed and in fact increases. The Membership Rewards brand-loyalty programme has been part of an overall marketing package skilfully orchestrated by American Express. The programme which was launched in 1991 now operates in over 27 countries and has over 5 million enrolees. American Express also has an incredibly high profile amongst its corporate customers. It currently provides a service to 89 of the Fortune 100 companies and over one million small businesses.

HISTORY

In the year 2000, American Express celebrates its 150th anniversary. Nowadays it is one of the world's most famous companies, famous for its charge card, travel services and financial facilities. The American Express Company originated as an express freight company. It was the result of a union between Wells & Co and other similar express carriers, Livingston & Fargo and Butterfield, Wasson & Co. American Express first operated under the company slogan "Safety & Dispatch" accompanied by a bulldog logo.

From the outset, American Express played an important part in people's lives - even saving them! During the American Civil War which dogged the 1860s, American Express transported vital supplies to Union army depots and facilitated the democratic process by issuing election ballots to troops in the field.

American Express first underwrote a money order in 1882, when it was realised that this was far safer than shipping sums of cash. This became an increasingly common practice from the mid-1880s onwards. American Express established banking relationships across Europe to transfer money from the immigrants based in the United States to their families in the Old World.

The company first moved into Europe through paying a British firm, Meadows & Co, to set up a one-man office at Liverpool Docks. Extending into Europe was key to American

Express becoming the world-famous organisation it is today. Before long, brochures were issued to its growing portfolio of European agents, stating the company's aims to "collect accounts, sell consignments, purchase goods for their patrons, and deliver goods for merchants" - also to - "pay money on Telegraphic Order at a moment's notice, between points thousands of miles apart and sell small drafts or money orders which can be cashed at 15,000 places".

Despite the increasingly high profile of American Express for its financial services, it was still chiefly a freight express business. However, as a major step towards facilitating greater, and easier travel in 1891, the American Express Travellers Cheque, the first of its kind, was introduced. This offered a solid guarantee that the cheque represented dollars and could be converted into a variety of currencies, thereby committing the long-winded money-changing process at international borders to bad memory. The beauty of this simple cheque was that it was automatically refundable should it be lost or stolen.

American Express freight offices in England, Germany and France also began selling tickets for railroads and transatlantic ships and offered travel information and itineraries.

One of the most famous American Express offices was opened in 1900, at 11, Rue Scribe in Paris. This became something of a Mecca, often a godsend, to tourists in Europe. The day war broke out, on 3 August 1914, around 150,000 Americans were trapped in Europe, many in awkward situations. Offices across Europe were jammed with Americans frantic to get home. In Paris, the line for counters was a hundred metres long, and six people deep. Money was posted to points all over Europe to help those further afield to make their way home. In many places, the locals were hoarding and trading in American Express cheques

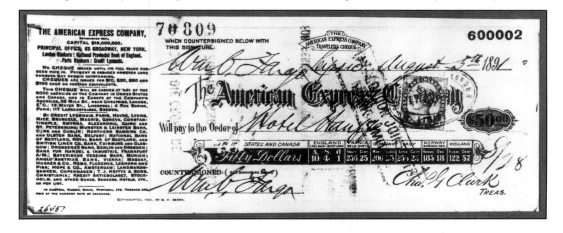

rather than trust in their own currency. In its role as a freight carrier, the company was inundated with baggage left in the rush to flee Europe. Whatever the crisis, and no matter how difficult the obstacles, American Express managed to reunite families, travellers with long-lost baggage, and secure a safe exit for thousands of people. In 1915 the Manchester Guardian dubbed it "The Romantic Company" in view of its shunting messages between prisoners of war and their families.

After the war, American Express increased its travel organisation and extended its international financial operations in Latin America, Europe and the Far East. American Express actually arranged the first around-the-world leisure cruise in 1922. Even during the depression of the 1930s, American Express continued to cash its travellers cheques despite the fact that most US banks were closed and their assets frozen.

The famous green American Express charge card didn't make an appearance until well after the Second World War, in 1958. Since then, American Express has expanded rapidly into various areas of financial and travel services. American Express even started its own publishing business in 1968. In 1986, American Express set up new headquarters at the World Financial Centre in New York - a fitting location for a company with the global prestige and financial heritage of American Express.

THE PRODUCT
The American Express Company operates in three core businesses: travel, finance and communication. Throughout the world, American Express employs around 71,000 people. Its main businesses are American Express Travel Related Services, American Express Financial Advisors and American Express Bank.

American Express Financial Advisors offer financial planning and investment advisory services to individuals and businesses in the United States. American Express' banking arm has three major businesses; correspondent, commercial and private banking and consumer financial services.

American Express Travel Related Services is by far the largest business in the American Express organisation and in fact generates around half of all American Express' profits. This is the most famous sector of American Express in that it operates American Express Card products as well as a world-wide network of American Express Travel Service and Representative Offices.

Although most famous for its charge card, American Express is now aiming to provide a portfolio of products - traditional charge and credit

cards, stored value cards and new products such as debit and smart cards. During 1995 the company made significant strides in broadening the number of products offered. For example in the US an Optima Card for students was launched as well as two co-branded cards with Hilton and Delta respectively. A credit card was also launched in the UK, with other markets set to follow in 1996. American Express will continue to customise its products for specific groups, rather than trying to meet the needs of the masses.

RECENT DEVELOPMENTS
Recent years have seen a variety of loyalty programmes and extra services added to the American Express product portfolio. The American Express travel business has extended massively through a deal in 1993 which secured the acquisition of Thomas Cook Group Ltd and Thomas Cook Partnership which rendered American Express the world's largest business travel agent.

In the same year, American Express was awarded the contract for the US federal government's travel and transportation payment system. A deal which amounted to the biggest corporate card account in the world. This meant around 900,000 federal civilian and defense employees would now be American Express Cardmembers.

Also in 1993, American Express launched an easier-to-read format for monthly bills which offered more comprehensive information on expenditure and also clearly communicated American Express' special services. In general, a more personalised approach was instilled which reflected the spending habits of each individual customer.

PROMOTION
The Blue Box American Express corporate logo made its debut in 1974 and

has since gone on to become one of the world's most familiar. American Express has always keenly supported its quality service and products with effective advertising which has produced at least two particularly famous and universally-recognised slogans: "American Express - that'll do nicely" and "Don't leave home without it".

Many TV campaigns have become famous, and featured celebrities. Campaigns focus on the benefits of owning an American Express Card above any other. Sticky situations are unstuck with the brandishing of an American Express Card or travellers cheques. The many perks and privileges afforded by American Express Card ownership were underscored in the 1987 "Membership has its privileges" campaign and the "Quality People" campaign, first introduced in 1993 highlighted the classy image of the American Express brand, in addition to the wide range of globally-available services it could provide. Testimonies from successful people, the likes of Anita Roddick and Rocco Forte, have further accentuated the exclusivity of the American Express brand.

BRAND VALUES
American Express is an exclusive brand. It is an achievement in itself to own one. American Express guarantees an efficient, quality and reliable service at all times. It is a global brand, which maintains a prestigious appeal throughout the world. American Express also has a "romantic" history, which has established itself as the undoubted Superbrand it is today.

Andrex

THE MARKET

Toilet tissue may not seem a particularly glamorous product but it is undoubtedly an essential household purchase and is second only to washing powder as the biggest selling and fastest growing household product in the grocery market. In fact, according to research from AGB, toilet tissue is three times larger than washing up liquid and fabric conditioner and up to five times larger than household cleaners and air fresheners. This places a value of £607 million per annum on the UK toilet tissue market.

UK consumers buy more toilet tissue per capita than any other country in Northern Europe, often for 'secondary' usage, such as make-up removal and nose-blowing. This is because UK toilet tissue is generally softer than elsewhere. In fact, some 98% of the UK toilet tissue market is for soft, (with 80% coloured) - a huge increase on 1957, for example, when soft toilet tissue accounted for just 25% of the total market.

Nielsen/Scott company estimates have shown that UK toilet tissue customers are prepared to spend more compared to Europeans. The average price per 100 sheets on the continent is 9p, and 12.8p in the UK.

ACHIEVEMENTS

Andrex has driven the UK market for soft toilet tissue since the 1960s, when demand for a softer product became the norm. Up to one and a half million toilet rolls are sold in the UK every day - a phenomenal achievement when you consider that Andrex is also one of the most expensive premium brands on the market. The premium sector now represents around 60% of the total market.

Andrex has enjoyed its position as the leading toilet tissue brand for over 34 years and, according to figures from AC Nielsen, is also the UK's 6th biggest grocery brand. It has become a well-known household name, largely through consistent high profile advertising. The famous 'Andrex Puppy' adverts have won over the public's hearts since 1972, with Andrex TV commercials voted national favourites in 1988 and 1991. The puppy's antics ensure that the brand's advertising enjoys a strong showing in Marketing Magazine's Adwatch prompted recall chart, as well as the Millward Brown 'Awareness Index'.

HISTORY

Andrex was first developed in 1942 as a disposable gentleman's hankie and was sold exclusively in Harrods, London's most famous, elegant department store. This tissue was produced at St Andrews Mill, in Walthamstow, north-east London. Andrex had to battle its way into a leading position in the toilet tissue market, as up to that point, tissue was chiefly sold through chemists and was a harder paper product, often known as 'shinies'. Famous brands included Bronco and Izal.

Andrex was boosted by Hollywood, when the film stars demanded studios stock a softer toilet tissue rather than the ubiquitous 'shinies'.

In 1957, Andrex produced the first coloured toilet tissue, a pink variant, and by the 1960s, Andrex was at the forefront of the UK toilet tissue market. A full range of coloured products was unveiled in 1966.

Toilet tissue soon became a common grocery purchase. Notably by 1991, over 81% of sales were being generated through multiple grocery outlets.

The first of the famous Andrex puppy commercials was screened in 1972, leading to mass awareness of the brand. In 1978, Scott, the manufacturers of Andrex, were awarded Royal Warrants of Appointment.

Consistent product innovation, such as the launch of a 9 roll Andrex in 1987, have added to the brand's premium positioning and has maintained Andrex' leading position in the UK market, with a 30% value share.

THE PRODUCT

Andrex markets its soft toilet tissue in a variety of pack sizes and colours. Currently available are 2 roll, 4 roll and 9 roll packs, with tissue variants in white, pink, blue, green, peach and honeysuckle.

Interestingly, Andrex is one of the most expensive toilet tissue brands on the market and yet still inspires the greatest brand loyalty amongst its consumers. Some 39% of customers buy Andrex over and above any other toilet tissue brand. Scott is constantly improving the Andrex product, particularly in terms of softness and thickness, to continue justifying its premium price point and emphasise its quality brand credentials.

RECENT DEVELOPMENTS

In recent years, Andrex has successfully managed to head off the threat form retailer's own brands and rising competition from other toilet tissue brands - often despite their higher advertising spend. This has been achieved by ensuring product quality is utmost, as typified by the launch of 'New Feel' Andrex in 1985.

A growing area of concern was the surge in popularity for so-called 'green' products, made from recycled paper, which had taken 20% of

PROMOTION

Few advertising icons have come to embody their brand's core values as perfectly as the Andrex puppy.

Andrex advertising has featured the lovable Labrador puppy since 1972, spawning some 75 commercials. In the public eye he has become inextricably linked with the brand itself - the puppy's 'softness' and 'strength' have come to symbolise the qualities that keep Andrex ahead of the market. Central to all Andrex advertising is the puppy with an accompanying by-line which always uses some combination of 'Soft', 'Strong' and 'Long'.

Interestingly, when the TV campaign was first conceived back in 1972, the puppy was not an automatic first choice as the Andrex advertising icon. Originally, a young girl was to be seen trailing a roll of Andrex toilet tissue around her home. However, the regulators of TV advertising at the time, felt that this could encourage children into bad, wasteful habits, so the mischievous cuddly image of the yellow Labrador puppy was suggested instead.

The puppy's heart-warming antics have continued to represent the Andrex brand in a variety of forms outside of the keynote advertising campaigns, particularly through merchandising. Typical promotions have included a Puppy calendar and the eternally popular soft toy. Scott estimates that to date around 450,000 toy Andrex puppies have been sold. The Andrex puppy has also been a potent symbol as part of the Guide Dogs for the Blind Appeal.

BRAND VALUES

Andrex has prospered from its positioning as a premium quality product, with a matching price point, through consistent investment in product innovation and an impressive advertising track record. Indeed, the Andrex puppy is one of the most enduring advertising images of our age, representing a seamless synergy with the 'soft', 'strong', 'long' qualities which typify the Andrex brand. It has been a remarkable achievement when one considers that toilet tissue is a relatively uninspiring, low profile product - albeit a household necessity. Classic advertising teamed with exceptional product quality lie at the heart of Andrex' success.

Things you didn't know about Andrex

○ On average, around 1.5 million rolls of Andrex are sold in the UK each day, enough tissue to encircle the world nearly one and half times.

○ Since the Andrex Puppy advertising campaign was initiated in 1972, Andrex has increased its volume share of the UK market from just under 5% to over 30%. (Source: Nielsen).

○ According to the AGB Superpanel, Andrex is the UK's second biggest brand.

○ The tremendous popularity and brand recognition engendered by the Andrex Puppy TV advertising campaign has led to 'spoof' campaigns from other brands, most famously by Hamlet Cigars.

○ Andrex 'Little Boy' TV commercial was the first to show Andrex toilet tissue in situ.

the market by 1991. In response, Scott's advertising pitched Andrex as an environmentally-friendly brand, explaining that Scott was a major 'planter' of trees. This was in addition to Andrex' mass production facilities converting to Non Chlorine Gas Bleached pulps during 1991.

In spite of an ever more hotly contested marketplace, Andrex has retained its brand leadership and remains the fastest-selling toilet tissue brand. Scott Worldwide, the parent company of Scott Ltd which produces Andrex in the UK, is now exporting many of Andrex'

core brand values and notably the famous Andrex puppy to Italy and Spain, to promote the premium Scottex brand.

Constant innovation is key to Andrex' success. One of the latest off-shoots of the Andrex brand is Andrex Moist, a moist toilet tissue launched in the UK in 1991. Sold as a tub of 40 wipes, with an accompanying refill pack, Andrex Moist is soft, thick and hypo-allergenic, particularly useful for use on sore or irritated skin. In this sector, Andrex Moist has already secured an impressive 60% market share.

BBC

THE MARKET

For years, the UK broadcasting market has been dominated by the BBC, the nation's publicly-funded broadcasting service, and ITV, its commercial broadcasting rival, comprising regional franchises, with Channel 4, a relative newcomer to terrestrial broadcasting. A further channel, Channel 5, is also due to enter the market.

However, with the convergence of media technologies (the information superhighway), satellite broadcasters (BSkyB), and cable operators offering a plethora of alternative channels and programming, the terrestrial TV offerings are threatened like no time before. Digital compression in TV and radio broadcasting will create an even greater choice of channels - potentially up to 30 TV channels and 200 radio stations.

ACHIEVEMENTS

The BBC is not just a public institution. It is the nation's memory bank. A repository of collective emotional responses. As the UK's national TV and radio broadcaster, its comprehensive and much-acclaimed news-coverage has involved us at key junctures in history-making. Through the BBC we have shared the highs and lows of our greatest sporting moments. It has delivered an incredibly wide and varied range of entertainment programming for 70 years, bringing us countless memories and hours of enjoyment.

True to say, the BBC draws the nation together, as shown by the TV audience's turn-out for those extra-special occasions. For example, in 1995, half of all TV viewers watched the VJ Day commemorations on 19 August, and the FA Cup Final drew 71% of the audience.

The BBC's pioneering attitude and expertise in broadcasting and production - not just TV and radio programming, but films as well - has earned it a string of well-deserved accolades. Through commissioning and broadcasting new music, drama and literature, the BBC is a notable contributor to the Arts. In moments of crisis, the BBC is the nation's first port of call. BBC commentary is renowned for its impartiality and independence. Its high-class journalism is praised for its objective, intelligent analysis of the issues that matter for all of us.

The BBC is also respected overseas, where its World Service radio service and World Service News TV service are a lifeline to expatriate British communities. Programming is broadcast in numerous languages, including Arabic, Serbian, Chinese-Mandarin, Urdu and Russian.

The BBC is truly 'Aunty' to the British nation; an essential part of our social fabric - respected and loved by audiences the world over.

HISTORY

The BBC was first awarded a Royal Charter to provide broadcasting services in the UK in 1927 - thus becoming the British Broadcasting Corporation. Prior to this, it had been known as the British Broadcasting Company, when it was first formed in October 1922.

In its early days, the BBC was concentrated solely on radio broadcasting. After all, the TV market hadn't then taken root. But even as far back as 1924, the BBC was forging its role as a national institution. 1924 was the year when the 'pips' - the time signal still used on the hour for its national radio services - were first introduced.

Aside from its public status, throughout its 70 year history, the BBC has acted as a pioneer in broadcasting services. In 1930, the BBC started broadcasting from Westminster with its

programme The Week in Westminster - still alive and well on Radio 4 today. In the same year, the BBC provided broadcasting services to the regions and used female announcers from 1933 onwards.

Just the year before, in 1932, the BBC moved into its headquarters at Broadcasting House, in Central London, where it is based to this day. The first major live outside broadcast was transmitted in 1937, on the occasion of George VI's coronation. The European Service, a multi-lingual radio programme was first broadcast in 1938. The forerunner of the BBC World Service had been launched in 1932, when it was originally known as the Empire Service.

Throughout the Second World War, the BBC was truly the voice of the nation. More than that, its radio service was one of the chief providers of news and moral sustenance across Europe, during the years when Nazi occupation cast a long, dark shadow over the continent. Key historical moments have been recorded for posterity including the declaration of war from Prime Minister Neville Chamberlain and King George VI, and later, Winston Churchill's speeches to the nation. But of course, not all was gloom and doom during the war years. Radio comics played an enormous part in pepping-up the nation's spirits and light entertainment arrived with the first broadcast of Desert Island Discs in 1942.

The BBC television broadcasting service, first started in 1939, but closed down during the war years, resumed in 1946. Rapid change and growth in broadcasting led to the establishment of the National Broadcasting Councils for Scotland and Wales in 1953. This was the same year, that the BBC transmitted pictures of Queen Elizabeth II's coronation, live from Westminster Cathedral.

Over the years, the BBC's live programming has recorded some of the nation's, if not the world's, most important moments - including the first live television pictures from the moon in 1966.

In 1964, the BBC's second channel, BBC2 was launched. Despite its involvement in testing since 1954, full colour TV transmission didn't officially begin until 1967, and even then, a full national roll-out for both the BBC and ITV, wasn't comprehensive until two years later.

The introduction of BBC services with which we are now so familiar, such as the Ceefax information service, Breakfast time television and Daytime television, weren't launched until much later - in 1974, 1983 and 1986 respectively. The most recent addition to the BBC's bouquet of broadcasting services has been World Service Television, started in 1991.

The heart of the BBC's television services is centred at Television Centre in White City, West London, first opened in 1960. National radio is based at Broadcasting

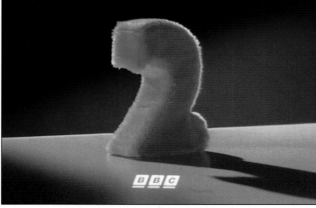

Broadcasting House. From here, Radio 1 was first introduced in 1967, and the former networks renamed Radio 2, 3 and 4. A new radio network, Radio 5 started in 1990, and was relaunched as Radio Five Live in 1994.

THE PRODUCT

The BBC operates two national TV channels - BBC1 and BBC2. Programming is sourced from 11 separate divisions.

Drama, produces over 400 hours of original drama each year. This can range from full-length feature programmes, to major theatrical works to classic series, such as the massively popular Eastenders, Z-Cars or Casualty, or one-offs, like Pride and Prejudice. Four regional drama departments are based in Birmingham, Northern Ireland, Scotland and Wales.

BBC Features produces journalistic programmes and topical entertainment, such as Crimewatch UK and Have I Got News For You.

The Presentation Department is responsible for the transmission operation of BBC1, BBC2 and the BBC Worldwide Television Channel, the marketing and promotion of programmes on-screen, programme announcements and public service information. It is also responsible for the BBC Weather Centre and Children's BBC.

Music and Arts produces 225 hours of Arts-based programming each year such as Omnibus and The Late Show, plus 100 hours of music.

The Entertainment group is split into Comedy and Variety. Up to 600 hours of programming are developed each year, offering us game shows, sitcoms and annual events such as the Children's Royal Variety Performance.

The BBC's children's programmes department produces 1,000 hours of TV a year, including Live and Kicking, Blue Peter and Newsround.

TV Sport & Events brings us our key sporting events, ranging from the FA Cup Final to Wimbledon. With its flagship sports programme, Grandstand, BBC Sport offers 1,400 hours of programming each year.

Science & Features produces the likes of Horizon and Tomorrow's World.

Documentaries produces programming at the cutting edge of investigative journalism, such as Inside Story and 40 Minutes.

The Acquisition Group controls the purchase of outside programming, which can cover anything from Neighbours to full-length feature films.

Finally, the Community Programme Unit, ensures the public can exercise its own editorial control from time to time, through programmes like Open Space and Grapevine.

The BBC is renowned for its high quality news-coverage. Its News & Current Affairs department spans five units: News Gathering; BBC Westminster; TV Daily News Programmes; Television Weekly & Special Programmes; and News And Current Affairs Radio.

A separate department oversees educational programming, mainly through Open University output and a number of educational books, videos and magazines.

The five main national radio networks target the widely varying needs of the national audience. Radio 1 chiefly offers popular music; Radio 2, offering music and chat, is aimed at a mature audience; Radio 3 provides a full repertoire of classical music, discussions and drama and originates 2,500 hours of live music, often recordings of the BBC orchestras and musicians; Radio 4 offers news, documentaries

and entertainment features; Radio 5 combines news-coverage with sports.

The BBC has got the nation covered through BBC Midlands & East; BBC Scotland; BBC North; BBC South; BBC Northern Ireland; and BBC Cymru/Wales as well as its local radio and regional TV services.

RECENT DEVELOPMENTS

By virtue of its Royal Charter, the BBC is funded by each TV-owning household's payment of a compulsory licence, which currently stands at £86.50 per annum. Accountability is an increasingly crucial issue. The BBC strives to ensure that its programming is of the highest quality, deserving of its licence-fee.

However, external pressures and an increasingly crowded broadcasting market mean that the BBC is looking to diversify its interests in the commercial sector, without resorting to a commercialisation of its programming with constant commercial breaks. Its commercial considerations have been gathered under the wing of BBC Worldwide - previously BBC Enterprises. This division sells BBC publications, videos and programming - indeed, the BBC is now more famous than ever for exporting its programming abroad.

During 1995, BBC programmes garnered illustrious prizes from around the world. These included an Oscar, five international Emmys and it swept the board at the Prix Italia and RTS Awards.

On the home front, the BBC held firm against its chief terrestrial rival, ITV, whose market share slipped, while BBC2 was the only channel to gain audience share, despite the greater choice of programming in the market.

It was a successful year for BBC radio, with Radio 2 picking up the Sony Station of the Year award. BBC Radio had about 31 million listeners in 1995.

PROMOTION

A combination of three letters - BBC - has come to represent a legend not only in broadcasting but as a worldwide brand. The BBC has become extremely skilled in its management of the famous trademark both in terms of promotion and protection. It is used both creatively, as illustrated in its imaginative idents for BBC2, and consistently. The logo is

ubiquitous, seen on flags, microphones, cameras, screen, in print, vehicles, merchandising, buildings, books, videos and magazines throughout the world.

Trailers for both programmes and corporate messages are becoming increasingly more sophisticated and entertaining. The Mel Smith and Griff Rhys Jones film in 1993 featuring skilfully crafted 'morphing' images, received considerable accolade including a D&AD nomination. The follow-up campaign in 1994 featuring Julie Walters was also well received and attracted considerable publicity.

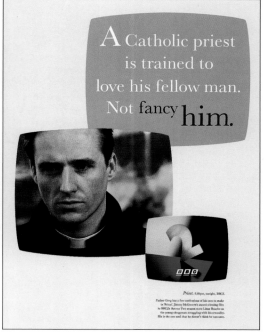

In recent years the BBC has become more adventurous in its use of external media. Posters and press have been used to promote programmes and services in addition to the considerable promotion on the BBC's own airwaves.

Radio Times has also acted as an invaluable promotional tool.

BRAND VALUES

The BBC lives by its motto: "To Educate, Entertain and Inform". This is part and parcel of the BBC's public service tradition, which is deeply engrained in the organisation. Top quality programming, unbiased and responsible news-reporting, a common ground drawing the British nation together as a whole, excellence and fairness - these are the tenets that the BBC stands for. The BBC is a heritage brand, which has become something of a legend.

Things you didn't know about the BBC

❍ The most often seen person on TV is Carol Hersee - the girl on the BBC2 test-card.

❍ The BBC licence actually only costs 23p per day, or in other words, 50% of a daily newspaper, 10% of a day's video rental, or 15% of a day's cable TV viewing.

❍ Most complaints made to the BBC are about changes to the advertised schedule. There are relatively few calls complaining about sex and violence in BBC programmes.

❍ First broadcast in 1951, Radio 4's The Archers is the world's longest-running soap. The first words uttered, (by Dan), were "Well Simon. What d'you think?".

BIRDS EYE WALL'S

Working Together For The Best

THE MARKET

With increasingly demanding lifestyles, more working women than ever before and a greater number of single person households, mealtimes have become less formal occasions, where convenience is often paramount.

The frozen food market has benefited from this trend. The UK frozen food market is now worth £3 billion. About 99% of consumers regularly buy frozen food. One company in particular has found its way into consumers' shopping trolleys. Around 85% of consumers buy Birds Eye which enjoys a 20% share of the total frozen food market.

In 1995, Birds Eye's product range comprised of more than 150 frozen food items.

Wall's produces ice cream and frozen desserts for what has become a highly lucrative and popular consumer market. In the same way that the frozen ready meal often replaces the traditional meal occasion, take home ice cream and frozen desserts have become ideal substitutes for home baking, or are commonly consumed as a tasty single portion snack, bought at newsagents, kiosks, cinemas and theatres.

The ice cream market is worth £1 billion. Wall's has a 63% share in the impulse market and 32% for take home ice creams.

Unsurprisingly, children are eager customers, spending up to 88% of their pocket money on ice cream, crisps and sweets (Source: Wall's Pocket Money Monitor 1996). Children represent 20% of the population but account for more than 40% of ice cream sales from newsagents and corner shops.

ACHIEVEMENTS

Birds Eye was the first UK company to manufacture and market frozen foods. The company has become synonymous with frozen foods with a string of top-selling brands and products, including Fish Fingers which Birds Eye first launched in Britain in 1955. Since then, an estimated 16 billion Fish Fingers have been sold.

Wall's has proved equally innovative in the ice cream market. It was the first company to produce soft scoop ice cream that can be served straight from the freezer. Today, 17 out of the Top 20 best selling impulse ice creams are from Wall's. To meet this demand, Wall's operates Europe's largest ice cream factory in Gloucester.

Wall's ice cream isn't just enjoyed by the punters. It has received critical acclaim. In 1994, Cadbury's Crunchie from Wall's received the ADAS/Sunday Telegraph supreme award for marketing and innovation excellence.

HISTORY

The original Clarence Birdseye, an American scientist and explorer, conceived the idea of commercially frozen food while on an expedition in Labrador in the 1920s. The idea came to him after eating with the Inuit (Eskimo) in Canada's Arctic region. He realised that fish and meat, once thawed, still retained its freshness after months of freezing.

On his return to the USA, Birdseye patented a freezing device known as The Birdseye Plate Froster.

In 1930, a group of Massachussets shopkeepers started selling 'Birds Eye' branded frozen fish, meat and vegetables. Clarence Birdseye continued to pioneer his quick freezing business under the auspices of the General Foods Corporation.

The Birds Eye brand was launched in the UK in 1938 by Frosted Foods Ltd, part of General Foods. The outbreak of the Second World War temporarily halted production, but under the ownership of Unilever, Birds Eye resumed operations in 1945 with an added urgency to make up for the country's post-war food shortages.

The second half of Birds Eye Wall's stems from Wall's, Britain's oldest and best known ice cream brand. Wall's originated in the 18th century as a London pie-maker. Legend has it that a young office clerk first suggested the company diversify into ice cream products to keep employees in work during the slack summer months. By 1922, Wall's was manufacturing ice cream at the site of an old friary in Acton, West London. Ice creams were sold in the streets from refrigerated boxes perched on tricycles. 'Stop Me and Buy One' became a national catchphrase. By 1939, 8,500 tricycles selling Wall's ice cream were trading their wares in streets up and down the country. Sweet shops and cinemas soon followed suit selling Wall's ice creams from refrigerated units.

The Wall's ice cream and meat divisions eventually parted company. However, Unilever which owned Birds Eye, realised that Birds Eye

and ready-made meals; and Hull, where all coated fish products, apart from Fish Fingers are handled in addition to the freezing and packing of vegetables.

THE PRODUCT

Birds Eye offers something for everyone, producing frozen food products to delight the whole family and individual meals. Some of Britain's most popular food brands come from Birds Eye, including Birds Eye Original Beefburgers and Birds Eye Peas. Wall's also markets top-selling ice cream brands such as Magnum, Cornetto, Solero and Viennetta.

Overall, Birds Eye Wall's operates in six key markets: Vegetable Products, with its frozen peas, vegetables, vegetables-in-sauce and potato products; Fish Products, with the Fish Cuisine and Chunky Cod Steaks brands; Meat Products, offering a range of chicken dishes plus Steakhouse burgers and grills; Prepared Dishes, including Panflair; Savoury Bakery and Ice Cream together with Frozen Desserts.

Birds Eye Wall's continues to innovate new products to grow the market. In 1995 alone, the company launched 24 new frozen food products and 17 new ice cream products.

RECENT DEVELOPMENTS

In 1995, Birds Eye responded to the remarkable growth in the cook-in-sauce market, which has grown by 127% in the past five years, with the launch of Panflair. Panflair is a meal in sauce product, which has to be cooked for ten minutes on the hob after the addition of milk or water.

Further innovations have included Chicken Marinades, Fish Cuisine Medley, another 'cook on the hob' style product, Chicken En Croute, Crispy Chicken Dippers and Toffee Viennetta, a variant of the popular Viennetta dessert brand.

In recent years, Birds Eye Wall's has concentrated its attentions in the field of poultry and fish through innovation centres located at the head office at Walton.

Birds Eye Wall's has increasingly turned its attentions to the business opportunities presented in the European continent. In 1995, about 19% of its total output was exported abroad.

PROMOTION

Birds Eye TV advertising for its Fish Fingers brand has launched one of Britain's most familiar faces, in the form of Captain Birds Eye. Prior to his appearance on our TV screens in 1967, Birds Eye's Fish Fingers advertising had chopped and changed between different slogans and settings. The arrival of Captain Birds Eye changed this. His friendly, weather-beaten face was popular with children, and he was easily associated with the seaside.

Played since 1967 by John Hewer, now 72 years old, Captain Birds Eye has become an advertising legend. The advertisements have been relayed in 14 countries, including Portugal, Dubai, Japan, South East Asia and the Caribbean. Outside of the UK, he is known as Captain Iglo - however his first name remains a mystery.

A roving Birds Eye Food Show also tours the country offering samples of new products to consumers.

In 1995, Birds Eye peas were advertised on TV for the first time in six years, introducing the

new VIP (Vitamins in Peas) guarantee stamp. This campaign has been based on research showing that the Birds Eye freezing technique actually locks in the freshness and goodness of the vegetable, from the moment the pea is harvested and then frozen, until it is marketed and sold.

Besides TV advertising, Birds Eye Wall's supports its ice cream brands with point of sale promotions located at amusement parks and theatres, sampling and PR campaigns.

BRAND VALUES

Birds Eye Wall's is a brand name that consumers know that they can trust.

The two house brands are so strong with their separate identities that consumers often think that Birds Eye and Wall's are two different companies. However, premium quality, added value products and innovation are at the heart of both brands.

Birds Eye has a reputation for being the frozen food expert and has become a firm family favourite with legendary products like fish fingers and peas. Great care is taken in the selectivity of raw materials to ensure all Birds Eye products are of the utmost quality. "Only the best passes the Birds Eye test" is a key statement used in TV and press advertising to demonstrate the company's commitment to consumers.

With Wall's, consumers know that the most popular ice cream manufacturer in the UK has ice creams for every occasion, from children's novelty and teenage refreshment to family sharing and adult indulgence. A successful innovation is shown in the launch of Solero Tropical Fruits, which was created using specially patented Unilever technology in 1995. Solero is the fastest selling single impulse ice cream ever.

frozen food and Wall's ice cream shared compatible interests in freezing and refrigeration techniques so the two companies were merged in 1981 to form the Birds Eye Wall's brand.

Two recent landmarks in the history of Birds Eye have included the 40th anniversary of the Birds Eye Fish Finger in 1995, and the company's 50th pea harvest in 1996. Harvesting lasts for 42 days and nights, with up to 300 people working round the clock. In 1995, an estimated 359 billion peas were harvested.

Today, Birds Eye Wall's employs more than 5,000 people, of which around 4,000 are directly involved in making the products. Its head office is based at Walton-on-Thames in Surrey.

Birds Eye Wall's operates four manufacturing sites at Gloucester, producing ice cream and frozen desserts; Lowestoft, producing Steakhouse burgers and grills, chicken, and potato products as well as vegetables; Grimsby, preparing Fish Fingers

Things you didn't know about Birds Eye Wall's

❍ The common pea is now so ancient that no-one knows its original ancestor, although it is thought to have stemmed from the near East to Central Asia territory. Even so, the first pea ever found was in 9750BC on the border of Thailand and Burma.

❍ There are approximately 1,224 peas in a 1lb pack of Birds Eye peas and approximately 230 peas in an average 85g serving.

❍ In July 1995, Wall's produced enough ice-creams for every man, woman and child in the country to have two each .

❍ In 1995, 50,109 Birds Eye Wall's TV commercials were shown - equivalent to one advert every 14 minutes during daylight hours.

❍ More than 16 billion Fish Fingers have been sold which is enough to stretch to the moon five times over or circle the equator 48 times.

❍ John Hewer has played Captain Birds Eye in Fish Finger advertising since 1967 and is the longest running brand personality on TV.

❍ Wall's was the first company to print jokes on lolly sticks.

THE MARKET

The nature of the Do-it-Yourself (DIY) market has changed in the last few years, as brands from the Far East have appeared in the UK market. The DIY market was badly hit by the recession. Gardening, a market which is traditionally reliant on favourable weather conditions, and housework may themselves be considered essential, but demand for high-quality specialist tools dropped during the uncertain economic climate of the late 1980s. This was not helped by the sluggish housing market, traditionally, moving house is a key time for DIY.

It took until 1994 for the power tool market to enjoy a growth in total sales - the first time in 4 years.

Innovation and the recent launch of new products by manufacturers such as Black & Decker, means that the whole market is set to benefit. This year, Black & Decker expected the whole UK power tool market to grow by 14% on its previous years total sales, part of which can be attributed to the relaunch and introduction of new tools.

Another one of Black & Decker's important markets, hand-held cleaners, shifts 600,000 units per year in the UK. This is a growing market, as consumers move away from the traditional vacuum cleaner to the more convenient hand-held models. This sector experienced a total value growth rate in excess of 40% from 1991-1994, and showed the highest growth of any vacuum cleaner type.

Black & Decker has also recently moved into the manual staple gun market, which is worth over £2m per annum in the UK, and even more recently into the torch market, with the innovative Snakelight.

ACHIEVEMENTS

Black & Decker holds the distinction of being one of the most well-known brands in the whole world. Of 6,000 brands surveyed amongst 10,000 consumers, in the US, Black and Decker ranked seventh out of the 100 top brands in terms of brand name awareness, and was ranked nineteenth in Europe.

Black & Decker holds a large share of many markets in which it operates. In fact, it can be said that in some markets, Black & Decker is the market, as in the rechargeable hand-held cleaner sector, where Black & Decker held in excess of a 90% share in 1995.

Some of its newer and more innovative products have also performed remarkably well. The Black & Decker Powershot, a hand-held nail and staple gun, achieved a 30% share of the market in the first year of its launch in the US, and is set to replicate the performance in the UK, taking 15% of the market since its launch in 1995. This has had the added effect of boosting the whole market, as the introduction of the Black & Decker brand name into this market has made the whole product more accessible. Endorsement and the company's marketing has grown the total category.

The new 'Snakelight' torch has also performed, turning the exisitng torch market upside down. It has gained over 30% of the UK market, making it the brand leader in this market. This was achieved in the last quarter of 1995.

Black & Decker's latest 'VersaPak' range of ten cordless tools for the home and garden, is set to become one of the biggest innovations in the DIY market.

HISTORY

Black & Decker began in 1910, when two young Americans, Duncan Black and Alonzo Decker formed their own manufacturing company. To raise the initial capital needed for the fledgling enterprise, Duncan Black sold his treasured Maxewell-Briscoe car, whilst Alonzo Decker borrowed an equal sum. With their $1200 investment they leased premises in Baltimore, and began contract machine work.

The early Black & Decker products ranged from equipment for the US mint, to bottle

capping machinery. In 1914 the first hand-held power drill was patented. With its pistol grip, trigger switch, and universal motor, Black & Decker had now begun to produce the goods for which it would subsequently become world-renowned. Early successes such as this, and the Lectroflator - an electric air compressor used to inflate tyres - pushed sales to above one million dollars, which meant that the company could expand. Service centres were opened in Boston and New York, and a new factory was built in Towson, Maryland, in order to cope with the phenomenal growth. In 1922 another milestone was reached when the first subsidiary outside the United States was formed, in Canada, and in 1928 the first factory was built in the UK, in Slough. This factory produced a range of heavy duty tools including tappers, screwdrivers and grinders. The outbreak of the Second World War proved a testing time for the new UK business, though it aided the general war effort by manufacturing armaments from its factories. The scarcity of metals at the time forced a rethink in the design of its tools. Tools were soon being manufactured with plastic housings.

In 1946, it came to Black & Decker's notice that industrial tools were going missing - often ending up in workers' homes. This alerted Black & Decker to the possibility of a thriving home tools market. So, the company decided to make tools specifically aimed at the DIY market - a major decision that was to change the face of the company, and form its core business for the next 50 years.

The extraordinary growth in sales that this decision prompted, ensured continuous expansion. By 1957, sales had exceeded £25 million.

The 1960s saw further expansion, with the opening of new branches, both in Scandinavia, and in England, with the opening of new headquarters in Maidenhead.

At the end of the 1960s, Black & Decker turned its hand to 'space development'. In association with the National Aeronautical and Space Agency, Black & Decker devised a cordless zero-torque space tool, used on the Gemini project, and in the early 1970s, a Black & Decker moon drill was used to remove core samples from the lunar surface.

The 1980s provided a different kind of challenge. The poor world economic climate restricted growth in the power tool market. Black & Decker weathered the storm by introducing a wide range of innovative products, such as the Paintstripper, the hot air stripper, Dustbuster, a hand-held vacuum cleaner and Strimmer, a grass trimmer.

THE PRODUCT

Black & Decker produces a whole range of tools and products for the home and the garden.

In its garden products range, it can boast a

variety of mowers, (cordless, rotary and hover), spanning the whole market. Black & Decker successfully averted becoming embroiled in the rival advertising campaigns from its competitors in the 1970s and 1980s. The company also produces a range of rakes, and trimmers for grass, for edges and hedges, and chainsaws for trees.

A more recent addition to Black & Decker's roster of garden products is the innovative, multi-skilled 'Leafbuster', a blower/vacuum for the garden. This machine is designed to blow leaves into piles, collect these piles, and shred garden debris into a mulch, which forms better compost.

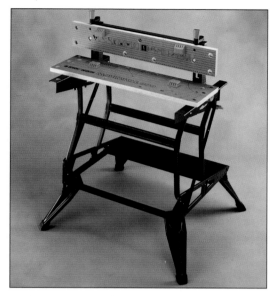

For the house, Black & Decker produces a range of hand-held vacuum cleaners, the 'Dustbuster' range, which vary in their power and uses. There are also tools to help with DIY, such as the Powershot nail and staple gun, used for affixing anything to wood, plus a range of hand-held drills, and multi-purpose tools, such as the Black & Decker Workmate workbench.

In 1994 Black & Decker launched the Snakelight, an adaptable, flexible light that can be bent to rest in almost any position, and can even be hung around the neck.

RECENT DEVELOPMENTS

Black & Decker's recent relaunch under the 'New Generation' banner, signifies a new era for the brand, one which, it is hoped, is the beginning of a renaissance in the DIY industry, that is slowly recovering from the recession. This New Generation of DIY tools, with new packaging, and a new advertising strategy, is the culmination of a massive three year research and development programme, in which the company has spent £500,000 on end-user research alone.

The most immediately visible difference in New Generation power tools is the new jade coloured casing, replacing the former black tool casing. Extensive research of over 500 different colours found jade was a colour which signified reliability, quality and durability. In addition, tools are designed with special textured grips, soft feel triggers and a host of other useful features, such as Twistlok keyless chuck.

The packaging too has changed, with the power tool products now coming in fully recyclable, cardboard boxes. Package design incorporates a full picture of the product, with clear line drawings, and pictograms, highlighting the tool's key features and benefits.

The most recent development from Black & Decker however, is the introduction of the VersaPak range of cordless tools for the home and garden. The range of ten tools, including a variable speed drill, the Snakelight torch and a grass shear, are powered by rechargeable cylindrical battery 'sticks', meaning that the consumer will only need to invest in batteries

and a charger once. Apart from the environmental benefits gained by using rechargable batteries, the batteries themselves have been designed to be fully recyclable. Black & Decker has set up a Europe-wide network of collection points for used batteries, which will eventually be reprocessed at a special plant in France.

PROMOTION

Black & Decker has always had an innovative approach to promoting itself, and its many products. One of the earliest examples of this was shown in 1928, when they capitalised on the novelty value of flight and air travel by acquiring an airplane. This was a specially outfitted 6-person monoplane, and was used as a flying showroom to demonstrate how their power tools could be used in the reconditioning of aircraft engines.

Black & Decker also recognised the advantage of mass-media coverage at a very early stage, and carried full page advertisements in the Saturday Evening Post, a popular US newspaper of the time.

The company's first foray into network television came as early as 1955, with a series of TV advertisements for its power tools. It continues today to have a high profile through its TV advertising, especially in the US. Its UK promotions have also focused on in-store demonstrations and videos, and direct marketing campaigns, including the recent magazine 'Possibilities'.

Black & Decker has historically been one of the biggest promotional spenders in the DIY sector, and committed £4.5 million to advertising in 1995 alone.

The company has recently launched a massive new campaign to coincide with the New Generation theme. A distinctive lighthouse symbol forms the central theme to the New Generation TV advertising campaign in Europe. This new campaign represents a doubling of the company's promotional spend.

BRAND VALUES

With its range of tools for the home and garden, Black & Decker has come to represent three main values: quality, durability and reliability.

With all its tools, whether it is lawn mowers for the garden, or drills for the house, Black & Decker's prides itself on the technical

superiority of its products. Nowadays, this has become especially important, given that tools from the Far East, previously regarded as inferior, have been significantly improved.

Black & Decker has always shown a high degree of innovation. The company has introduced a number of completely new tools into the home, such as the Workmate workbench, the Multisander, a three-in-one sander, the Reflex Strimmer grass trimmer and the Snakelight torch.

Black & Decker has succeeded in changing gardening, and other household tasks which were previously regarded as chores, into hobbies enjoyed by millions.

Black & Decker continues to put the excitement back into power tools, as shown by its latest innovation with the VersaPak range.

Things you didn't know about Black & Decker

○ As part of Black & Decker's 75th anniversary celebrations in 1985, a time capsule, including all sorts of company memorabilia, and products, was placed in the company's newly renovated buildings at Towson. It will remain sealed until 2085.

○ 8 out of 10 households in the UK own at least one Black & Decker product.

○ The Black & Decker Workmate - the multi-purpose workbench - was invented by Ron Hickman, designer of the Lotus Elan sports car, in 1961.

○ Over 50 million Dustbusters - the hand-held household cleaner - are sold worldwide per year.

○ The power products sector is one where customers like the reassurance of a premium product. The best-selling Black & Decker Dustbuster, for example, is not the £20 model, but the Dustbuster Turbo unit at over £30.

○ Black & Decker operates 41 service stations countrywide.

○ Black & Decker offers a 2 year guarantee on all of its products with a 3 year guarantee on gardening products.

○ Black & Decker's tool production plant at Spennymoor is the biggest of its kind in the world.

THE MARKET

The UK new car market rose to 1.95 million units in 1995, but is still short of the all time high of 2.3 million units in 1989. The car market proved once again to be a reliable indicator of the fortunes of the British economy. The prospects for the market over the next five years show growth to around 2 million units being achieved again. Since 1993, there has been a structural change in the market with increases in company car taxation causing more people to consider the opportunity to purchase their own car.

In addition, the increase in availability of new finance schemes for private and business buyers has been a feature of the market.

It is, however, true to say that company cars remain the dominating influence on the market accounting for possibly around a half of cars sold.

Imported cars continue to take a share of around 50% of all cars sold in the UK.

ACHIEVEMENTS

BMW is one of the most famous car companies in the world, to the extent that one in 10 of every new cars sold in the luxury car market today in Great Britain bears the famous blue and white roundel.

BMW has an enviable reputation for leading edge design, technology and engineering which together with skilful marketing has contributed to sales in the UK trebling since 1980. If BMW's sales had grown at the same rate as the rest of the UK car market, around 300,000 BMWs would have been sold between 1980 and 1995. In fact, BMW outperformed the market and sold over 550,000 cars. The UK is BMW's third largest market after Germany and America.

15 years of consistent advertising have given BMW brand values which focus on understatement and exclusivity derived from the car itself. BMW does not rely on borrowed values. This advertising has consistently won awards, culminating in the IPA Advertising Effectiveness Grand Prix Award in 1994 which demonstrated that strong creative advertising can sell cars as well as building an image.

BMW does not rely on heritage to promote its products, relying instead on a forward looking approach which is based on contemporary appraisal of the product and its market.

HISTORY

Bayerische Motoren Werke (BMW) was founded in the early 1900s as an aircraft engine manufacturer. From this, the "spinning propeller" logo was derived.

The company is now best known for its motorcars and motorcycles, although through a link with Rolls Royce it is also responsible for the manufacture of aircraft engines once again.

BMW's role in manufacturing aircraft engines was previously truncated by the post Second World War Treaty of Versailles.

BMW's renaissance really started only in 1966 when the BMW 1502 was introduced. This car is largely credited with introducing the concept of the sports saloon.

During the 1920s and 30s BMW did, however, have a number of notable successes including the classic

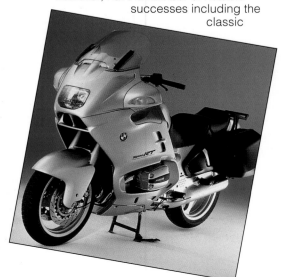

BMW 328 which started production in 1936 and in 1940 won the famous Mille Miglia, a 1000 mile road race around Italy.

In 1955 BMW Motorcycles won an incredible 57 world records and in 1983 BMW developed a power unit for Brabham which helped Nelson Piquet to win the Formula One motor racing championship.

In 1980, when BMW established its wholly-owned subsidiary, BMW (GB) Ltd, some 13,000 BMWs were sold in Great Britain. In 1995, this had grown to a new record total of 55,000 sales. The product range has been considerably expanded since then but continues to provide cars which incorporate outstanding quality, technology, performance and, of course, exclusivity, truly cars which deserve the title, "The Ultimate Driving Machine".

THE PRODUCT

BMW cars epitomise the finest design, engineering and quality available in motoring today. The core values that are used to promote the brand accurately reflect the product itself.

Quality, technology, performance and exclusivity are the cornerstones of BMW's reputation. Research and Development is an absolute priority for the company. BMW is thought to spend a higher percentage of its turnover on Research and Development than any other company. Its Research and Development Centre in Munich is home to over 5,000 designers and engineers.

From this strong base, BMW designs cars that develop a well established theme. Revolution is not a word within the BMW vocabulary. There is no need for this type of approach because BMW has always been at the cutting edge of technology and hence its cars are always in the vanguard of automotive design and engineering.

That difficult word "style" is often used to characterise the appeal of BMW and indeed there is a definite BMW style. By maintaining key motifs such as the classic kidney grille a BMW is recognised anywhere in the world. The clear differentiation between the model Series 3, 5, 7 and 8 also provides a simple route map for consumers. Many other manufacturers have sought to emulate this concept of house style but precious few have succeeded.

Innovation and technology go hand in hand at BMW. The company is renowned as an engine company and so many of its advances have been in the area of driveline technology.

When BMW talks of performance, the company means dynamic performance, more of a concern for BMW than mere straight-line acceleration or an ability to go around corners quickly, rather a view that a car should be balanced and harmonious in all of its areas of operation. The feel of a switch, the positioning of the steering wheel, the lighting of the instrument panel are just as important as the feel of the suspension and the engine. This is what makes one BMW feel so similar to the next. It is a strong belief in product pedigree, coupled with a desire to continuously push back the bounds of automotive technology that creates cars that can be truly described as unique.

With such a strong brand image and broad product portfolio it is sometimes all too easy to forget that BMW also manufactures fine motorcycles as well.

BMW has produced over one million motorcycles and every second one ever made is still in operation. The design philosophy inherent in the BMW motorcar is also apparent in its motorcycles. It is noteworthy that its classic twin cylinder horizontally opposed 'Boxer' engine has just been completely redesigned after a 60 year history of success. Once again, this points out the evolutionary approach that BMW takes to its products.

BMW now produces over 500,000 motorcars a year and in excess of 50,000 motorcycles. Whilst this makes BMW a modest player in comparison with the major international car and motorcycle manufacturers it should be borne in mind that none of BMW's products operate in the so-called mass market.

RECENT DEVELOPMENTS

By the middle of 1998, BMW will have launched completely new 3, and 5 Series cars together with outstanding new products such as the two-seater sports car which will be known as the Z3 'Roadster'.

The range of cars that BMW now makes is wider than ever before. By the time the Z3 Roadster is launched, it will encompass two seater sports cars, four seater convertibles, 3

door hatchbacks, 4 door saloons, 2 door Coupes and 5 door estates. In terms of engines there will be 4, 6, 8 and 12 cylinder petrol engines together with 4 and 6 cylinder turbo-diesel engines.

PROMOTION

Much of BMW's success in Great Britain is attributed to its marketing. Managers within the company are quick, however, to point out that the best marketing in the world cannot enhance a poor product and in the case of BMW the product's substance is absolute.

BMW's primary marketing weapon over the last fifteen years has been advertising. The campaign created by agency WCRS, has proved extraordinarily effective. Indeed, a paper describing the effect of the advertising since 1980 won the IPA's Grand Prix Award for advertising effectiveness in 1994. During the period covered, BMW's sales trebled in Great Britain against a backdrop in Europe as a whole which would have shown nearly a doubling in sales had it not been for this

consistent and concerted advertising campaign.

BMW's advertising avoids using people, situations or stories which detract from the car itself. Nothing must hint at fallibility. As Deyan Sudjic, Editorial Director of the design and architecture magazine Blueprint says "BMW is the first car company to treat us as grown ups, to move beyond giving its products the obvious lures of glittering chrome and superfluous styling mannerisms .... just as there is no such thing as a cheap BMW, there is no such thing as an ostentatious one .... it doesn't have to raise its voice to gain respect. And, like a well cut suit, it has an identity but does not seek to impose its personality on its user".

Initially the campaign relied on double-page colour spread advertising in the Sunday colour supplements to the point where readers came to expect that the first advertisement in the magazine would be for BMW. The so-called brand campaign was subsequently moved on to television with innovative 20 second commercials. BMW's "sniper" strategy targeted particular programmes and relied on a large number of individual commercials, each one centring on a different aspect of the BMW product, thereby creating a mosaic. A dramatic advertising campaign recently launched the fourth-generation BMW 5 Series.

Emphasising the high-contrast black and white film using a state-of-the-art technique known as 'solarisation'. The commercial depicted the latest BMW model balancing on one side of a huge set of scales, with the car's component parts resting on the other. This and accompanying advertisements in other media focuses on the car's technological improvements over its predecessor and new body shape.

Recognising the importance of new media, BMW launched a creative, practical and interactive presence on the Internet in January 1996. BMW's site (http://www.bmw.co.uk) is part of a strategy that offers genuine customer benefits, which complement and expand BMW's communications channels. For example, BMW is the first automotive manufacturer to create a database of available cars to a user-defined set of parameters. In addition, the site offers visitors entertainment in the form of a screensaver which can be downloaded to reveal the BMW Z3 Roadster, James Bond's new car.

MORE LITRES, LESS GALLONS.

BRAND VALUES

BMW has used the expression "The Ultimate Driving Machine" for over 15 years. This remark succinctly expresses BMW's brand position and is always played back by consumers in research as summarising exactly what they feel about the brand.

BMW sees no need to move away from its four core values of quality, technology, performance and exclusivity.

There is clearly a market for this proposition since 1996 and beyond is expected to show a consolidation of volume sales for BMW in Great Britain with total volume sales consistently exceeding 50,000 cars.

Things you didn't know about BMW

○ BMW runs a series of April Fool's Day advertisements which feature "almost" believable technical innovations, such as a steering wheel which changes side for continental driving, a mini-windscreen wiper for the BMW badge, a multi-lingual in-car computer which can interpret the language of the country you happen to be in and a convertible which can keep out the rain, even with its roof open. They may sound ludicrous, but over the years hundreds of people have fallen hook, line and sinker. They also play an essential part in BMW's brand strategy in reinforcing the understated humour of the ads which run year-round and are, at face value, relentlessly factual.

○ Sales of BMW in Britain are outperforming the overall car market.

○ There are over 500,000 BMWs on British roads.

○ BMW is the predominant feature of a mobile art collection: BMW Art Cars. This collection consists of professional artists, such as Andy Warhol, Ken Done, David Hockney and César Manriqe, decorating a different BMW as they choose.

○ In the latest James Bond film, Goldeneye, starring Pierce Brosnan, a BMW Z3 Roadster is used as Bond's new company car, replacing the previous famous Bond cars, such as Aston Martin and Lotus.

○ One of the world's fastest and most expensive production cars, the McLaren F1, uses a BMW 6-litre V12 engine, generating 627 bhp.

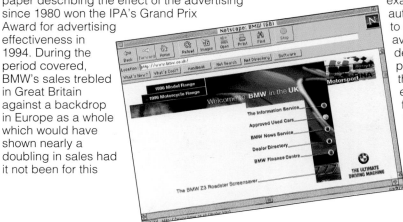

The BMW Z3 Roadster Screensaver.

THE MARKET

Since the last century, meat and vegetable extract pastes have been a popular feature in UK larders.

Prized for their versatility, nutritional value and strong flavour, meat and vegetable extract pastes are consumed on toast, as a sandwich spread, as a reviving warm drink and they can enhance a wide variety of dishes, from casseroles and stews to gravies.

In 1996, the total UK market for meat and vegetable extract pastes was worth £34,466,000m on a MAT basis (Nielsen. 20 Jan 1996). Together, two brands, BOVRIL, a meat extract paste, and MARMITE, a vegetable extract paste, took the lions share of all sales in this sector. Both brands are part of the CPC (United Kingdom) Ltd portfolio.

ACHIEVEMENTS

BOVRIL is one of the UK's best-known brands, with a history stretching back to the 1870s. Steered by innovative advertising, including a long series of well-loved poster campaigns, the meat extract paste has enjoyed consistent popularity.

The brand's heyday just goes on and on. Annual sales of BOVRIL paste are now worth approximately £10 million. The healthy association BOVRIL holds has as much relevance for us today as it did during the harsh years of two world wars and the Great Depression of the 1930s.

The fame of this brand has extended beyond the UK. It is sold throughout the world and is manufactured at Burton-on-Trent in England.

HISTORY

BOVRIL meat extract paste was first produced by a Scotsman, John Lawson Johnston, who was working for the French Government in 1871. Following the siege of Paris during the Franco-Prussian War, when the city had literally been starved into surrender, the French were wary of this ever happening again. Johnston was charged with the responsibility to stock up emergency supplies of canned meat for the French forts, to ensure they avoided a similar fate to Paris.

This commission gave Johnston the opportunity to develop a meat extract paste that he had already conceived in a laboratory. The resulting product was called Johnston's Fluid Beef.

In 1874, Johnston moved to Canada where he started commercial production of his meat extract at Sherbrooke, near Montreal. However, demand for the paste grew so rapidly, production had to be moved to a larger site in Montreal. Johnston's Fluid Beef was further popularised at carnival time, when free samples were distributed to the crowds.

However, a fire which destroyed the Montreal factory in 1884 precipitated Johnston's return to the UK.

He kickstarted production of his meat extract paste at 10 Trinity Square in London. Again, the

public were invited to sample his product for free at the Colonial and Continental Exhibition in South Kensington in 1886.

The paste was renamed BOVRIL, after Bo, meaning Ox in Latin, and -Vril, derived from

vrilya, the name given to mean 'life-force' in a novel, The Coming Race, by Bulwer Lytton. Johnston once admitted to a journalist that the name came to him "over a cigar".

The BOVRIL brand was boosted from 1893 onwards when a former employee, S. H. Benson, turned his hand to advertising, starting his own agency. BOVRIL was the first major brand he worked on.

Advertisements for BOVRIL have become famous with many of the brand's early posters valued as collectors items.

The success of the BOVRIL brand was not limited to the UK. Even as early as 1901, BOVRIL was being advertised as far afield as Africa, South America, Australasia, India, South East Asia and most of Europe. Using local agents, the producers of BOVRIL meat extract always ensured that advertising drew on local customs, culture and of course, language, to best promote the brand's distinctive taste and healthy properties.

The BOVRIL brand has continued to woo the British public with skilful advertising up to the present day, although sadly, the major poster campaigns were abandoned in the 1960s in favour of increased TV and press advertising.

The brand's long association with MARMITE, its 100% vegetarian yeast extract 'cousin', started in 1924, when Bovril Ltd's chairman, Sir George Lawson Johnston - a descendant of the company founder - merged some of the company's interests. Marmite Ltd eventually became a subsidiary of Bovril Limited. In 1990, both the BOVRIL and MARMITE brands were taken over by CPC (UK) Ltd.

THE PRODUCT

BOVRIL is a concentrated paste of meat and vegetable extracts. It is currently produced in two flavours: beef and chicken. It is also available as stock cubes.

BOVRIL is popular as a spread and as a drink. With its rich dark colour and meaty taste, the beef variant of BOVRIL is also commonly used as a cooking ingredient to 'beef up' stews, casseroles, sauces and gravies.

One of the basic raw materials of BOVRIL is yeast, which is the richest natural source of 5 B group vitamins including Folic Acid, which is essential for mothers-to-be as it helps prevent spina bifida. Other vitamins yeast contains include Thiamin, Riboflavin, Niacin and Vitamin B12.

RECENT DEVELOPMENTS

In recent years, the BOVRIL brand has 'sponsored' Bonfire Night. After all, what could be better on a cold November night than a cup of hot BOVRIL? This message has been relayed via radio and TV advertising and in-store promotions.

Overall, between 1994 and 1995, penetration of the BOVRIL brand declined from 7.4% to 6.9%, although the 65-plus age-group was shown to be as loyal as ever, with penetration actually rising from 9.4% to 9.9%.

PROMOTION

It is difficult to sum up the legacy of the advertising of the BOVRIL brand, which is almost a history of British advertising itself.

From the outset, the promoters of BOVRIL built a brand identity based on the virtues of its health-giving meat extract, using a stream of poster images and testimonials from the likes of Dr Livingstone. Early advertisements were largely educational in content, asserting the nutritional value over and above similar 'beef tea' products. This approach clearly proved efficacious as sales soared.

However, it was the outbreak of the Boer War which really underlined the advertising credentials of BOVRIL. The coinciding campaign enforced the view that BOVRIL was nothing less than 'Liquid Life'. Some 85,000lbs of BOVRIL was supplied to soldiers in Africa - a fact which was emblazoned in press advertisements. One advert even set out to show how Lord Roberts, Britain's general, and his men followed a route through South Africa which spelt out the word BOVRIL. In addition, "Bovril War Cables", a fleet of khaki-clad cyclists, distributed war news around London.

The advertising team working on the BOVRIL brand, headed by S.H. Benson, always capitalised upon testimonials from the famous and great. In 1904, the BOVRIL brand gained useful publicity from its use by Captain Scott (of the Antarctic) and five years later it was taken by Shackleton on another Antarctic expedition. His saying, "It must be BOVRIL" became the cornerstone of an advertising campaign.

A series of promotional stunts followed, which included an airship in 1913 and a "log rolling" championship, where the public were invited to balance on a 'log' of 'BOVRIL tins' for a full five minutes.

Shackleton's former testimonial, "It must be BOVRIL" took on fresh meaning during the years of the Great War from 1914 to 1918.

For gardeners with blue fingers.

Gone were the days of fun advertising and slapstick promotions. The healthy proposition BOVRIL held, in particular to ward off influenza (a major killer at the time) and chills was emphasised.

After the war, however, the mood changed again, and a new campaign, featuring a pyjama-clad man armed with his BOVRIL, coined the catchphrase, "BOVRIL prevents that sinking feeling". This originated from a 'Golfer's Score Book' which the makers of BOVRIL had produced as far back as 1890, written by a Mr Horace Hutchinson.

During the 1920s and 1930s, posters for BOVRIL were seen everywhere - at railway stations, on buses, in press advertising and cartoons. The product's battle on the public's behalf to fend off fatigue and illness strongly figured.

The Second World War curbed the output of BOVRIL paste, both in terms of advertising and in production. Any advertising was patriotic in tone, and in 1942, once supplies had dried up, a poster declared that BOVRIL "doffs the cap to the splendid women of Britain," who proved such a valuable force sustaining the home front.

Post-war advertising

introduced "Little BOVRIL", a friendly, little bull-calf. He contrasted strongly with a 'beefier' bull emblem used in previous advertising under the slogan "Alas! My poor brother". The "Little BOVRIL" character was put to good use in TV advertising, initiated in the 1950s, where he would magically come to the aid of harassed housewives.

The 1960s saw the revival of an old slogan, "Fitness without fatness", in keeping with the weight-conscious concerns of the British public. "Drink your health in BOVRIL" was a slogan accompanying TV advertisements at the time. Gradually, TV and press advertising took over from the traditional posters, in what was seen as a new promotional era, although the long-lived association of BOVRIL with sporting achievement continued.

The makers of BOVRIL have also become increasingly aware of the importance of promotion at point of sale, although emphasis has been placed on attractive shop window displays since the start of the century.

BRAND VALUES

The heritage of BOVRIL as a reliable, healthy food source has raised the brand to the status of one of Britain's best-loved brands.

Renowned worldwide for its distinctive taste, BOVRIL has been valued by the discerning public for over a hundred years. Its legacy of imaginative, often humorous, advertising has ensured it enjoys huge brand recognition. Despite the product's initial development in France in 1871, and its original launch in Canada, since arriving in Britain in 1884, BOVRIL has become a thoroughly British brand.

BOVRIL is a registered trademark of CPC International Inc.

Things you didn't know about BOVRIL

❍ Over five million jars of BOVRIL paste are bought every year. This amounts to an estimated 98 million mugs of BOVRIL drink.

❍ In British Columbia, Canada, BOVRIL is still known by its original name - Johnston's Fluid Beef. A similar product, BOVRIL Cordial, is the best-selling BOVRIL product in Canada.

❍ The longest and dullest advertising slogan for BOVRIL ever is thought to be "For over 40 years millions of men and women have proved the unique sustaining and energising powers of BOVRIL". This was devised in 1932.

BRITISH AIRWAYS

THE MARKET

The start of the 1990s proved to be a difficult period for the airline industry. A host of issues, including recession, increased deregulation, reduced air fares, and fierce competition wrought great changes in the airline industry as a whole. One of the most unsettling factors was the Gulf War in 1991, but this was an abnormal occurrence.

There are currently 800,000 international schedule passengers travelling by air each day. This number will increase as some of the most populous areas of the world, such as India and China, take to the skies as a convenient method of travel. Predicted long term growth isn't only limited to the world's untapped markets. North America, Europe and increasingly, the Pacific region, are still important markets in which a successful airline must stake a presence.

ACHIEVEMENTS

British Airways is the world's leading international passenger airline, and certainly one of the most profitable. In 1994/5 the airline's pre-tax profits amounted to £452 million (before £125 million investment in USAir) - its best ever performance. This was an impressive achievement in view of the troubles that have recently beset the industry as a whole.

British Airways carried a total of 35 million passengers in 1994/5. On its international scheduled services, British Airways carried 24 million passengers in 1994, amounting to 6.5 million more than its nearest international rival.

Through a series of global alliances, British Airways now covers some 492 scheduled destinations in 99 countries worldwide, and offers an average 7,000 departures per day.

In 1994, British Airways also broke records in cargo-handling. Some 660,000 tonnes were carried.

As the airline which has been repeatedly voted as the world's best airline by the readers of "Business Traveller" magazine, British Airways aims to ensure that such appreciation endures. British Airways has as its hallmark, quality of service, customer loyalty and a dedicated workforce committed to the continuance of the airline's operational and financial excellence.

HISTORY

British Airways, "The World's Favourite Airline", launched the world into the age of jet and supersonic flight. Its predecessor, Aircraft Transport and Travel Ltd (AT&T) launched the world's first daily international scheduled air service between London and Paris.

The first service operated from Hounslow Heath, (a far cry from Heathrow, although not in distance). The first cargo consisted of a single passenger, a bundle of newspapers, Devonshire cream and grouse.

Two more fledgling airline companies soon commenced flights to Paris and Brussels. However, in those days flying was more of an adventure than one of life's more pleasurable experiences. For instance, one pilot took two days for the two hour flight to Paris and was forced to make 33 emergency landings on the way.

In 1924 the four main British airline companies merged to form Imperial Airways. Services continued to Paris and Brussels, and were extended to Basle, Zurich and Cologne. During the 1920s and 1930s, flights started to move further afield to Egypt, the Arabian Gulf, Africa and Singapore.

The first service to Australia was initiated in 1935, in co-operation with Qantas Empire Airways. In the same year, a number of new airlines merged to form British Airways Ltd. This was now Imperial Airway's main rival operating out of Gatwick, however, following a Government review, Imperial Airways and British Airways Ltd were nationalised in 1939 to form British Overseas Airways Corporation (B.O.A.C.).

Under the auspices of BOAC, long-haul flights were instigated and the continent was served by a new airline, British European Airways (B.E.A.). Air travel was revolutionised in the 1950s with the introduction of the Comet - a passenger jet which halved previous flying times. After two tragic crashes which set back its progress by some years, BOAC was still the first airline to operate the jet transatlantic flight in 1958. Two BOAC jets flew simultaneously from London and New York, days ahead of their American rival.

In the following decade, the changes in the airline industry came thick and fast - firstly the package holiday was born. BEA took the

challenge head-on by establishing a charter airline BEA Airtours. BEA also claimed a first with its Trident aircraft making the world's inaugural automatic landing, allowing aircraft to land in poor visibility for the first time.

In 1967 the government recommended that a holding board be established to oversee both BOAC and BEA. A conglomerate of independents were formed into a second force airline. In 1970, following British Caledonian Airways merger with British United Airways, British Caledonian Airways was established. Two years later, both BOAC and BEA were bought together under the newly formed British Airways Board. The separate airlines became British Airways in 1974.

This new airline was to launch the world's first supersonic passenger service, Concorde in 1976. Three years later, the Government announced its intention to sell shares in British Airways. This finally happened in 1987. After having once been widely regarded as "Bloody Awful", British Airways had become "Bloody Awesome". The company had been in the midst of clawing itself back from debt but British Airways' financial situation was set for a massive turnaround. A new First Class service was launched in 1989, in the same year that the Boeing 747-400 entered service.

THE PRODUCT

British Airways has one of the largest fleets of any airline in the world, with over 283 aircraft currently in operation. The latest addition to British Airway's fleet is the Boeing 777, the world's largest twin jet, capable of carrying up to 400 passengers.

The most famous member of British Airways' comprehensive aircraft fleet must be Concorde, the flagship of the fleet. It is certainly unrivalled in terms of its sheer speed, and has crossed the Atlantic on several occasions in less than three hours.

All British Airways aircraft are equipped for convenience, comfort and reliability. A broad range of services ensures that all the needs of each type of traveller are catered for. Quality service, in-flight entertainment, varied healthy menus and added comforts such as the Well Being in the Air programme, which is designed to prepare you for the perfect flight, and to help you feel at your best on arrival, are featured on British Airways flights.

Friendly, comprehensive service isn't just reserved for the airborne, British Airways has also invested heavily in facilities on the ground. Specially trained staff, excellent check-in facilities and Fast Track at Heathrow and Gatwick ensure a faster, smoother and easier journey.

Frequent travellers who belong to the British Airways Executive Club worldwide loyalty programme also enjoy enhanced benefits and incentives, including access to a network of dedicated lounges around the world (Silver and Gold members), priority waitlist, recorded seat preference and Hertz Chauffeur Drive (UK).

In addition to its core airline operations, British Airways is also a significant player in the package holiday operators market. British Airways Holidays offers a selection of programmes, including longhaul holidays, city breaks and specialist golf holidays.

RECENT DEVELOPMENTS

In recent years British Airways has set itself the goal of becoming a truly global airline. Since 1990 British Airways has contributed to the setting up of a new international airline, Deutsche BA, with a consortium of German banks; acquired a stake in USAir, one of America's largest domestic airlines, and a stake in French independent TAT airlines. British Airways bought 25% of the Australian airline Qantas, as well as teaming up with Maersk Air, Brymon, CityFlyer Express, GB Airways and Manx Airlines Europe. In addition to being one of the world's biggest and most popular airlines, the "World's Favourite Airline" is now fast becoming a global player through these alliances.

A variety of new British Airways services and facilities have been introduced. In 1995, British Airways announced a £500 million drive to relaunch its Club World longhaul business brand and Executive Club frequent flyer brand, with an emphasis on 'comfort, personal service, flexibility and choice'.

The new service, simply called 'First' ensures passengers are more cocooned during their journey. In Club World, the space between rows of seats has been increased and redesigned "cradle" seats with a unique ergonomically-designed tilting base introduced. Passengers are now able to get a good night's sleep while flying. On Boeing 747s, 14 individual cabins offering a 6ft 6ins bed have been introduced.

The bed can be converted into a visitor's chair at the touch of a button. The compartments, complete with a personal entertainment system, pearwood finish, grey and silver trim, leather and textured fabrics, have been designed by design consultants Davies Barron and yacht interior experts Design Acumen.

World Traveller, the airline's main cabin on intercontinental flights, has also been relaunched with more comfortable seats and an interactive entertainment and information system providing 24 video/audio channels, video games, a telephone and shopping.

Ensuring that their customers never go hungry, British Airways now provides Club World

passengers with an in-flight larder full of nibbles. An à la carte restaurant service is also on board, offering haute cuisine. The menu was devised with the advice of top chef Michel Roux.

PROMOTION

British Airways has always been acclaimed for its advertising. TV advertising has embraced the airline's position as one which encompasses the world with its exceptional and friendly service.

Earlier advertising forged the patriotic identity of British Airways as something to be truly proud of, with the slogan "Fly the Flag", however the global reach of the brand today is such that British Airways' corporate identity constitutes a wholly cosmopolitan flavour as portrayed in their fully integrated global advertising campaign,

"Feeling Good" in October 1992. Nine years earlier, British Airways had launched its classic campaign "Manhattan Landing" which depicted Manhattan coming down to land.

The benefits of each sub-brand are communicated by means of TV, press and poster advertising, as well as by direct mail. This significant investment is supported by specific brand teams who pay attention to every aspect of customer service.

For example, British Airways' premium Club World service, with added features such as the cradle seat and in-flight larders, is highlighted in the 'Slingshot' campaign. A further ongoing advertising campaign, World Offers, promotes British Airways' UK sales, and was duly honoured at the prestigious Creative Circle Awards Ceremony in 1996.

In general, mass-media advertising highlights the overall image of British Airways, with direct mail campaigns identifying product and service benefits. British Airways recognises the needs of each and every passenger. This is underlined in the 'Masterbrand' campaign, which focuses on how British Airways provides an unrivaled service

- how it does not merely treat passengers as freight but realises that each of its passengers has hopes, dreams and ambitions of their own. This serves to highlight that British Airways is the World's Favourite Airline.

BRAND VALUES

British Airways' excellence is exemplified in the high quality of its services and the airline's consistent self-improvement and innovation. It is also the world's first truly global airline thanks to a series of solid alliances forged around the world.

The pioneering spirit of British Airways has always shone through and is a powerful driving force behind the brand. The airline has become particularly noted for its exceptional customer service, matched with the breadth of its network and total commitment to safety.

Things you didn't know about British Airways

- On average, a British Airways passenger checks-in every second, 24 hours a day, 365 days a year.

- A British Airways aircraft takes off or lands somewhere in the world every single minute.

- British Airways has more than 100 travel shops and offices in cities and airport locations around the world.

- British Airways shares its expertise by offering training and services to other companies through its subsidiary Speedwing Consulting in the areas of aircraft and passenger handling, engineering, training and information technology.

- Unlike many of the world's other leading airlines, British Airways is owned entirely by private investors - with almost a quarter of a million shareholders, including many of the company's own employees.

- British Airway's new "cradle" seats have been medically endorsed by Dr John O'Brien, a leading UK back specialist.

- British Airway's Club World in-flight "larder" facility offers snacks suited to everybody's tastes. Everyone enjoys Babybel cheese portions, hot croissants, Mars and Snickers bars. However, the Japanese favour the rice crackers and pot noodles, while the Americans seem to have the sweetest tooth, opting for popcorn and pretzels.

- British Airways has introduced nasal strips, which prevent snoring, on a number of its flights, to help ensure that everyone gets an undisturbed night's sleep.

THE MARKET

The $1.5trn global telecoms industry is undergoing sweeping changes.

Deregulation of the telecoms industry spells the end to closed markets and state-owned monoliths. The UK market was the first to open up to competition, introducing a duopoly between British Telecommunications and Mercury which lasted until 1991. The advent of cable operators, offering both telephony and entertainment services, has signalled a new competitive era for UK telecoms.

Throughout the world, similar changes are afoot. Early 1996 saw new US telecoms legislation freeing up the telecoms and cable markets. 1998 signals pan-European deregulation.

Telecom companies are having to review their status as traditional conveyors of voice and fax communications alone. International alliances and the potential delivery of interactive TV and online services are high on the agenda.

ACHIEVEMENTS

BT has transformed itself from British Telecom, the state owned, impersonal monolith into a high profile, dynamic international company, actively pursuing worldwide success.

BT was incorporated as a public limited company in the UK in 1984. It has more than 2.5 million shareholders and is listed in the Stock Exchange in London, New York, Toronto and Tokyo.

BT's vision is to become the most successful worldwide telecommunications group. The company's strategy is to increase revenues in the UK market - now the most open and competitive in the world, with more than 150 licensed operators; to expand into new services such as interactive TV and multimedia; and to expand overseas in chosen markets, both alone and through partnerships.

BT had a turnover of £13,893 million in the financial year to 31 March 1995, up from £13,675 million the year before. Profit before tax to the end of March 1995 was £2,662 million, compared with £2,756 million the year before.

In 1994 BT's UK operation became the largest single organisation in the world to receive company-wide registration under the international quality standard ISO 9001.

BT continues to build a global reputation as one of the leading players in the international telecommunications market. Over recent years it has built a series of partnerships which span the globe with a particular focus on North America, Europe and Asia Pacific.

BT has a 20 per cent stake in MCI, the second largest North American long-distance carrier. This deal led to the setting up of Concert, a $1 billion joint venture company which offers a one-stop communications facility for the world's major companies.

In Europe, BT is involved in joint ventures with Banco Santander, Spain's largest bank; the German industrial group, VIAG; and Banco Nazionale del Lavoro in Italy, with a

new company called Albacom. In Japan, BT struck deals with Nippon Information and Communication (NI+C), and the Marubeni Corporation. In India, BT formed an alliance with Wipro, a market leader in IT.

HISTORY

For many years, the UK's telephone service was provided by the General Post Office, which was a government department. In 1969, the Post Office became a state public corporation and was split into two separate entities. The corporation responsible for telecommunications took on the trading name British Telecommunications, or British Telecom as it was popularly called. Then, in 1984, British Telecom was privatised, and made its debut on the London Stock Exchange.

British Telecommunications plc was the first privatised company of its kind in Europe. Instantly it set about sweeping changes. In 1985, Cellnet, the British Telecom and Securicor joint venture cellular radio service was launched.

British Telecom began breaking new grounds by building the world's first undersea optical fibre cable laid to the Isle of Wight. An international optical fibre cable was to link the UK and Belgium in

1986. In addition, the first video-conferencing service was introduced from the UK to Canada, later extended to the United States.

In 1991, British Telecom was restructured and relaunched as BT, with a clear mission of putting customers first. The new Customer's Charter was announced and the half-way stage in switching local exchanges to digital working was reached.

In 1992, BT's 100,000th public payphone came into service. Malicious calls bureaux were set up throughout the country. The Videophone was demonstrated at the Ideal Home Exhibition.

THE PRODUCT

BT is one of the world's leading providers of telecommunications services in one of the fastest growing worldwide markets. Its main products and services are local, long-distance and international calls (with direct call connection to more than 230 countries): telephone lines, equipment and private circuits for homes and businesses; providing and managing private networks; and supplying mobile communications services.

BT spends approximately £2 billion every year on modernising and expanding its network.

Since privatisation, it has spent more than £20 billion. July 1995 saw a major milestone reached when all BT's old analogue exchanges were replaced, which paved the way for the launch of per second pricing. Today over 7,000 digital and modern electronic local exchanges serve all BT customers, giving them access to a range of network services including itemised billing, Call Waiting, Caller Display, Call Return and Three Way Calling.

BT is fully committed to research and development. It currently invests over £270 million per year in the development of products, network services and information critical to BT's future and to the ultimate benefit of its customers. These include optical fibre technology, ISDN (BT's Integrated Services Digital Network, which makes possible high transmission of high quality

voice, data, image and text, in any combination) and BT's interactive media services.

Faced with intense competition from more than 150 licensed operators - including Mercury Communications and cable companies - BT has consolidated its position as the only telecoms company capable of offering national coverage and local service with an unrivalled portfolio of products and services.

RECENT DEVELOPMENTS

On June 28th 1995, BT introduced one of the most radical changes to its pricing structure in 50 years with the introduction of per second pricing. Today customers pay for the exact time they use, apart from a minimum charge of 5p, whether they are calling a number in the UK or abroad. Weekend local rate calls cost just a penny a minute.

BT is at the centre of the explosive growth in mobile communications through BT Mobile and Cellnet - with over 2.4 million registered customers and the number swelling by approximately one per cent per week.

Significant progress has been made in the field of remote diagnostics through Camnet, a headset incorporating a video camera which relays pictures from a remote location down a high-speed ISDN line.

In April 1996 BT launched BT Internet, the access service which gives customers everything they need to get going on the Internet - software, a unique e-mail address, access via a local call nationwide to the full range of Internet services and 7 days a week Customer Service. In partnership with games publisher Gremlin, BT also launched its own video games network, Wireplay, which offers multiplayer competitions for up to 20 participants at once. Accessible to anyone with a PC and modem, Wireplay had 350,000 customers hooked up by the end of 1995.

PROMOTION

From day one of its privatisation, BT has dedicated itself to completely integrated branding at every possible level. The BT 'Piper' corporate mark was designed to symbolise the process of communication, in that the figure is both listening and calling. The logo represents a human figure, to ensure a sense of familiarity.

This accessibility is matched by BT's professionalism in everything it does. BT's public face combines confidence with a helping, guiding and responsive approach in all communications, whether it be by letter, bill or direct mail advertising.

It is the BT brand position of valued two-way communication, enabling people to build relationships through communications, that gives cohesion to the marketing communications.

The corporate campaign dramatised BT's vision to keep the world talking. The ad featuring Stephen Hawking, which emphasises the power of communications and the importance of new technology, won considerable acclaim and awards.

A more recent commercial features Sir Edmund Hillary talking to his son on the slopes of Everest, using Camnet technology.

In its personal customers campaign, BT portrayed itself as a guide to communication with the line 'It's good to talk'.

From the day the campaign broke, with press advertisements like 'Why can't men be more like women?' and 'Is it a coincidence that the animals who mate for life never stop talking to each other?', it was clear that no punches were being pulled. It wanted to spark debate, provoke reaction and get people talking about communicating, even if they weren't doing it yet.

The first phase gave way to the TV-led campaign featuring Bob Hoskins as an invisible guide, highlighting good and bad communications techniques, and showing how matters can usually be improved by a simple

change of attitude.

Speaking for himself rather than BT, he confronted gender, age and other barriers to break those barriers down, thereby improving the quality of their lives. Love him or hate him, Hoskins worked - in the first three months of the campaign, an estimated 155 million calls were made on business and residential lines. "It's good to talk" also entered Britain's collective consciousness, with Lenny Henry, Spitting Image and Drop the Dead Donkey all using it to good effect on national TV.

For its business customers, BT positioned itself as the guide who could help steer them through the telecommunications maze, with a campaign featuring the theme 'Work smarter, not just harder'. The ads create a soap opera about a company. In each ad 'communications' is the hero coming to the rescue with innovative solutions to common business problems. One of the messages conveyed was that 'Communications can help me get more out of my working day'.

For global customers, BT ran the 'Let's Talk' campaign, focusing on BT's world class portfolio, which helps businesses to gain competitive edge, and establishing the brand identity as the platform for joint ventures. The highlight of the year was Telecom '95 at Geneva where BT was a major exhibitor with other multi-nationals in the global telecommunications industry.

BRAND VALUES

BT's mission is 'to provide world-class telecommunications and information products and services, and to develop and exploit its networks at home and overseas so that it can meet the

requirements of its customers, sustain growth in the earnings of the group on behalf of its shareholders, and make a fitting contribution to the communities in which it conducts its business'.

At the heart of the BT brand is the importance of effective communication. BT's brand values are based on the idea of creating an environment where communication can operate most effectively, and people can conduct meaningful, productive dialogue.

As the experts in communication, BT today is practising what it preaches to make it the driving force in the global telecommunications industry. With BT, better communications mean better relationships, better business and ultimately, a better world.

CHANEL

THE MARKET

Haute Couture - exquisite, made-to-measure and highly exclusive - can only be found in Paris.

Yet, while luxury perfume, jewellery or fashions remain the perfect gift, indulgence or expression of style, the influence of the great designer houses and luxury goods manufacturers will continue to be felt around the world.

For that touch of exclusivity, quality, premium skincare/make-up products are in demand, as shown by their market value, in 1995, of £400 million. In 1995, the UK luxury ladies fragrance

market was worth £380 million, with the mens fragrance market valued at £170 million.

For sheer class, a luxury watch or designer fashion is unbeatable. The main players in the luxury ladies watches market are few, and include the likes of Rolex, Cartier, Patek Philippe and CHANEL. Truly exclusive designer clothes can only be purchased from selected outlets. CHANEL, for example, only has two shops in the UK, both in London.

ACHIEVEMENTS

The seasoned adage "fashion fades, but style lasts forever," is at the heart of CHANEL's enduring success. It is an incredible story, a virtual fairy-tale. It is the story of how one single innovative Frenchwoman had a vision of a new society, a new woman.

This vision has revolutionised the world of haute couture and forged a style and brand which has become synonymous with elegance and glamour the world over.

As the brand's creator, Gabrielle Chanel (better known as Coco Chanel), once said: "In a quarter of a century I created fashion, because I was living in my own era. The secret is to do things at just the right moment. I created the most well-known style in the world, because fashion is ephemeral, but style is eternal".

Classic CHANEL style is engendered in all CHANEL's branded products ranging from

perfume, with CHANEL No.5, make-up, jewellery, handbags through to the ubiquitous little black dress, adored by women spanning all generations and cultures.

One Chanel-devotee, Andre Malraux, once said, "Chanel together with de Gaulle and Picasso are the greatest figures of our age". The force of her personality is embodied in the empire she developed from a millinery boutique in Deauville to offices stretching across the globe, with the celebrated salon on rue Cambon and the Ritz Hotel at the Place Vendome in Paris at the heart of it all.

Chanel possessed a strikingly powerful personality. Petite and dark-haired, she exuded a magnetism and exacted a respect which enabled her to rub shoulders with the cream of society and rule her domain with a tight grip. Her life-story was lauded with a musical, "Coco", which hit Broadway, New York, in 1969, with the famous actress Katherine Hepburn in the starring role.

Since her death in 1971 at the age of eighty-eight, the CHANEL empire has stayed true to the tenets of its founder. Masterminded by Karl Lagerfeld, the classic, timeless designs which made Chanel's name, continue to thrive and evolve.

HISTORY

The woman who came to define style had surprisingly humble beginnings. Unlike her suave, urbane image, Gabrielle Chanel was brought up in the French countryside. The daughter of a peddlar, Chanel was born on 19 August 1883 in Saumur. Her mother died of tuberculosis when she was just twelve years old leaving Gabrielle in the hands of an orphanage. In 1900, she moved to a convent and from there she went to Moulins where she started working in the trousseau and layette trade.

But Gabrielle had an artistic streak. She longed to be a professional singer. In 1908, while working and singing part-time in Vichy,

Gabrielle met a young officer, Etienne Balsan, who invited her to his country estate where he enjoyed a genteel existence. This proved to be a fortuitous moment in the history of Chanel. It was here that she was first dubbed "Coco", met a host of celebrities, well-placed members of society - all Etienne's friends - as well as Arthur (Boy) Capel, a brilliant businessman, who was instrumental in setting her up with her very own shop, designing and selling hats, in Deauville.

From hats, Coco soon graduated to clothing, applying the principles of simplicity, "less is more," to her designs. A second Chanel shop was opened in Biarritz in 1915. The outbreak of war changed women's fashions irrevocably. With the men on the frontline, women's styles had to be more practical, in line with their increased contribution to the war effort. Coco did this exceptionally well. Her fashions were soon featured by a US magazine, Harper's Bazaar. Her international reputation was underway.

After Boy Capel's death in 1919, Coco turned to new friends to guide her through her grief. One such friend was Misia Sert, a famous pianist, who whisked her into a social circle known for its high-brow intellect and creativity. Coco befriended the likes of Diaghilev, Picasso, and Stravinsky, and a Russian emigre, with whom she had a passionate affair. This liaison awakened her interest in antique Russian and Slavic decor, jewellery and perfumes - an interest which spilled over into her designs.

In 1921, with the talented perfumer, Ernest Beaux, Coco devised a new scent, the evocative CHANEL No.5. Chanel opened up for business in Paris, at 29 Rue du Faubourg Saint-Honoré. Her reputation, both as a formidable woman and the foremost couturier of her age, was gaining ground. The launch of the Chanel little black dress in 1926 sealed this status. At the time, American Vogue described it as the "Chanel Ford". An "English" look crept into her designs. This was partly due to the influence of her new lover, one of the richest and most powerful men in England, the Duke of Westminster.

By 1928, Gabrielle Chanel was widely

acknowledged as "the first lady of France". She was dressing the Hollywood greats - Gloria Swanson, Greta Garbo, Marlene Dietrich - but despite her star's dramatic rising across the Atlantic, Coco chose to stay in France, living in a sumptuous villa, where she was attended by a succession of brilliant admirers.

Times changed. The Second World War forced an exile in Switzerland as the German army occupied France. It took many years ... until 1954, when Coco had turned 70, for Chanel to revive the famous, simple look. By then, the newly-crowned master of French haute couture was Christian Dior, but the Americans still turned to Chanel for simple, practical elegance. Before long, Chanel was back in business.

The famous Chanel fitting-rooms at rue Cambon were soon crowded with aspirants to the Chanel look. The nearby Hotel Crillon was famous for being full of American ladies whenever Chanel presented her latest collection.

Even after her death at the Ritz Hotel, where Coco was a permanent guest, the spirit of Chanel lingers on, breathing new life into the company year in, year out.

The product range continued to grow and similarly high design standards were endorsed by a new and talented designer, Karl Lagerfeld, who assumed the mantle of Mademoiselle Chanel in 1983.

THE PRODUCT

Quality and style are resonant throughout CHANEL's product range. CHANEL offers women the 'total look.' First there is the suit, described by designer Philippe Starck as "the one and only modern suit". It has gone down in the annals of fashion history as an absolute classic, offering quality in both fabric and design. Coco Chanel abided by two basic principles, discipline and thoroughness. To this day, the company adheres to Chanel's golden rules, "Always remove things, never add". "No buttons without button-holes". "The inside must be as perfect as the outside".

Jean-Marie Rouart, a writer, succinctly says, "Fashion fades, but the CHANEL suit lasts forever". This timeless quality has been achieved through simple, elegant design and conscientious attention to the fitting. When a lady wants a haute couture suit from CHANEL, she is encouraged to have at least two fittings, to ensure the garment is perfectly matched to her

personal style and body shape.

The classic CHANEL handbag, known as "2/55", the handbag's birth-date, was first designed by Albert Monnot. The bag was formed in jersey, overstitched in a diamond pattern and lined with gros-grain. Chanel conceived the handbag's chain and leather strap which has become so characteristic of a Chanel handbag, along with the double C's logo as a clasp.

CHANEL shoes were primarily two-tone - beige with a black toe-cap. To this day, all CHANEL shoes are hand-sewn and all-leather.

A wide range of make-up and skin-care products has been introduced over the years to ensure that women can enjoy the high quality CHANEL experience from top to toe.

And of course. The perfume. CHANEL has spawned some of the most famous, almost legendary brand names in the perfume market, with the likes of CHANEL No.5, CHANEL No.19, COCO (dedicated to the company founder), Cristalle, and for men, Egoiste, Antaeus and Pour Monsieur.

The original, CHANEL No.5, was created in 1921 with the master perfumer Ernest Beaux. The main floral notes in CHANEL No.5 are May rose, ylang-ylang and jasmine from the French town of Grasse, the centre of the French perfume industry. Beaux submitted two lists of samples to Chanel to choose from, numbered 1 - 5 and 20 - 24. She opted for No.5 - which then became its name. Later, CHANEL No.19 was named in honour of her birthdate - the 19th of August.

Coco Chanel was a great believer in bold jewellery. "A piece of jewellery can never be mean," she said.

RECENT DEVELOPMENTS

CHANEL continues to introduce spectacular new designs, modern extensions of Chanel's vision.

Since 1987, notable additions to the must-have CHANEL range have included three collections of ladies watches - Première,

Mademoiselle and Matelasseé, all retain the exquisitely simple style advocated by the company's founder.

Première reflects the shape of the classic perfume bottle stopper, Mademoiselle, a perfect square and Matelasseé, with its quilted face re-interprets the stitching on the famous handbags. Most recently, a collection of fine jewellery has been created as a natural extension of the company's luxury products - Chanel's love of jewellery with innovative designs.

In May 1996, CHANEL launched a new fragrance, ALLURE.

PROMOTION

Aside from the huge press and consumer attention given to CHANEL's fashion shows, where some of the most beautiful women in the world today model CHANEL's latest collections, the fashion house has pursued an effective advertising campaign, reaffirming the basic classic values and beauty of the CHANEL brand. As Jacques Helleu, artistic director at Chanel says: "Perfect lines. Captivating shapes. Films designed to convey eternal truths in the space of sixty seconds". A succession of famously beautiful faces have been used to capture the Chanel myth, including the French actress Carole Bouquet and the legendary Hollywood film star, Marilyn Monroe.

BRAND VALUES

Coco Chanel once said: "When I started work in the profession, my ambition was not to create things I liked, but to stop the fashion for things I didn't like". The result was luxurious simplicity, quality of design and manufacture, discipline, timelessness. This has been recognised and consistently delivered by the modern, post Gabrielle Chanel. As Karl Lagerfeld said in 1993: "The spirit of Chanel must be part of today's life, it is a phenomenon of here and now, of this day and age".

CHANNEL FOUR TELEVISION

THE MARKET

Traditional British broadcasting is entering an era of rapid transition. Digital technology is set to bring about sweeping changes throughout the industry, offering - through cable, satellite and digital terrestrial technology - a greater choice of channels than ever before. This presents established terrestrial broadcasters with a huge challenge, as they are forced to combat competition in an increasingly crowded market whilst maintaining their own high standards, public service remit and audience share.

The viewer is unlikely to spend any more time in front of the TV screen, since the British already watch more television than any other nation. But broadcasters are now not only competing with each other, but with video games, pre-recorded videos, the Internet, online services - and many other leisure activities. And cable and satellite are gradually biting into the market share of the terrestrial channels. According to BARB, the UK body which audits television viewing figures, satellite and cable channels accounted for 8.5% of UK channel share in 1995. The commercial ITV network, including its breakfast service GMTV, took the largest share with 37.2%, followed closely by BBC1 with 32.2%. BBC2 took a 11.1% share with Channel 4 (and the Welsh fourth channel, S4C) holding 10.9%. Unlike the cable and satellite channels, ITV and Channel 4 are wholly dependent upon advertising revenue; ad sales are only a small proportion for cable and satellite, whose share is spread thinly among a very large number of satellite channels.

ACHIEVEMENTS

Channel 4 is the only fully public service broadcaster in the world that relies entirely on commercial revenue and operates without a penny of licence fee or government subsidy.

From its launch in 1982, it swiftly achieved worldwide recognition as the first "publisher broadcaster", with no in-house production (except for its own viewers' answerback show, Right to Reply), but commissioning most of its programmes from independent producers. This pioneering model has been so successful - and efficient - that it has been adapted by other broadcasters in the UK and around the world. Its reliance on independents effectively created the independent production sector in the UK,

which has since successfully fought for guaranteed access to ITV and the BBC channels, which previously made most of their programmes in-house.

Channel 4 was charged by government with a specific public service remit to innovate in the form and content of programmes, and to cater for tastes and interests not served by the main commercial channel. Its success in carving itself a distinctive and lucrative niche in the UK broadcasting market has been achieved by fulfilling that remit with a diversity of programming. It was never conceived to compete for the mass audiences reached by BBC1 and ITV. It serves a much wider range of viewers than most cable or satellite channels: around 85% of the nation watch something on Channel 4 each week. But in interpreting the remit to serve interests neglected by the main commercial channel, it attracts a larger proportion of young and upmarket viewers in its total audience than its larger commercial rival. They are light viewers of television in general, and of ITV in particular, so the channel is not only fulfilling its remit but offering advertisers an audience that they find hard to reach on ITV.

Channel 4 sells its programmes and gains recognition for them round the world. In 1995 it won premier international awards for entertainment (the Golden Rose of Montreux for Don't Forget Your Toothbrush), documentary (the Prix Italia for The Betrayed) and drama (an International Emmy for The Politician's Wife). It has won even wider recognition for the Channel 4 Films it commissions and finances - either wholly or in part - many of which achieve critical and commercial success in the cinema before their transmission in Channel 4's 'Film on Four' strand, including Four Weddings and a Funeral (the most commercially successful British film of all time), The Madness of King George, Trainspotting (financed solely by the channel) and The Crying Game. The channel has won a number of Oscars over the years for feature films and animation - and in one year attracted more Oscar nominations than all but one Hollywood studio.

HISTORY

Channel 4 was created under the 1981 Broadcasting Act and launched on air on 2 November 1982 as a national TV broadcasting service covering the whole of the UK except Wales. For the first ten years, the service was operated by the Channel Four Television Company Ltd, a wholly-owned subsidiary of the Independent Broadcasting Authority (IBA), later the ITC. It was funded by a subscription levied on the ITV franchise-holders, in return for which the ITV companies were entitled to sell the commercial airtime on Channel 4 in their own franchise areas. Channel 4's subscription income was set as a proportion of the total advertising revenue on both ITV and Channel 4 - it was not dependent upon the revenue which the channel itself attracted.

However, the 1990 Broadcasting Act determined that from 1 January 1993, Channel 4

should sell its own airtime in competition with ITV. It would retain exactly the same public service remit yet rely entirely on its own commercial revenue. Channel 4 itself was reconstituted as a public corporation without shareholders, broadcasting under a ten-year licence from the ITC. Responding to government concern that the channel might not be able to sustain both its revenue and its remit, the Act established a safety net under which the ITV companies would be required to top up the channel's revenue if it failed to achieve a 14% share of total terrestrial commercial revenue, though that commitment was limited to 2%. However, the Act's Funding Formula declared that if the channel were successful it would have to pay half of its revenue over that 14% share to ITV and put a further 25% into a statutory reserve. Channel 4 has thrived commercially increasing both its audience share and - even more - its revenue, so it has had to pay ITV increasing sums every year, £74 million in 1995 (more than the cost of an entire quarter's programming). Far from sustaining its remit, this rogue formula has proved the only threat to its remit and curb on its success, diverting £169 million in the first three years to ITV shareholders that might otherwise have been invested directly in British programmes.

THE PRODUCT

Channel 4 sustains its remit and revenue with a diversity of programming to suit all viewers at some time or another, but with a particular appeal to the young and upmarket. Channel 4's highest-rated transmission in a decade, in November 1995, amassed over 12 million viewers for the TV premiere of Four Weddings and a Funeral, but the channel was equally proud to attract more than six million viewers in total for a series of campaigning shorts about sign language during the week, Four Fingers and a Thumb, drawing on the film's imaginative use of sign language through the hero's deaf brother.

The nightly hour-long Channel 4 News with its commitment to serious analysis of British politics and international issues defines the channel's brief for serious journalism in peak-time, supported by the investigative strengths of the weekly series Dispatches, commissioned from a different specialist team each week. It has an unequalled commitment to factual programming in peak-time, for example Witness, the only peak-time strand on British TV devoted to religious documentaries about personal and religious belief, the science strand Equinox, and programmes reflecting people with disabilities in Inside Out. Other factual strands, such as Cutting Edge with its accessible documentaries from golf-clubs to shop-lifting, can prove among the channel's most popular programmes. And its educational programmes also provide distinctive approaches to gardening, cookery and other popular subjects.

Innovation is not confined to minority programmes. The Big Breakfast pioneered a completely new and unprecedented format, and target audience, for breakfast TV, quite distinct from either serious news or the lightweight sofa-bound coverage of other commercial broadcasters around the world. From that success, its presenter Chris Evans went on to develop an equally innovative approach to game shows with Don't Forget Your Toothbrush that won several awards for innovation as well as attracting format sales around the world.

Since its opening week, Channel 4's most consistently popular programme has been Brookside, the thrice-weekly soap which proved hugely influential through its commitment to contemporary issues and determination to shoot on location, based in a group of real Merseyside houses. Its drama

series like The Politician's Wife by Paula Milne or Alan Bleasdale's Jake's Progress take risks with adult subjects.

Channel 4's most internationally-successful sub-brand is Film on Four in which it premieres the feature films it has backed - wholly or in part, over 300 to date.

And the channel has also encouraged creativity of British animation, launching the career of Nick Park with Creature Comforts, his first Oscar winner, and pioneering an animated soap-cum-sitcom, Crapston Villas. And it has promoted new or unfamiliar sports in Britain, American Football, cycling (with annual daily coverage of the Tour de France), NBA Basketball, Kabaddi and Sumo.

The channel has always sustained its particular youthful appeal with a policy of specific commissions, whether the late-night notoriety of The Word or Eurotrash, or the novelty of Moviewatch where the critics are the young people who form the majority of today's cinemagoers. It sustains its commitment to multicultural programmes across the schedule with current affairs (Devil's Advocate and Africa Express), entertainment (the highly-successful Desmond's and its spin-off Porkpie) and even feature films (Salaam Bombay and Bandit Queen). And its Independent Film and Video department has not only encouraged film-makers from outside the mainstream but mounted many seasons reflecting gay life and culture.

RECENT DEVELOPMENTS

Channel 4's sustained campaign against the iniquities of the Funding Formula has won the prospect that payments will be phased down after 1997 and probably stopped entirely by 2000. The channel is eager to retain more of its own earned income to invest more in British programming and reduce its reliance on repeats and American imports, however successful they have proved. Its advertising sales department has not only eliminated the discount at which the channel was traditionally sold, but can now charge a premium for some

particularly attractive target audiences it can deliver. The success of feature films, such as Four Weddings and a Funeral (in which C4 had a 30% stake) and Trainspotting (for which it invested and recouped the entire £1.7m budget) allows the channel to expand its investment in British feature films.

PROMOTION

Channel 4 promotes itself not just on-air and with extensive editorial coverage in newspapers for its original and controversial programming, but with a continuing commitment to paid-for advertising in newspapers, on radio but particularly with high-profile poster campaigns for major drama series and other programmes, from the documentary series The Nick, to The Girlie Show. The channel supports many arts events, including sponsorship for the Turner Prize (now the most publicised event in the British arts calendar) and for Glyndebourne, linked to exclusive transmission deals. The channel's wholly-owned subsidiary Channel 4 International commissions Channel 4 Books through deals with publishers linked to specific programmes. It also distributes Channel 4 Video releases and licenses magazines linked to Brookside, Channel 4 Racing and other popular programmes, while the channel's educational support services offers reading lists, booklets, telephone counselling and other services, and the channel is developing its own Internet web-site as an extension - and encouragement - to viewing.

BRAND VALUES

Channel 4 is valued around the world for the quality and distinction of its programming and feature films. It has one of the most readily recognisable and established logos in European media. It has a reputation for audacity and originality which attracts some controversy from mid-market tabloids, but also guarantees that its programming will avoid the conventional or the bland - which supports its youthful, radical image with viewers and advertisers.

Things you didn't know about Channel 4

❍ In 1995 the channel's Duty Office answered 133,613 telephone calls (a 19% increase on 1994) of which 10% contained critical comment, and received 47,348 letters (an increase of 8.3%); of these, 14% were critical.

❍ The channel's largest-ever number of calls of praise was elicited by its exclusive live relay of the original Three Tenors Concert from Rome at the end of the 1990 World Cup. The largest number of protest calls came in the days before the network TV premiere transmission of Martin Scorsese's Last Temptation of Christ in the summer of 1995.

❍ Feature films apart, Channel 4 International's highest earner to date has been its share (with Chris Evans' Ginger Productions) in selling the format rights of Don't Forget Your Toothbrush around the world - and to BBC1!

❍ Some would say that Channel 4's most important off-screen artistic contribution was its enlightened commissioning of Sir Richard Rogers and his Partners to design the new Horseferry Road headquarters - a building that rivals Rogers' much larger Lloyds Building and Beauborg in Paris, and has won numerous architectural accolades.

CHIVAS REGAL 12

THE MARKET

Scotch Whisky is one of Britain's most important exports. According to research company Datamonitor, whisky is the most popular spirit in Europe. The UK has the largest whisky market. Whisky also tops the spirits market in the Asia-Pacific region.

Based in London, The Chivas and Glenlivet Division is a division of The Seagram Spirits and Wine Group. It is responsible for the production, business development and strategic development for The Seagram Company Ltd's Scotch Whisky brands, including Chivas Regal, The Glenlivet, Royal Salute, Glen Grant and Passport. It also oversees strategic marketing and international expansion for Seagram's North American Whiskies, including Bourbon, Canadian and American.

ACHIEVEMENTS

Enjoyed in more than 150 countries, Chivas Regal is the world's leading premium Scotch Whisky (according to research company Canadean in 1995) and one of the few truly global spirit brands.

During the past 25 years, Chivas Regal has experienced and continues to experience tremendous growth. In 1957, sales totalled just 100,000 nine litre cases; in 1993, worldwide

sales volume rose 10% from the previous year to more than 3,500,000 cases. As proof of this brand's global appeal, its sales are evenly spread across the geographic regions of Asia Pacific, North America, Latin America and Europe, as well as Duty Free.

HISTORY

It is remarkable that with so many malt and blended whiskies to choose from, one Scotch whisky stands above other premium whiskies in popularity. Chivas Regal is the preferred brand of discerning drinkers.

But what makes it the world's favourite premium Scotch whisky?

Firstly, a word of warning for those who would consider the question lightly. The word whisky comes from the Gaelic 'Uisge Beatha'. It means nothing less than the 'water of life'.

Whisky from Scotland has been respected, appreciated and consumed around the world for generations. But since its introduction in the last century, Chivas Regal has outpaced all other luxury premium Scotch whisky brands, setting its own unique standards of quality, taste and integrity.

There are many factors that contribute to the brand's pre-eminence. A good starting point is the Chivas family's heritage. The name 'Chivas' can be traced back over 500 years in the area between Aberdeen and Speyside, the heartland of malt whisky distilling. In 1836, young James Chivas left his home region of Strathythan to seek work in Aberdeen, the burgeoning port and industrial centre of North East England. The move was to have far reaching consequences.

James began work at a well-respected grocers and wine and spirit merchants, eventually taking over the business and beginning a partnership trading in Stewart & Chivas. In less than two years, he had earned a Royal Warrant which appointed him 'Purveyor of Grocery to Queen Victoria.' The new Queen and her consort, Prince Albert, having discovered a passion for Scotland, started a fashion among English aristocrats for all things Scottish. Stewart & Chivas were at the forefront of suppliers to this growing market.

In 1857, James's brother John joined the business and the company prospered, supplying luxury provisions to the gentry at large. At the same time they began to lay down large stocks of the very best whiskies, gaining a reputation for their skill and excellence in blending. They introduced their own blended Scotch whisky which found a ready and appreciative market in England for its well-rounded flavour. Other brands followed. A traveller of the time said: "we

have never tasted finer, mellower or more exquisitely flavoured whisky than that which Chivas Brothers hospitably put before us during our sojourn in Aberdeen. The memory lingers still". Extravagant praise indeed but even this was soon to be surpassed.

In the 1890s the company created what was to become a de luxe blend, unparalleled in the history of whisky making: Chivas Regal.

It met with instant success. Chivas Brothers' reputation as pre-eminent blenders reached new heights.

In a speech to his employees made in 1904, Alexander Smith, a partner in the company, said that he wished the name of Chivas Brothers to be associated with "the best service, the best quality - in effect, to become the equivalent of a hallmark of excellence". Things don't change: this is the guiding principle of Chivas Brothers today.

In 1950 Chivas Brothers took the significant step of buying its own distillery. But this was no ordinary malt distillery. This was Strathisla, the oldest working distillery in the Highlands, which produces the predominant malt Scotch whisky in Chivas Regal, known since it was first officially sold in the 1880s, as 'mellow, mountain dew'.

The physical and spiritual home of Chivas Regal, Strathisla is arguably the most picturesque of all distilleries. Its dignified louvred pagodas, cobbled courtyard, waterwheel and warm stone buildings are set deep in perfect Scotch whisky making country.

A nearby spring supplies the purest of Scottish Highland water while golden barley is

If it seems a little bit harder to open than your other scotches, it's because you probably closed it a little bit tighter than your other scotches.

Scotland's Prince of Whiskies

grown and harvested from the rich soil of the Scottish plains. Malted barley plus yeast act naturally together but, controlled by the skilful hands of the distiller, still man and warehouseman, produce the magic, mellow spirit of pure gold which is the heart of Chivas Regal.

THE PRODUCT

For a premium blend such as Chivas Regal, the transformation of its fine malt and grain scotch whiskies takes a minimum of twelve years, and each is a superb example of Scotch Whisky in its own right. At the heart of Chivas Regal is Strathisla Single Malt Scotch Whisky, which is described as having a "complex array of haylike aromas, with a sweetness and smoothness that produces a well rounded and pleasant nutty finish" [Colin Scott, Master Blender, The Chivas and Glenlivet Group].

Chivas Regal itself is described as "smooth, with a honeyed richness, round and full bodied, slightly smoky with a long, lingering finish". [Colin Scott.]

At Strathisla, original methods of production are still employed and respected. Distillery Manager Norman Green explains: "Our single malt Scotch whisky is made using the same methods that have been used for 500 years. However, not only do we retain original methods, we have restored the structural splendours of this magnificent distillery". The public are invited to visit the distillery. Guests are invited to the Dram Room where they can 'nose' a selection of malt whiskies and then enjoy a 'wee dram' of Chivas Regal or Strathisla Single Malt Scotch Whisky.

In summary, Chivas Regal is a triumph of the blender's art, as many different malt and grain Scotch Whiskies of different ages and characteristics are combined to produce a Scotch Whisky of great complexity and subtlety.

RECENT DEVELOPMENTS

The glory of Chivas Regal is that the brand, first developed in the 1890s and largely unchanged since then, provides a consistent, high quality taste experience year on year. This is the continuing responsibility of The Chivas and Glenlivet Group's Master Blender.

PROMOTION

Chivas Regal has a strong advertising heritage - the icon for which is probably the legendary 'Father's Day' advertisement. This moving piece of work was written by David Abbott, one of the most respected copywriters in the world, and has won numerous awards.

On January 12 1995, The Chivas and Glenlivet Group, unveiled details of its new global advertising campaign for Chivas Regal. Impactful and mould breaking, the new campaign, tag lined "You Either Have It Or You Don't" plays on the inherent attributes of the world's number one Premium Scotch Whisky.

Because I've known you all my life.

Because a red Rudge bicycle once made me the happiest boy on the street.

Because you let me play cricket on the lawn.

Because you used to dance in the kitchen with a tea-towel round your waist.

Because your cheque book was always busy on my behalf.

Because our house was always full of books and laughter.

Because of countless Saturday mornings you gave up to watch a small boy play rugby.

Because you never expected too much of me or let me get away with too little.

Because of all the nights you sat working at your desk while I lay sleeping in my bed.

Because you never embarrassed me by talking about the birds and the bees.

Because I know there's a faded newspaper clipping in your wallet about my scholarship.

Because you always made me polish the heels of my shoes as brightly as the toes.

Because you've always been there when I've needed you.

Because you still hug me when we meet.

Because you still buy my mother flowers.

Because you've more than your fair share of grey hairs

and I know who helped put them there.

Because you've remembered my birthday 38 times out of 38.

Because you're a marvellous grandfather.

Because you made my wife feel one of the family.

Because you wanted to go to McDonalds the last time I bought you lunch.

Because you let me make my own mistakes and never once said "I told you so."

Because you still pretend you only need glasses for reading.

Because I don't say thank you as often as I should.

Because it's Father's Day.

Because if you don't deserve Chivas Regal, who does?

The advertising proposition is a simple one, placing in people's minds the thought that "Chivas Regal is special and so am I". The executions - both in print and TV commercial format - are simple and striking with a subtle sense of humour. The campaign was developed for The Chivas and Glenlivet Group by TBWA London.

Alisdair Ritchie, Chief Executive, TBWA London says: "This striking new campaign demonstrates that global campaigns do not have to be dull. This is a beautiful example of simple images reflecting an idea which is witty, and relevant to every country Chivas Regal sells in".

BRAND VALUES

Many people around the world enjoy Chivas Regal. They range across different ages, cultures, religions and countries. They consume the brand on many different occasions. However, Chivas Regal consumers are united by an attitude to life. In a difficult world, they want to rise above mediocrity. As a result, they share a number of specific aspirations: to be fashionable; to be smart, intelligent and witty; to achieve and demonstrate status; and to have and serve the best.

They want the brands they choose to reinforce these values. Chivas Regal is special and distinctive and therefore is highly appealing to its consumers.

You either have it   or you don't

Things you didn't know about Chivas Regal

- Only a handful of people know the secret of the composition of Chivas Regal.

- The heart of Chivas Regal is Strathisla Single Malt Scotch Whisky, produced at Strathisla, the oldest working distillery in the Scottish Highlands.

- Whisky comes from the Gaelic 'Uisge Beatha' meaning 'water of life'.

Club Med

THE MARKET

In a holiday market dominated by cut-throat price promotions, centralisation of the giants, greater standardisation of the budget holiday package and ever increasing competition, it is becoming more and more difficult to please "The Consumer".

Once, not that long ago, the world was big and full of unknown corners. Today, thanks to the media available, the world has shrunk and its most intimate, exotic and exclusive spots have become familiar sights.

The "Consumer," gearing up to the next Millennium, demands, at the very least, value for money, new experiences, beautiful surroundings, good food. In short, a quality escape from the realities of everyday life. Social demographic changes such as the increasing number of single parents and lone travellers, increasingly affluent mature travellers as well as a growing trend towards late booking all play an increasingly important role in the type of holiday the consumer will choose and the level of service demanded. Those companies able to adapt their marketing, product and destinations will survive and flourish, those who flounder will fail.

ACHIEVEMENTS

Club Med is the only truly global organisation, dedicated to giving people a chance to escape the pressures of everyday life into a man-made and carefully maintained Utopia, in which people and interaction are the most important aspects. Its unique philosophy makes it much more than just another tour operator or hotel organisation. It gives its members a chance to recharge their batteries and to start living again. In real terms, Club Med is the original, the largest and most comprehensive of the world's all-inclusive holiday organisations.

In 1995 it ranked as the world's 13th largest hotel chain, employed over 25,000 people worldwide, of which 9,000, from different nationalities, work as GOs - "Gentil Organisateurs" - in the Club Med village resorts. In 1995, Club Med organised holidays for over 1,325,300 people of which over 250,000 were children. To book a Club Med holiday it is necessary to become a Club Member, making Club Med the world's largest and most cosmopolitan Club in the world. In 1994, Club Med welcomed its 20 millionth member!

HISTORY

The Club's concept was born in 1950 when Belgian diamond cutter, water polo champion and ex-resistance fighter Gerard Blitz decided to offer a unique escape from the depressions of post-World War II Europe. After he came back from a camping holiday with a group of

friends he placed two small advertisements in the "Samedi Soir" and "L'Equipe" newspapers advertising the first all-inclusive holidays. The response was overwhelming - 2,300 people - and the beginning of Club Méditerrannée. The very first village consisted of a number of army surplus tents, supplied by the Trigano family, in Alcudia, on the Balearic Island of Mallorca.

Although Blitz had the idea, it was actually Gilbert Trigano who had the vision, business sense and necessary drive to develop the company. Gilbert Trigano retired in 1994, handing over the reins to his son, Serge Trigano, who will be taking Club Med into the next century and beyond.

The first of Club Med's famous straw hut villages opened in 1954 on the island of Corfu.

This village, Ipsos, still features strongly in the Club Med straw hut programme and is extremely popular with sporty-minded "twenty and thirty something" singles and couples. Not much has changed since the early days. The Polynesian style huts are still there, albeit with concrete floor and single light bulb and the bar beads are still in use.

THE PRODUCT

The beads, huts and lotus-eaters might still be around, but nowadays they exist alongside smart-cards, luxury accommodation and a clientele varying in age from babes in arms to nonagenarians. The average age of a Club Med member is in the 35 - 40 bracket and around 65% come as part of a family. A very high proportion of club members, around 70%, return year after year to either soak up the sun, meet like-minded people, indulge in some golf, tennis or watersports or whizz down the ski slopes.

1956 saw the opening of Club Med's first ski village, Leysin in Switzerland, making Club Med one of the world's oldest ski tour operators. Nowadays, the programme features 20 Winter-sports destinations in Switzerland, France, Japan and the USA. The formula is all-inclusive in all villages, with the exception of Meribel where a new "A La Carte" concept is being tested. All, but two, villages have childcare facilities and some even take babies from four months upwards.

To be able to go on a Club Med holiday, one has to become a "GM" - "Gentil Membre" - and pay a joining fee of £8, and an annual membership fee of £6. However, once you are a "GM," holidays are all-inclusive and one price covers: return flights and transfers, full board, sports facilities, qualified instruction, children's clubs, evening entertainment as well as fully comprehensive travel insurance.

The Winter sports holidays also include an area lift pass and ski and/or Snowboard lessons. The only extras are special courses such as intensive sports training, green fees, excursions, telephone calls, drinks at the bar and special beauty treatments.

The key to its success, and its over-riding strength is the complete and utter dedication of Club Med's staff - "GO" or "Gentil Organisateur". It is the commitment of these very special people that differentiates Club Med from anything else. Club Med employs around 9,000 "GOs". They are a team of multi-lingual, multi-talented and multi-national hosts and hostesses who are responsible for everything that happens in the village, from food to accommodation, from sports to entertainment, from happiness to health. "GOs"

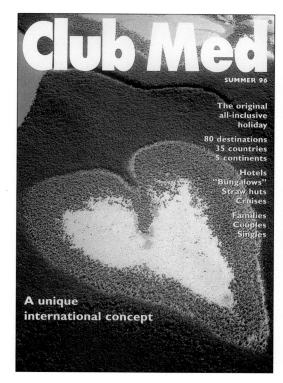

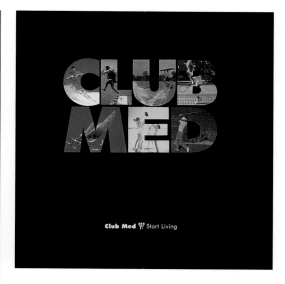

Club Med ♥ Start Living

Things you didn't know about Club Med

- ○ Club Med runs the largest water-sports club in the world with 1,600 wind-surfers, 1,500 sailing boats, 85 water-ski boats, 250 kayaks, 1,200 diving tanks and 2,000 pairs of flippers.

- ○ Club Med runs the largest Tennis Club in the world with over 800 tennis courts, 8,000 racquets, 44,000 balls and around 300 qualified tennis instructors worldwide.

- ○ With 36 village resorts featuring golf facilities in 16 different time zones, Club Med is the largest Golf Club in the world using 9,000 golf clubs. 84,000 golf balls and over 150 golf professionals. In 1995, some 76,000 Club Med guests played golf for at least one hour per day during their holiday.

- ○ Club Med guests are served over 20 million meals during which some of the following items are consumed: 21 million croissants, 4.1 million baguettes, 23 million eggs, 2.7 million kgs of meat, 500 tons of seafood and over 3.5 million litres of wine.

- ○ Club Med operates the world's largest sailing cruise ships, the Club Med I and II. Specially designed with the comfort of the "GMs" and ecology in mind, they have set a benchmark in the international cruise industry. Each ship can accommodate about 440 guests and 190 staff.

- ○ 1994 saw the opening of Club Med's first ecology reserve and the "Gilbert Trigano Research Laboratory" in Rio das Padras, Brazil. The nature reserve is some 12 km square.

- ○ Club Med employs a team of underwater gardeners to clean up the lagoons and coral reefs around Bora Bora, Polynesia. Once areas are cleaned they are re-planted with plants from the underwater nursery.

- ○ Club Med Cherating in Malaysia jointly operates a Giant Turtle egg hatchery programme increasing the turtle's chances of survival and growing into a mature Giant Turtle with a weight of up to 900 kilos.

---

are at the service of all, but servant to none. They participate in all aspects of village life and might be sports instructors by day, table companions at meal times and entertainers in evening shows. Each team is headed by a "Chef de Village". The GO team only remains in a village for the duration of one or two seasons before moving on to the next of Club Med's 110 village resorts anywhere in the world.

RECENT DEVELOPMENTS

Club Med's corporate development plan is targeting a figure of 2 million customers for the beginning of the next century versus 1.3 million today, implying a growth rate of around 7%. After a financially rocky period between 1990 and 1993, Club Med has re-focused on its core business, streamlined its expenditure, invested in quality and pushed through a more aggressive marketing plan, and since 1994 has seen a return to profits.

Club Med has started an extensive renovation programme for around 20 of its 110 villages, mostly in the Europe/Africa zone. Its corporate and conference facilities, available in about 30 villages world-wide are being continually upgraded and most sales offices now have dedicated Corporate Departments. Extensive growth and development is planned in the Far East. Sales offices are set up and new villages are being developed in China, Indonesia, Japan and Vietnam, to name but a few. Other areas of development are the Americas, with the scheduled opening of Club Med's first village in Cuba, the opening of the first dedicated Club Med Casino and the building of a new landing strip on Columbus Isle, Bahamas.

PROMOTION

Club Med's strategy of globalisation and segmentation will continue and is reflected in a changing customer split and profile. French "GMs" worldwide now only account for 30% as opposed to 45% in 1985! American "GMs" account for around 20% while the Asian share stands presently at around 16%, but is growing steadily. The Club Med brochure is currently translated into 10 languages and has a circulation of around 3 million in Europe alone.

New technologies have been welcomed and the Club Med brochure can now be found on the Internet (http://www.clubmed.com/) as well as on CD-ROM.

To be able to handle the planned increase in members, home shopping facilities and other new developments leading up and continuing

into the 21st Century, Club Med has invested over £50 million in a new world-wide reservation and information system which, apart from handling the business, allows sales staff to respond immediately to customers' requests, as well as integrate marketing data with cost analysis and track sales trends.

The present communications strategy for Club Med is designed not only to draw in new consumers to the brand, but to provide a clearer and easier insight into the benefits provided by Club Med to existing as well as new clients. The aim is to provide a consistent brand message across Europe. To position Club Med as the holiday club for the global citizen and to differentiate it from any competitor or imitators by re-affirming its ideology: the truly unique and inimitable essence of Club Med.

The communications focus on an emotional rather than a rational level. Club Med is not something you go to, it is something you are part of and it is part of you. The central thought and end line of the present advertising is "Club Med. Start Living". This strap line encapsulates the unique and key element of the Club Med philosophy and attitude towards life. At the same time, it is a strong, motivating call to action. The emotionally focused communications are designed to appeal to people who want to get the most out of life. The images created evolve from the stimulating environment of the Club Med village life and the basic philosophy of the company - to create an environment where people can live life to the full and recharge their batteries without any concerns or worries.

Club Med's television campaign dramatised in an involving way the philosophy of Club Med, provoking viewers to find out more about Club Med. The supporting press advertising campaign focuses on different elements of the Club Med philosophy, suggesting how consumers can benefit from them.

BRAND VALUES

Club Med is unique, and is the one and only truly global tour operator committed to people's happiness and relaxation.

Its research and development in all areas, ranging from technology to environmental issues, makes Club Med a leader in the global leisure industry as well as in many other fields.

Total commitment to the happiness of its members is what has kept Club Med's heart "throbbing" throughout the years and will keep it going well into the next century.

THE MARKET

The importance of the soft drink market can never be underestimated. Not only is it huge now, but it still has enormous potential to grow. Adults today grew up with soft drinks. For them, a soft drink has become as common a form of liquid refreshment as a traditional hot beverage. The same applies, to an even larger extent, with the children of today, who are growing up in a soft drink culture and consequently have greater expectations from an increasingly sophisticated market. At present, carbonates make up over half of the soft drinks market, with cola flavoured carbonates accounting for a large portion of the carbonates sector. The UK soft drink market is currently worth around £6.6 billion.

ACHIEVEMENTS

Quite simply, Coca-Cola is the most valuable and powerful brand in the world, as borne out by the annual valuation of the World's Top Brand Names in Financial Review (August 1994). Coca-Cola sells nearly half of all soft drinks consumed throughout the world. In 1995, Coca-Cola held an enormous 47% share of the world-wide soft drink industry. In so many countries, the Coca-Cola drink is the market leader, often taking second place in the rankings with its diet formula or with Fanta, the company's orange carbonated flavour. How does Coca-Cola achieve and maintain this position of pre-eminence?

First and foremost, Coca-Cola is the best-recognised commercial trademark in the world today. Three independent surveys conducted by Landor Associates in 1988 confirmed this. In response, a business magazine in the US stated "Coca-Cola is so powerful it's practically off the charts". The company has pursued a winning policy, ensuring Coca-Cola's ubiquity, with powerful global advertising and a well-organised, all-pervasive distribution system. This strategy is based on the company's belief that every day, every single one of the 5.6 billion people who populate this planet is going to get thirsty, and the onus is on Coca-Cola to ensure that it is available to satisfy this need.

The dedication of Coca-Cola sellers around the world is quite remarkable and bears testimony to the company's determination to provide a "pause for refreshment" at any time, anywhere. A fine example is the father and son team, travelling 7000 kilometres a week through some of the world's toughest terrain, the Australian Outback, to deliver Coca-Cola products to isolated pockets of civilization dotted throughout the wilderness. Or the 73-year old Filippino man who refuses to budge from his selling post in his local town market until he has managed to sell at least 50 cases of Coke every day. The

distributors are supplied by a comprehensive network of bottlers peppered across the globe, who ensure Coca-Cola maintains a world-wide presence. In fact, Coca-Cola's bottling system is the largest, most widespread production and distribution network in the world. As a consequence, Coca-Cola has been able to take full advantage, establishing a firm foothold in new and emerging markets. Today, you can buy a Coke from Beijing to Delhi, from Moscow to Mexico City.

However, Coca-Cola has not stopped at being the best-selling soft drink the world has ever known. By virtue of its singularly powerful brand personality, Coca-Cola has become a vehicle for promotion in its own right and is the backdrop to a number of highly successful artistic and sporting events - The Olympics

included. In addition, Coca-Cola merchandise is widespread and fashionable.

HISTORY

The syrup that was to become Coca-Cola, was first manufactured in 1886 in a three-legged brass pot in the backyard of Dr John Styth Pemberton, a pharmacist in Atlanta, Georgia. Dr Pemberton took his new product to a local pharmacy where it was considered good enough to be sold at 5 cents a glass. Somehow, the syrup got itself mixed with carbonated water, resulting in a drink pronounced as "Delicious and Refreshing". This became a popular slogan associated with Coca-Cola, the name dreamt up by Pemberton's partner Frank M Robinson.

Despite some minor advertising - including the first shop signs declaring - "Drink Coca-Cola" - Pemberton never realised the potential of his creation. Before his death in 1888, he sold his interest in Coca-Cola to a wised-up Atlantan business-man Asa G Candler, who soon assumed complete control. He finally achieved sole ownership in 1891. Candler was a confirmed believer in the power of advertising. He fervently plunged into the world of mass-merchandising, ensuring the Coca-Cola trademark was depicted on countless novelty products such as fans,

calendars, clocks, ornate leaded glass chandeliers and urns. He distributed thousands of coupons offering a free glass of coke. Colourful signs promoting the brand were displayed on trolley cars and in shop windows. His efforts were well-rewarded. Just three years after the official incorporation of The Coca-Cola Company in 1892, Candler was proud to announce that Coca-Cola was now drunk "in every state and territory in the United States". A major leap considering that in its first year on the market, Coca-Cola had sold on average a mere nine drinks per day.

Expansion was so impressive that in 1898, a new headquarters was housed in a large building in Atlanta. Candler naively described the three-storey building as "sufficient for all our needs for all time to come". Needless to say, the building was too small after just a decade.

Marketing concentrated on the pressing need to vanquish pale imitations of the increasingly famous Coca-Cola brand – conversely, a sign of its success. Advertising boards declared the stern warning "Demand the genuine" and "Accept no substitutes". Equal in importance to the marketing of Coca-Cola however, was the question of distribution. The origin of today's vast Coca-Cola bottling system stems from 1894 when a local shopkeeper installed a bottling device at the rear of his store and proceeded to trade crates of Coke up and down the Mississippi River. The first major bottling plant was inaugurated soon after.

Coca-Cola made great strides under the guidance of Robert Woodruff who was elected president in 1923. Woodruff instilled some of the main tenets of Coca-Cola's quality and internationalism into the corporate thinking. He insisted on a high standard of product, packaging and service and focused on the importance of the bottled market. As a result, bottle sales soon exceeded fountain sales for the first time. His main objective was to ensure the accessibility of Coca-Cola, introducing the take-home carton concept and the installation of Coca-Cola vendors in key positions at major sporting venues. The introduction of the metal open-top cooler enabled Coca-Cola to be served ice-cold in retail outlets and with the onset of refrigeration, to be stored in the workplace. A distinctive soda fountain glass and the introduction of automatic fountain dispensers, hastened Coca-Cola's brand recognition.

And not only in the States. From 1926 onwards, bottling operations were opened abroad by Coca-Cola's foreign department, renamed The Coca-Cola Export Corporation in 1930. Coca-Cola ensured a major marketing presence at the Olympic Games in 1928 with a troop of vendors signalling its arrival on the international scene.

At the outbreak of the Second World War, Coca-Cola was bottled in 44 countries, including some of those countries then considered to be the enemy. Ironically, the war favoured rather than hindered Coca-Cola's development as a world brand. American soldiers, all over the world, demanded huge quantities of their favourite drink, which in turn introduced the locals to their first taste of Coke. Coca-Cola was therefore well-placed to seize the opportunity for growth the post-war boom promised. Coca-Cola's post-war message contrasted strongly with the preceding conflict. It was based on global friendship, harmony - in effect a message for all time.

Since the war, Coca-Cola has successfully introduced other branded products to the Coca-Cola family and has been able to offer the consumer a wider choice in size and style of packaging. In the wake of staggering advances in the communications industry, Coca-Cola has launched highly-successful advertising campaigns, which although varying in style, have never failed to relay Coca-Cola's essential brand values. It would seem the company could do little wrong. In 1982, diet Coke was introduced, the first extension of the Coca-Cola and Coke trademarks. It was a stunning success. By 1984 diet Coke had become the top low-calorie soft drink in the world.

THE PRODUCT
Coca-Cola itself is a drink which needs no introduction. Diet Coke is its obvious sister-product in a low-calorie format. Most interesting however, is the legendary secrecy that has been built up around the product's formula. The Coke taste has certainly effected an emotional resonance with many of its long-time consumers, as typified by the hue and cry that met the change in Coke's formula in 1985. Coca-Cola duly responded with the re-introduction of its original product under the title "Coca-Cola Classic". Caffeine-free Coca-Cola and Cherry Coke have been also been introduced in recent years.

RECENT DEVELOPMENTS
Coca-Cola has expanded its world-wide share of global soft drink sales. World-wide unit case volume just keeps on growing. Coca-Cola Foods is the largest marketer of juice and juice drink products in the world. Minute Maid has become a leading fruit beverage trademark.

In 1995, The Coca-Cola Company gained over $27 billion in market value reaching a phenomenal $93 billion. By market value, Coca-Cola was rated the fourth-largest US-based company and the sixth largest company worldwide. (Source: Financial Times, FT500 Survey of the World's Top Companies January 1996).

PROMOTION
Coca-Cola's TV advertising campaigns have produced a number of famous slogans and jingles ranging from "Things go better with Coke" (1963), "It's the real thing" (1942 and 1969), "Coke adds life" (1976), "Have a Coke and a smile" (1979), "Coke is it!" (1982), "Can't beat the feeling" at the end of the 1980s, and the "Always" campaign introduced in 1993. Radio and television have provided Coca-Cola with endless valuable opportunities to spread the Coca-Cola theme. Coca-Cola sponsors major events and radio\TV programmes. The Coca-Cola trademark is a crucially important marketing tool, inspiring

recognition wherever it is positioned, whether it be on a billboard, bottle or T-shirt.

Coca-Cola has always been associated with high-quality packaging. The graceful, "sexy" curves of the Coke bottle have been admired since their inception in 1916 when the contour bottle replaced the straight-sided design, thereby distinguishing Coke from its competitors. Acknowledging its importance to the heritage and authenticity of the brand, the bottle-shape was eventually awarded registration as a trademark by the US Patent Office in 1977, an honour bestowed upon only a handful of packaged products by that time. And rightfully so, it would seem. Coca-Cola's own research has uncovered a consumer preference for the contour bottle as opposed to the straight-sided variety, by a margin of 5-to-1. (The famous signature flourish of "Coca-Cola" was registered in 1893, and the short and sweet "Coke" in 1945).

Following a change in legislation, in 1995, the famous contour bottle became the first 3D depiction of a trademark to be registered in the UK.

However, The Coca-Cola Company never rests on its laurels even though in many ways Coca-Cola hardly needs promoting - it is everywhere, at anytime.

BRAND VALUES
In many ways, Coca-Cola's brand values are encapsulated in its marketing messages. Slogans like "It's the real thing", and "Coke is it!" articulate perfectly the core elements of Coca-Cola. It's the first, authentic, truly genuine article. Coke is portrayed as a life-giving force. Not only does it quench your thirst but it rejuvenates, inspires, instils youth and vitality. And Coke is fun, ...youthful, wholesome fun. Coke is also a global force, extending a harmony of purpose across boundaries, as typified by the famous 1971 TV advertisement which brought together children of various nationalities to sing "I'd like to buy the world a Coke". Coca-Cola has no frontiers.

THE MARKET

Beer-drinking is a major British pastime. However, the popularity of traditional English real ales and beers has been clouded by the growing prevalence of lager. Standard lager is now the largest part of the UK beer market, accounting for total sales of over 6.8 million pints a day.

The lager market itself can be divided into four groups: Premium packaged lager; premium draught; superstandard (lager with 3.8% - 4.2% Alcohol By Volume - ABV) and standard lager (less than 3.8% ABV). In 1995, superstandard lagers held the greatest market share in both the on and off trade with 42%, followed by standard (26.4%), with premium draught (13.7%) and premium packaged lagers (13.2%) virtually neck-and-neck, according to Stats MR.

ACHIEVEMENTS

Foster's can truly claim to be the UK's favourite lager. It is drunk by more UK consumers than any other lager and enjoys the highest brand awareness and enormous sales - currently topping one million pints a day. Combining sales of Foster's standard lager with Foster's Export and Foster's Ice, the brands have a standing value of £860m in the UK. This amounts to a staggering 1.5 million barrels a year, distributed through 20,000 outlets. Foster's has the widest distribution network in the UK of any lager brand.

And of course, Foster's is not just available in the UK. It is sold in around 100 countries worldwide and is Australia's best selling beer. Here, in the UK, Foster's is the fastest-growing lager brand with an approximate 17% share of the total lager market.

The quality of Foster's lager has always been highly-praised. Foster's won its first award, the International Brewing Award, as early as 1888, and repeated this feat as recently as 1994, when Foster's came first in the Brewing Industry International Awards, fending off 42 rival draught lager brands.

Foster's innovative advertising has earned the brand a 'cult-status', an achievement which has translated into sales. The latest TV campaign, "Search for the Amber Nectar", inspired sales of an extra 50 million pints of Foster's in one year alone.

Overall, Foster's is probably Australia's most famous brand, the world over. It is certainly one of the world's most exported brands and looks set to continue this record of success.

HISTORY

Despite its positioning as thoroughly Australian, Foster's Lager was devised by two Americans - the Foster brothers - who arrived in Melbourne, Australia, in 1886, flanked by an American German brewing expert and a refrigeration engineer.

Together, they brewed the Foster's lager prototype, a German-type bottom fermented lager, in 1888. This was the first lager of its kind to be brewed in Australia. Prior to this, the fashion had been for English-style ales.

In that same year, 1888, Foster's lager received its first brewing accolade - the International Brewing Award, awarded at the Centennial Exhibition in Melbourne.

Foster's lager soon made a name for itself as

a high quality lager. So much so, that German brewers in Melbourne were prosecuted for attempting to pass their own beers off as Foster's, by swapping the bottle-labels. The Foster Lager Brewing Company took pains to ensure that its lager was always delivered to the customer in optimum condition. As this meant 'ice cold', during the 1890s, every Foster's stockist was issued with a free daily supply of ice to keep the lager extra-cool.

Towards the end of the nineteenth century, The Foster Lager Brewing Company teamed up with other major Melbourne brewers to form Carlton & United Breweries Proprietary Ltd. The group pinned a lot of its hopes and marketing clout on Foster's Lager. The Foster's Brewing Group soon became known as the parent company of Carlton & United.

Foster's first step to international fame and fortune was in 1899, when it was exported to South Africa. As the century progressed, the UK market, with its increasingly large Australian expatriate community, also offered Foster's an excellent opportunity to expand internationally. By 1976, Australia's Financial Review was able to report that Foster's "was no longer a drink devoted to Australian bigots". Indeed, its popularity abroad wasn't solely committed to the UK. The largest single consignment of foreign

beer to ever enter New York was one million cans of Foster's in 1976. Within just a year, ten million litres of Foster's were being sold in the USA.

In 1981, a distribution deal was forged with UK brewers Watney, Mann & Truman, meant that Foster's lager could be sold on draught throughout the UK. Canned Foster's, brewed under licence in the UK, debuted in 1984.

Three years later, the Foster's Brewing Group acquired the major UK brewer Courage, with its comprehensive, nationwide distribution network. From this point on, Foster's became Courage's leading lager brand.

Bolstered by extensive marketing, which included a celebrated TV campaign featuring the little-known Australian comedian Paul Hogan, Foster's had soon secured a 6% share of the UK draught beer market.

Foster's was then relaunched in 1993, with updated can designs bearing striking new graphics; bar-founts (the Foster's Draught name was renamed to simply Foster's, emulating the global Foster's can design); an increased alcohol content from 3.6% to 4.0% ABV; and a multi-million pound advertising campaign. Spectacular sales have since lifted Foster's to the number one spot in the UK's preferred choice of lager.

THE PRODUCT

Foster's lager is 4.0% ABV and is only brewed from Australia's Pride of Ringwood hops. It is available on draught, in either keg or tank. To ensure customers receive their Foster's in tip-top condition, pubs and clubs are issued with guidelines detailing the temperature at which Foster's should be served (8 °C), and how Foster's should be stored and served. A body of trained technicians carry out check-ups to make sure these rules are adhered to.

Foster's is now brewed outside of Australia in the USA, Canada, Ireland, Germany, Sweden and China. In the UK, Foster's is brewed under

licence in Berkshire, Tadcaster and Halifax.

Foster's is available in the UK on draught and in 440ml cans, four-packs and twelve-packs, and 33cl bottles known as 'stubbies' from 20,000 on-trade outlets spread across the country.

Recent additions to the Foster's range are Foster's Ice and Foster's Export. Launched in 1994, Foster's Ice is only available in 330ml bottles. It has a 5.0% ABV and is currently the top-selling "ice" beer in the UK. Foster's Export is also 5.0% ABV. It is a full-strength premium lager and is brewed to the same recipe as the original Foster's lager introduced into the UK during the 1970s. Foster's Export is available in bottles and 375ml cans.

RECENT DEVELOPMENTS

Since relaunching the Foster's brand in the UK in 1993 as the 'Gold Standard' lager, business has boomed, with sales of draught Foster's up by more than 100 million pints, plus a 100% rise in off-trade sales year on year.

The launch of Foster's stylish "ice" beer, Foster's Ice, in 1994, has further strengthened the Foster's portfolio. Foster's Ice is already well-positioned as one of the most popular premium lagers on the UK market and is the 4th best selling bottled beer in the UK. This kind of success has been replicated with Foster's other quality brand, Foster's Export, formerly known as Foster's Lager Export Strength.

PROMOTION

Successful marketing has proved key to Foster's success. A year after the product's first launch, in 1889, a marketing campaign was already underway. The Foster Lager Brewing Company labelled 360 cases of safety matches with the slogan, "Drink Foster's Lager," and installed beer-engines in numerous Melbourne hotels where the lager was first served.

Since then, the much-acclaimed 1980s TV advertising campaign, with Paul Hogan, the Australian comic, acting as spokesman for the brand, and a string of promotions, have maintained the marketing momentum behind the

SEARCH FOR THE AMBER NECTAR.

Now with added nectar. 4% ABV.

brand. Inadvertent advertising came from Barry Humphries - the Australian satirist, better-known as media celebrity Dame Edna Everage - who created a cartoon strip "The Wonderful World of Barry Mckenzie," in which the leading character was constantly yearning for an ice-cold Foster's.

Courage has invested up to £25 million in Foster's latest round of advertising, viewing Foster's as their most important lager brand. In 1993, Foster's launched a new series of advertisements, entitled "The Search for the Amber Nectar". Directed by Ridley Scott, the commercials star Slake and Beanbag, two comic characters roaming the Australian outback, "sometime in the future" (a post-apocalyptic world, reminiscent of Mad Max), looking for "a more noble way of life". This search is instigated by Slake - the more heroic of the two - as his old father shares nostalgic memories of a drink described as "the golden throat charmer," "the legendary larynx wobbler," which was "like an angel crying on your tongue". Slake and his sidekick, an ex-gentleman's outfitter, undergo a number of adventures in their quest.

This became the largest radio promotional campaign ever mounted in the UK and Europe. For those who didn't make it to Australia, Foster's brought a little bit of Australia to them, through 24 roadshows held in pubs and clubs, hosted by outback hero Harry McCabe. Famously Australian pastimes, such as Koala Dunking, Sydney Surfing and Sheep Throwing were part of the fun. Poster and press advertising was featured in major publications, including The Sun and The Mail.

Foster's has also built-up a high profile at key sporting events worldwide. These have included Formula I Grand Prix, Australian Rules Football, and sponsorship of the Oval Cricket Ground. Foster's signage is featured at all major Test Cricket grounds. Outside of sport, Foster's signage, depicting the distinctive blue and gold livery associated with all Foster's products, is located at prime 'city' spots such as Piccadilly Circus in London, Times Square in New York and Hong Kong.

BRAND VALUES

Foster's spans all generations of lager-drinker, but is largely targeted at 18 - 34 year olds. Its popularity with young people speaks volumes about the brand. Foster's is truly Australian. It has a quirky 'No Worries' attitude to life, and is warm, witty and subtly clever - as its advertising will bear out. Foster's aim to be the 'Gold Standard' of lagers is based on its top quality proposition, its clear visual differentiation from other brands and its clean, refreshing flavour.

On top of TV advertising, Foster's offers promotional support packages at point of sale, including free offers, a coolbag with every special 6-pack or a T-shirt in every 12-pack, for instance, and holiday competitions, such as 'Destination Australia.' In association with airline Qantas, 'Destination Australia' offered Foster's drinkers the chance to win a pair of seats on one of three special Foster's flights to Australia, by picking up one of 10 million special "passports" found in 11,000 venues across the country. The passport contained clues to help answer questions set by 28 commercial radio stations.

Gillette

THE MARKET

The male grooming market is one of the fastest growing sectors within the toiletries industry as a whole, with a year-on-year growth of 1.9 per cent. The male grooming market was worth £387 million in 1995, more in value by £100 million than any other sector of the toiletry market. Four key categories account for over 90 per cent of this market; blades & razors, shave preparations, mass market male fragrances, and male anti-perspirants and body sprays.

Over the past ten years, men's attitudes to their personal health and appearance has changed dramatically. This change has made them reconsider their attitudes to personal "Grooming". In fact 90 per cent of men now use some form of male grooming product, 75 per cent of whom wet shave. A man's bathroom cabinet is likely to be filled with almost as many products as a woman's.

In answer to men's changing grooming habits, an enormous number of new products specifically formulated and designed for men have been launched. It is not only the growth of new areas that has promoted this change in attitudes to male grooming, but also a change in shopping trends. Ten years ago, two thirds of men said that women bought their toiletries for them. Nowadays, 72 per cent actually purchase their own, meaning that companies have been forced not only to alter their products but also their style of advertising. Research shows that men now want to use high performance products such as after shave conditioners, pre-shave gels and deodorising body sprays.

The male grooming market is forecast to continue to grow rapidly over the next five years, and as it does, so it will become increasingly more complex and sophisticated.

ACHIEVEMENTS

Founded in 1901, the Gillette Company is the world leader in male grooming products, a category that includes blades and razors, shaving preparations, post shave conditioners and electric shavers.

Gillette also holds the number one position worldwide in selected female grooming products, such as wet shaving products and hair depilation appliances, anti-perspirants and body sprays.

The Company is the world's top seller of writing instruments and correction products. In addition, the Company is the world leader in toothbrushes and oral care applications.

Gillette manufacturing operations are conducted at 57 facilities in 28 countries, and products are distributed through wholesalers, retailers and agents in over 200 countries and territories.

In the UK, only Gillette has the leading market sector presence in all three wet shaving categories. First, and the largest sector in the market, is blades and razors, where Gillette dominates this area of the industry with 66 per cent of the market share, and by 80 per cent by value of male shaving systems. The second category is shaving preparations, where Gillette is also the market leader with a 52 per cent share of the market. The third category is the post shave conditioners category where Gillette is also the number one manufacturer with 20 per cent of the market.

The Company has constantly been at the forefront of the shaving market, introducing and patenting many innovations that are now taken for granted by customers. These include the adjustable razor, a fully contained cartridge, the pivoting head, Lubrastrip, spring mounted twin blades and soft, flexible microfins, all contributing to Gillette's powerful market share.

HISTORY

In 1895, King C Gillette had the idea that was to revolutionise shaving. The idea? A disposable steel wafer blade.

He began work on a prototype and a campaign to interest people in the concept. He was met with disbelief: everyone said it was impossible to sharpen a thin piece of metal enough to make a razor blade.

King C Gillette persisted, however, and finally met and recruited William Nickerson.

Nickerson, who had been trained as a chemist at the Massachusetts Institute of Technology, was a highly imaginative thinker and inventor who had once developed a light-bulb manufacturing process that even Thomas Edison had said was impossible.

It was his verdict that it was technically possible, which led to the formation of The American Safety Razor Company in 1901. New processes for hardening and tempering steel and mass production machinery were developed. In 1902, the business changed its name to The Gillette Safety Razor Company and, in 1903, the first razor went into production. In that first year just 50 razor sets were sold - a far cry from today, when Gillette sells 300 million in Britain alone!

In 1904, the company received its first US patent for the safety razor and sales increased to a staggering 12 million blades. Since that time, Gillette has patented almost all the major innovations relating to shaving. During the 1960s and 1970s, Gillette engineers were the first to patent a special polymer coating on the blade edge. This was followed by the first system razor, the Techmatic, in 1967. This was a continuous band razor which meant that the customer no longer had to touch the blade. GII followed in 1971 and brought with it the concept of twin blade shaving. This was followed by the Contour razor, and then in 1986, the Lubrastrip. This was followed in 1991 by the world's first

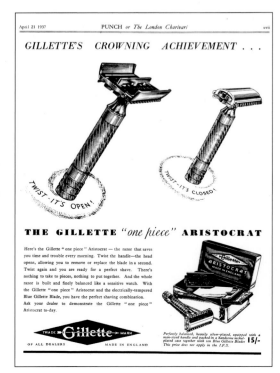

razor with spring mounted blades, Sensor.

Finally, in 1994, SensorExcel was introduced with five, flexible microfins preceding the blade, causing the skin to be stretched gently for a really close, smooth shave.

In 1993, Gillette revolutionised the female shaving market with the introduction of Gillette Sensor for Women, the first product specifically designed to meet women's shaving needs.

1996 has seen the launch of GilletteSensorExcel for Women with a larger Lubrastrip for moisturisation, a non-slip handle even when wet and spring mounted twin blades with five, soft flexible microfins positioned in front of the blades to protect the skin while gently lifting stubborn hairs.

When Gillette, at the time a prosperous travelling salesman, first conceived the idea of his blade in 1895, he was already well known in radical political circles. The year before, in a book titled "The Human Drift", he proposed a sweeping plan to reorganise the entire world as a gigantic corporation that would be owned and managed by the people. Gillette evidently had hopes that the scheme would usher in an earthly paradise, and went on to spend much of his life promoting his peculiar version of Utopia. But, perversely, the world was more interested in the clean, close comfortable shaves that Gillette's razor gave them than his philosophy, so his curious economic and political notions have been all but forgotten.

King C Gillette had thought he might be remembered as one of history's social and economic reformers. Instead he is recalled as the inventor of the safety razor with its disposable blade and as the founder of the major American corporation that bears his name.

THE PRODUCT

The Gillette Company has always been famous for its razors and blades, in particular its latest systems razor for men - SensorExcel. The razor introduces a revolutionary new technology to shaving.

The Sensor razor was first developed in the UK in 1979 by Dr John Terry. Development continued for a further ten years in the USA, costing over £100 million, before the launch in 1989. Today, Sensor has taken over 26 per cent of the value of the systems blade market.

However, never satisfied with the technology as it stands, Gillette continues to stretch science to the limit. SensorExcel has set a new benchmark in shaving technology and performance. Its revolutionary spring mounted twin blades, Lubrastrip technology, five soft flexible microfins, combined with the new Flexgrip handle, offers men a closer, smoother shave. The microfins precede the blades and gently stretch the skin, causing the beard hairs to spring upwards, enabling them to be cut further down the shaft, with greater comfort

than ever before. The results of consumer research, independently conducted by Gillette, demonstrated the advanced technology of SensorExcel. Overall Gillette dominates with over 54 per cent of the value of the total systems market with SensorExcel alone taking over 16 per cent.

RECENT DEVELOPMENTS

To respond to the changing male attitudes to grooming, the first Gillette Series range was launched in 1993. The first Gillette Series range, Cool Wave fragrance, which was a result of three years of research and development by the company's designers, includes 13 high performance products. All Gillette Series products are available in three invigorating and fresh fragrances - Cool Wave and Wild Rain and now Pacific Light. In 1996 Gillette added Gillette Series Pacific Light fragrance to the range, which incorporates skin benefits and is one of

the first new products to bring a light and subtle fragrance to the mass market. Gillette Series, via new product launches, will add a further estimated £10.3m to the male toiletries market.

Gillette Series Pacific Light, unique Alcohol-Free Splash, refreshes like a splash whilst instantly soothing and moisturising without stinging - making it very appealing to the 86% of after shave users who use a splash. Pacific Light After Shave Gel delivers 30% more moisturisation than current Cool Wave and Wild Rain.

1996 has also seen the introduction of Gillette Series Moisturising Shower Gels, available in the three refreshing world-class fragrances, suitable for both hair and body with a rich non-greasy lather. An estimated 15.6 million men shower in the UK. Gillette Series Shower Gels will add around £6.2 million to the estimated £14 million male market.

On the female side, just three years after Gillette revolutionised the female shaving market with the introduction of Gillette Sensors for Women, the first razor designed specifically to meet women's shaving needs, Gillette introduces the most advanced wet shaving system for women for softer, smoother legs - SensorExcel for Women.

The interest this created has since forced Gillette to broaden its range with the launch of a new female grooming product. Gillette Satin Care Shave Gel is the first non-soap based moisturising shave gel created for women and includes moisturisers and skin conditioners that provide maximum comfort for the customer.

By supporting the female shaving portfolio with a £2.5 million advertising and press campaign, Gillette is further set to build its volume share in the blades and razors business,

while making a significant breakthrough into the female shaving preparations sector.

Gillette Satin Care was voted winner of the prestigious award of New Woman 1995 "New Best Bodycare Product". While on the male shaving side, Gillette SensorExcel was awarded New Woman 1995 "Best New Men's Grooming Product or Product Range".

PROMOTION

Gillette is committed to building its technologically advanced, high performance branded products through consistent and heavyweight marketing investment. This commitment can be demonstrated by its year on year increases to TV advertising and sampling. The investment in 1996 will be no less than £20 million.

Increasingly, many consumers choose to make their purchasing decisions at the point of sale. Gillette is committed to offering its customers display solutions and effective promotions that are designed to accelerate its mutual sales growth.

BRAND VALUES

The Gillette Company celebrates world class products, brands and people. These three factors account for their global achievements. Their world-class products are distinguished for their quality, value, safety and effectiveness. Their world-class brands are the names by which people the world over know and trust Gillette. Their world-class people are the nearly 33,000 Gillette employees worldwide whose skills and dedication ensure the Company's progress.

Gillette is a world leader in the production of blades and razors. The Company's progress and brand values are reflected in its success in new technology and innovation. Gillette is renowned for its leading edge products, which are technologically advanced and offer consumers superior performance. The male image is sporty, masculine, clean, and immaculately groomed. The female image is modern, energised and an understander of women's needs. Gillette knows what it takes to make men and women look and feel their very best by continually producing technologically advanced grooming products.

The following are registered trademarks of Gillette:
GILLETTE; LUBRASTRIP; TECHMATIC; GII; CONTOUR;
SENSOR; SENSOREXCEL; FLEXGRIP; COOL WAVE; WILD
RAIN; PACIFIC LIGHT; SATIN CARE.

Things you didn't know about Gillette

❍ The annual production of Gillette razor blades is enough to go round the world 12.5 times.

❍ The average male will spend 139 days of his life shaving.

❍ Shaving does not remove a tan. Tans are caused by melanin deep within your skin. If anything, shaving enhances a tan by removing flaky skin that hides a tan's glow.

❍ Gillette actually introduced the first razor for women in 1903 called the Milady Decolleté.

❍ In 1918 the United States government decided to issue every soldier and sailor with his own shaving equipment and the Company shipped 3.5 million razors and over 36 million blades to the armed forces.

THE MARKET

As a staple part of any family's diet, bread is top of every home's shopping list and naturally forms one of the largest food markets in the UK today. Wrapped sliced bread is by far the most popular sector of the bread market and is valued at around £1.1bn. In addition, the rolls and baps sector of the bread market is also gaining in importance and is worth £600m. Estimates from research company AGB show a 6% growth year on year in this sector.

Medical opinion asserts the dietary benefits of fibre, of which all bread is an excellent source. It is now recommended that we eat an average of six slices of bread a day.

ACHIEVEMENTS

Hovis is Britain's most famous bread brand. In fact, Hovis is the number one bread brand in the UK with a 28.3% share of the branded bread market. Hovis produces bread for most sectors of the market, including brown, white, wholemeal, and wheatgerm. Since its introduction into the white bread market in 1991, Hovis has become the fastest growing white bread brand in the UK with a current year on year growth of 45%.

In the last six years, Hovis sales have more than quadrupled, as the brand has extended from its original wheatgerm variety to encompass a range of premium quality products in all sectors of the bread market. It is now not only well known for its famous wheatgerm bread but is brand leader in wholemeal, and is even the fastest growing white bread brand and the biggest brand in bread rolls.

Market research from AGB shows that Hovis is one of the UK's top ten consumer brands, enjoying sales of £130m. Consumers recognise Hovis as being synonymous with high quality. Hovis has developed many products for the modern, busy society, including the Hovis Cobble, a premium quality, square shaped roll which fits neatly into a lunchbox.

HISTORY

For most of the 19th Century, brown bread was considered the basic food of the lower classes.

This all changed in the early nineteenth century, however, when Richard 'Stoney' Smith, a flour miller from Stone in Staffordshire, decided to put his belief that wheatgerm was a healthy component in any diet into practice. He saw his goal as being to preserve the goodness of the wheat germ, while ensuring that the bread was longer-lasting. He devised a flour which he felt

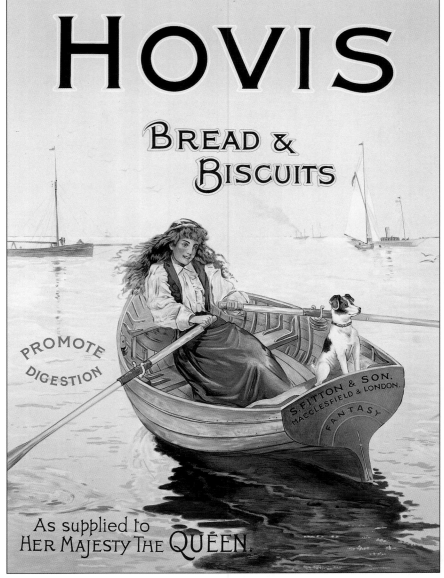

matched his requirements. He took this to a milling company in Macclesfield, called S.Fitton & Son. Together, they registered 'Smith's Patent Germ Flour' in 1887.

Yet 'Smith's Patent Germ Flour' wasn't deemed a particularly inspirational name. In 1890, both Richard Smith and Thomas Fitton, a descendant of the mill-owner who had first bought Smith's brown flour, launched a competition to decide on a suitable name for their product. After some deliberation, one potential name, 'Yum Yum', was soon discarded.

Eventually, a student from London, Herbert Grime, claimed the £25 prize money, with his Latinate idea of 'hominis vis,' meaning 'the strength of man' - which was soon abbreviated to the simpler-sounding Hovis.

With a good name and a good marketing tale to tell, sales of Hovis bread flour became one of the success stories of Victorian British enterprise. In 1896, Thomas Fitton bought Imperial Mills on the Embankment by the House of Lords. There had been a mill on the site for many years, and that is why Millbank is so called.

As the business grew, so the Hovis Bread-Flour Company Limited was formed. 'Stoney' Smith died in 1900 and is buried in Highgate Cemetery in London.

In 1928, Cecil Gordon Wood joined the board of Hovis and the company began a rapid expansion. Hovis soon became a formidable household brand name with a string of mills, and domestic and overseas milling establishments. Intelligent advertising, plus the dissemination of Hovis tea-shops across the land, had certainly served to popularise the Hovis brand name. However, the Hovis Company underwent particular strain during the second world war, including the destruction of its Manchester Mill in 1940. Under the terms of the national emergency, the government took complete control of all Hovis' proceedings, but Hovis ensured that Britain never went short of bread. In addition, they also helped on the front line too, providing a Spitfire, appropriately named 'Hominis Vis' to the Royal Air Force.

The succeeding post-war years saw Hovis fortunes thrive through a merger with the McDougall Trust in 1957, to form Hovis-McDougalls Limited and the formation of Rank Hovis McDougall Limited in 1962. The company went from strength to strength until 1979, when control of Hovis Limited was vested in Rank Hovis Limited. The Rank connection had started with Joseph Rank in 1875, when he started his own chain of flour-mills in Hull, London, Barry and Birkenhead.

Together, the Rank Hovis partnership was formidable, leading the way in UK flour-making for many years to come.

The Hovis millers at Rank Hovis celebrated their centenary year in 1986, and have continued to provide top quality flours for its bakers ever since, consolidating the brand's leading position in the UK market as the best flour for the most popular branded bread.

THE PRODUCT

Hovis bread is valued for its highly nutritious content. It is an important source of vitamin B as well as containing important natural minerals such as iron, magnesium and phosphorous.

Traditional Hovis bread is still available, however, there have been many additions to the Hovis range. In 1989 Hovis began producing a wholemeal variety, and following its success Hovis entered the premium white bread market in 1991 with its Hovis White loaf. In 1994, the Hovis Cobble, a square shaped premium white roll embossed on one side with the famous Hovis name, was a welcome addition to the £600m roll and bap sector. Following the huge success of the white Hovis Cobble, a brown variant and a Hovis Granary© Cobble have also been introduced.

RECENT DEVELOPMENTS

A number of new and innovative Hovis products have been developed and launched in recent years, constantly adapting to changing trends in the market.

Most recently, in 1995 the Half 800g Hovis loaf was introduced. As the name implies, this is not in fact a 400g loaf, which has smaller slices than an average 800g loaf, but is a half sized loaf with full size slices. This loaf is available in white, brown, or Granary©, and was developed to reflect the growing number of one and two-person households in the UK.

PROMOTION

Hovis has been a distinguished advertiser for the whole of its 110 year history. Hovis has also been inventive in its approach. At the turn of the century, as cycling became hugely popular, thousands of Hovis Cycle Road Maps and Guides were published to promote the bread and to indicate those cafeterias where it might be enjoyed on the road. In the 1920s, Britain's strongest man, Thomas Ince, was called upon to tour the country boasting of the body-building qualities of Hovis flour.

Hovis was among the first exhibitors at the Daily Mail Ideal Home Exhibition and the Hovis bakery remained a memorable feature of that event for many years.

In the early years of the twentieth century, bakers' shop fronts were adorned with Hovis gold-lettered 'V' signs, tea-shops advertised "Tea with Hovis", and tea tricycles carrying this slogan were introduced to serve seaside promenades.

Many famous artists were commissioned through the years to create Hovis advertisements, including Mabel Lucie Attwell, Heath Robinson, and Tom Eckersley.

One of Hovis' most memorable advertising slogans, "Don't say Brown say Hovis," was first used in 1924 and was given greater visual emphasis with the advent of commercial television in the 1950s. Hovis was among the first to use the new medium, and their short, black and white advertisements featuring George Benson and Kenneth Connors were notably humorous.

A much-praised series of Hovis commercials with a nostalgia theme followed in the '70s.

Those images of the baker's boy pushing his bike up cobbled Gold Hill to the sound of Dvorak's New World Symphony, and the Coronation street party (directed by celebrated film-directors Ridley Scott and his brother Tony) remain forever in the memory. They won more than 36 international awards, and parodies of the Gold Hill commercial entered the repertoires of many comedians.

After 20 years of the famous "sepia tinted" television advertising campaign, Hovis introduced a new major creative development in 1994.

The new "Raised the Hovis Way" campaign focuses on specific products. With voiceovers by the popular actress, Julie Walters, set of course against the well known strains of Dvorak's New World Symphony, each advert features a familiar mealtime scene and a gently amusing endline. For example, in "Egg" we see a soft boiled egg spilling over the egg cup when dipped with a Hovis White 'soldier' before ending with the line "Yes, I hate it when that happens".

The "Raised the Hovis Way" campaign has since been extended across the Hovis product range and now includes television adverts for Hovis Wholemeal, Hovis Cobble and Hovis Half 800g.

BRAND VALUES

Hovis is viewed as a branded representative of goodness and quality. In both its original wheatgerm form, and with newly-developed modern flours, Hovis continues to build its already impressive brand recognition. Hovis flour has spurred the founding of a comprehensive range of bread products for any mealtime occasion which arises in modern life. The Hovis brand has succeeded in marrying its worthy sense of tradition with a continuing relevance to the modern shopper.

Things you didn't know about Hovis

❍ The founder, Richard Smith, died in 1900, and is now buried in Highgate cemetery. His grave is marked by a special headstone in remembrance of his particular contribution to the British man's diet.

❍ Early Hovis advertising encouraged the consumer to ask for Hovis by name - "Don't say Brown say Hovis" - was the catchphrase.

❍ During the Second World War, Hovis donated a spitfire to the RAF, called Hominis Vis, Latin for "the strength of man", which in a shortened form, was the root of the brand-name Hovis.

❍ The first Hovis advert appeared in 1888, in the form of an analyst's report on the nutritive value of bread baked from germ flour. Professor William Jago said "the prepared germ meal and flour yield a bread far superior in nutritive value, flavour and texture".

❍ Hovis TV advertising has won over 36 international awards, including a prestigious Gold Clio in 1974.

❍ Dvorak's New World Symphony has become synonymous with Hovis advertising.

❍ 110 years after Hovis flour was first introduced, Hovis is the number one bread brand in the UK.

RAISED THE HOVIS WAY

SINCE 1886

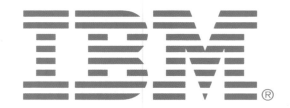

Solutions for a small planet™

THE MARKET

It is incredible to think that a few decades ago, a computer was the preserve of selected educational establishments and the military. Hugely expensive, cumbersome-looking and with pitifully slow processing-power, computers were barely in the public domain.

In recent years, we have witnessed the dawning of a technological revolution, where computers are used at home, at work, even on the move, and increasingly, to 'log on' to the Internet, a global network of computers. Highly sophisticated, but reasonably priced, PC penetration into the home is growing at a rapid rate.

In the UK, a GfK survey showed that in 1994, up to 3.3 million households (approximately one in seven) owned at least one PC. Another survey, from Zenith Media, revealed that around 510,000 UK homes had a multimedia PC (with a CD-Rom drive and able to access the Internet) at the start of 1995. This market is growing at a tremendous rate. It is predicted that by 1998, around 7 million households will own a CD-Rom equipped PC.

ACHIEVEMENTS

IBM has traditionally been one of the world's truly great Superbrands. The name IBM has always been associated with high quality technological products. Research has shown IBM's standing as a clear market leader.

IBM however, has just survived a period of immense instability and uncertainty. It had enjoyed an unrivalled position at the top of the computer market, throughout the 1970s and 80s, and through the introduction of the Personal Computer, the PC, had revolutionised the world of computing.

IBM was so pre-eminent, that all software and applications produced during this time had to be IBM compatible.

However, a flood of IBM 'clones' changed the face of the market. Up to 50,000 companies

were suddenly competing against IBM, often with cheaper machines.

IBM responded to the challenge by creating autonomous businesses, which it was felt could be more responsive to different market sectors. The downside of this, however, was a 'dilution' of IBM's unified, core brand values.

Throughout this period, constant research showed that IBM was still the most easily recognised computer company, both by business and consumers, although this was not being reflected in sales. The company then set about re-affirming its strengths as a brand, emphasising its global reach and reputation for high quality reliable products. This contrasted with its former image as unapproachable, expensive and difficult to do business with.

On 1 April 1993, Louis V Gerstner was appointed as Chairman and CEO of IBM. He decided that IBM had to shed its old, unapproachable image and identified the need for IBM to adopt a common global advertising identity, operating across the whole company. In 1994, all IBM's existing advertising agencies around the world were replaced by Ogilvy & Mather.

The resulting advertising campaign, launched in the UK in January 1995, delivered the simple message 'Solutions for a small planet', meaning whoever you are, wherever you are, IBM has a solution for you. The global campaign was run in 40 different countries, and had the same recognisable format, giving IBM a single brand identity in the global market. The campaign went on to win three 'Clios' (international marketing awards).

There is no doubt that IBM's repositioning has proved a major achievement, ensuring the company's very survival. IBM has definitely turned the corner, and with a vastly improved sales performance and an invigorated reputation as a world leader in technological innovation.

HISTORY

IBM has a longer and more illustrious history than one might think from such a technologically driven company. The corporate history of what is now IBM started in 1911 with the creation of the Computing-Tabulating-Recording company. However this company had a history stretching back to the 1880s. Three companies merged to form CTR in 1911: a New York clock manufacturer, the International Time Recording Company (ITR); the Computing Scale Company; and Herman Hollerith's Tabulating Machine Company.

CTR became a holding company for any other companies that produced components or finished products for machines which generally were used for measuring, (either units, portions time or weight). This included cash registers, weighing & measuring machines, time recorders, and accounting machines with punch cards. In 1917 the new Canadian division of the operation was called International Business Machines. In 1924, CTR adopted this name universally, because it was felt that this better reflected the varied and changing nature of the business.

IBM moved into Europe, setting up branches in France and Germany, although expansion was restricted in the UK by existing marketing and licensing agreements.

The UK operation evolved very differently to its US parent company. IBM's UK ancestry began with the British Bundy Clock Company, the UK arm of ITR, the founding New York company. The name ITR lived on in the UK until 1951, with the British ITR operating alongside IBM UK.

After the Second World War, the ITR and IBM partnership was merged to create IBM United Kingdom Limited in 1951. This new company took control of all existing operations in the UK.

Other milestones in IBM's development in the UK were the creation of development laboratories in London in 1956, which were then moved to Hursley in Hampshire two years later. A second manufacturing plant was established at Havant in 1967, and a new UK headquarters was built at North Harbour, Portsmouth in 1976.

THE PRODUCT

IBM virtually initiated the personal computer (PC) market. Its PC range includes the 'ThinkPad' portable computers and the new Aptiva Family PCs. The Aptiva range, launched in Spring 1996, has all the latest multimedia features, including Internet access using a 28.8 kbps modem. Also available from IBM are Speech Dictation machines, home PCs that type for you as you speak!

IBM also produces a full range of printers for business use. This range has been boosted by two new inclusions, a full colour laser printer, and a black & white printer that can also print three extra colours.

The IBM Magstar Tape Drive is another recent addition to the IBM data storage product range. It can store 10 gigabytes of uncompressed data into a standard cartridge, and its improved data compression techniques can allow for an increased capacity of 30 gigabytes.

IBM is dedicated to the idea of a universally connected world where people and organisations from all over the globe can get in touch with each other. The development of network connected computers, making full use of the Internet, has shown IBM's world leading expertise in this field. The company was the worldwide information technology sponsor of the 1996 Olympic Games in Atlanta, using its vast expertise in this area to provide comprehensive administrative support behind the scenes during the competition. Over 6,000 IBM touch screen PC's were installed at the Games to provide a constant supply of up-to-date information, collected and stored by IBM.

Other products in IBM's network range include Internet Connection Servers, for managing text, images, video and audio, and OSA 2 Adapters which link servers directly to high-speed networks, enabling them to run applications such as Video-on-demand.

IBM also supplies the technology that will take finance and banking into the next century. It has a range of new products to improve banking efficiency, from its VisualHomeBanker, an online banking service, to an Automated Teller Machine (ATM) that works with smart-card technology, and allows you to 'load' your cash card with money, and use it as a new form of electronic payment.

RECENT DEVELOPMENTS

1995 was a landmark year for the AS/400, proving to be the most popular multi-user commercial server in the world. With 14 PC and UNIX applications using this platform, IBM pushed ahead of rival platforms. At the CeBit 95 conference, the AS/400 re-affirmed its position as the world's most popular mid-range commercial business computer, and consistently outperformed its competitors in both price and performance. Currently, around 360,000 AS/400 platforms have been installed worldwide.

However, IBM didn't just enjoy success with the AS/400. Overall, sales were up by 30%. IBM regained its status as a company operating at the cutting edge of new technology and was acclaimed by the information technology (IT) industry as one of the best companies to forge a partnership with.

PROMOTION

IBM's most recent advertising campaign, developed by Ogilvy & Mather, which began in 1995, was designed to highlight IBM's brand strengths, global reach, and leadership in the IT market. The main focus of the campaign was to present these competitive advantages in an accessible way, giving them a warm, human angle, showing that technology could be enjoyed by anyone, anywhere in the world - not just the developed West. 'Unusual people in unexpected situations' was the main visual idea

"But you've got to get faster on the keyboard."

running through the whole series of advertisements. This combined hard product information on the screen, in the form of subtitles, with seemingly incongruous 'international' settings. Thus two elderly French gentlemen are seen strolling along the Seine accompanied by accordion music, in a scene that could be from a French 'Art' film. Yet, the subtitles reveal that the two men are actually discussing the storage capacities of their respective hard drives. Other advertisements have shown 'net-surfing' nuns and Buddhist monks contemplating the ease of global communications.

This advertising campaign has also translated to poster format, and has featured a Russian woman tapping into stock exchange details to check on the international tractor market, and a camel-mounted Arab, using software on his IBM Thinkpad to navigate the desert.

IBM also ran several print campaigns in the UK national press in 1995. These featured black & white photographs of faces from different cultures, which were used to highlight specific IBM products and services. For example a native American endorses the upgradability of the AS/400 range, which allows him 'freedom to embrace new ideas, yet preserve the old.'

Taking a traditional situation, and giving it a new technological perspective - often with humorous overtones, was a consistent thread running throughout the campaign. The advertisements showed that technology is not something to be afraid of. In fact, it can provide solutions to everyday problems, an idea which could be translated into a multitude of languages and cultures without losing any of its potency.

BRAND VALUES

The transformation of IBM from a struggling giant of the computer industry to its present role as a user-friendly industry leader has represented a major shift in its core brand values.

IBM led the market at a time when computers and technology were generally associated with professors and men in white coats. IBM seemed to epitomise this market perfectly: it was reliable, technically-advanced, yet somewhat aloof.

The PC meant that for the first time, computers were accessible to everyone, and a degree in computer science wasn't a requirement to operate one. Faced with greater competition, IBM started to lose touch with this new market. The brand had to re-invent itself to survive.

IBM's global marketing campaign, 'Solutions

Location: 29°N. 31°E. Route: 2nd left at Pyramids.

for a small planet,' spearheaded a new positive direction for the once-ailing computer company. It has succeeded in conveying the friendlier face of information technology, stressing its everyday practical applications and the benefits of easier global communications.

In recent years, IBM has shown it can maintain its leading role in the IT market. Yet, whereas IBM was once perceived as cold and distant, IBM has now shown that it is in touch, both with its market and the people it serves.

Things you didn't know about IBM

○ IBM's ancestry can be traced back to 1875. The modern company has grown from humble beginnings as the Willard Bundy Clock Manufacturers in New York.

○ IBM is working with Bayer AG to produce a 'Health Smart Card' which will be able to electronically store all your health details, including X-rays taken throughout your life.

○ New wireless technology means that computers can be linked to a network without being attached to cables. It is possible to access the Internet whilst sunbathing on a beach, or sitting on a train.

○ Through its education centres, IBM has trained over one million students to use desktop PC applications worldwide.

○ IBM's Deep Blue computer, which recently competed against Garry Kasparov for the ACM Chess Challenge title, is capable of examining 200 million positions a second, or 50 billion positions in three minutes.

THE MARKET

ICI is one of the most international companies in the chemical industry.

Its 8,000 plus products compete in a variety of different international markets.

Its main areas of business can be broadly categorised as paints, materials, explosives, and industrial chemicals, including both polymers and titanium dioxide. It also competes in a variety of specialised local markets around the world.

In 1995, the paint market was a tough place. But ICI consolidated its position as the world leader with the purchase of a major US paint company, the Grow Group, and early in 1996 of Bunge Paints, the leader in South America. Consumers in Europe and North America remained very price-conscious, but sales remained buoyant in Asia, where volumes grew by 20%, and ICI increased its market share as a result of major expansion in Malaysia, China, Thailand and Indonesia.

ICI's materials division competes in three main markets; acrylics, films and polyurethanes. 1995 saw an improvement in all three markets, with a significant increase in demand, and profits up by over 150%.

ICI is the world's largest producer of commercial explosives, but the explosives market has had a difficult year, due to an increasingly competitive market chasing fewer customers. This was particularly noticeable in the UK, with the demise of the coal industry, formerly a big user of explosives technology, and the USA.

The industrial chemicals markets in which ICI specifically competes include polymers and titanium dioxide, used in paints and plastics. Both of these markets showed encouraging signs of growth, although it slackened in the second half. Prices rose and the Chemicals & Polymers business announced major investments in the UK, as well as in growing Asian economies such as Taiwan and Pakistan.

ACHIEVEMENTS

Innovation in science can be regarded as more than just discovery or invention. It is the consequence of a moment when the perceived qualities of a new material and a particular need are magically combined. This thinking has been behind the main technological inventions that ICI has brought to the industrial world in the last 70 years.

ICI's invention of polythene and its related products have contributed greatly to the profound social revolution which has taken place in the western industrialised countries. Plastic housewares, self-service shopping (impossible without the plastic film to keep food fresh), affordable home fridges and

freezers small enough to fit in modern houses, and the whole do-it-yourself culture of the last forty years would not have been possible had it not been for ICI's innovation. ICI (Imperial Chemical Industries PLC) holds leading positions in the paints, materials, explosives and industrial chemicals markets. Total group turnover in 1995 was £10,269 million, making it one of the largest chemical companies in the world.

ICI has certain key areas of strength. In paints and industrial coatings it is the world leader. In the industrial explosives market, ICI explosives is the leading supplier of industrial explosives and initiating systems.

ICI is the largest producer of methyl methacrylate (MMA), a key component in the manufacture of resins and surface coatings for bathrooms and kitchenware. ICI is also a leading manufacturer of ozone benign replacements for CFC's. It has production plants for them in the UK, USA and Japan, and is the only company with such a global production spread. ICI is also the second largest producer of titanium dioxide pigments, used to produce whiteness in paper, plastics and paints: the largest polyester film producer and the second largest manufacturer of PTA, the basic ingredient for polyester fibres and other products.

HISTORY

ICI began as a business enterprise on 1st January 1927. It was formed from a merger of four of the largest, and most important chemical producers of the time. In 1926, the leaders of the largest chemical companies from Britain, Germany and the USA met in New York hotel rooms to engage in discussions that would ultimately determine the

control of the vast, lucrative markets around the world. The main players in these meetings were: Brunner Mond; Britains largest alkali manufacturer, Allied Chemical & Dye Corp of the US; Nobel Industries, the British explosives business; and IG Farbenindustrie, a powerful consortium of German companies that threatened to give Germany supremacy in the world chemical market.

It was for this reason that these meetings had been held. The British and US companies realised that the threat of a German monopoly made some kind of deal imperative, either by forming an alliance with the Germans, or by forming a defensive pact against it.

The result of these meetings was that a large, British-led group of companies decided to merge and form a single entity. The new company acquired, by exchange of shareholdings, four of the companies involved in the meetings: Brunner Mond, Nobel Industries, United Alkali, and British Dyestuffs Corporation. The amalgamation of the four companies was typed out on four sheets of Cunard Line writing paper as they sailed back to Europe on the RMS Aquitania. This agreement formed a company representing some 5,000 products, and £100 million in assets. It's name, Imperial Chemical Industries Ltd was decided by Sir Alfred Mond, of Brunner Mond, and Nobel Industries' Sir Harry McGowan during the crossing.

The rivalry between the ICI group and its German counterpart IG Farben intensified in the period leading up to the Second World War.

At the time, one of the major breakthroughs for ICI was the discovery of 'Polymerisation', the production of polythene. This major scientific breakthrough, was made by an ICI research scientist - Eric Fawcett. Even though the

discovery had not yet been patented, Fawcett announced his feat at a Cambridge University conference. Luckily for ICI, one of the attendees, a German scientist Hermann Staudinger, firmly refused to believe that 'Polymerisation' was possible.

However, as the potential commercial reverberations of this discovery sank in, IG Farben attempted to prise the secret from ICI. In return, ICI wanted to extract information on the Germans' polystyrene and rubber products. But after weighing up the pros and cons of such an exchange, ICI decided to hold on to its secret.

One ICI historian has since remarked: 'There cannot have been many business propositions in history which have broken down with such advantage to Britain".

More recent developments in ICI's history have included the demerger of the company into two separate entities. This historic decision was taken by the board meeting on 25th February 1993, and involved splitting the group into ICI and Zeneca, the bioscience business. This came into effect from 1 June 1993, and Zeneca immediately became the fourth most profitable drugs business in the world.

THE PRODUCT
ICI operates in various, diverse markets. It manufactures nearly 8,000 different types of product.

ICI Paints is a world leader in decorative paint, coatings for food and drinks containers and refinish paints for damaged vehicles. It has become a world leader in this area, through its innovative technology and marketing of strong brands such as 'Dulux' and ICI Autocolor.

ICI Materials produces chemicals and related materials from which products can be made. It specialises in acrylics, which are used for coatings, lighting products and vehicle components; high-performance plastic films, with a multitude of purposes, including packaging and data storage; and polyurethanes, used for applications such as insulation, seat cushioning, shoe soles and adhesives.

ICI Explosives is the world's leading supplier of blasting services, including industrial explosives and initiating systems, essential in the mining, quarrying and construction industries.

ICI Explosives develops the explosive component which expands an in-vehicle air bag on impact.

The ICI industrial chemical area is divided into two sections: Chemicals & Polymers (C&P); and Tioxide. C&P is one of the world's largest manufacturers of industrial chemicals. It manufactures pure terephthalic acids (PTA), 'Melinar' PET resins, and Klea, CFC replacements, as well as surfactants (surface effect chemicals) and chlorine products.

Tioxide is the world's second largest producer of titanium dioxide pigments, which are used to give whiteness and opacity to a wide range of products such as paints, plastics and inks.

ICI's regional businesses operate in areas where ICI's strengths offer clear competitive

advantages. ICI invests in strong businesses in selected local markets. So, for example, the company invests in fertilizers and crop care in Australia, rubber chemicals in India, and forest products in Canada, but not world-wide. Within these markets, ICI aims to excel against local and international competition.

RECENT DEVELOPMENTS
With such a large company producing so many different products, there is a constant need to track and keep ahead in each market that it operates in.

One such development has recently come from ICI's Autocolor division, which produces paint used to re-spray car bodywork. The vehicle refinishing market specifically requires a product with a long shelf-life which is able to satisfy the demand for thousands of different car colours, past and present. Therefore, the ease by which colours can be mixed is crucial. A range of water-based basecoat paints called 'Aquabase,' have been produced, which meet this need, but also feature a much reduced level of organic solvents, compared to standard paints. This development ensures that companies using Aquabase can cut the costs of complying with new environmental legislation, as fewer organic solvents in the atmosphere mean a safer and healthier workshop environment.

Other new developments from the Paints Research & Development department have been the first solid emulsion paints, and water-borne spray lacquers for the insides of drink cans, while ICI was the first company to produce commercial alternatives to CFCs. ICI polyurethanes' new vacuum packs are cutting the size and improving the energy efficiency of fridges and freezers.

PROMOTION
ICI operates in a wide range of markets, and therefore has to maintain its common 'umbrella' identity, to successfully encompass its vast and diverse array of products, and over 400 trading companies which form the ICI group.

To retain a strong association with the ICI Group, the famous ICI symbol is used. This logo was adopted from the original Nobel Industries symbol. When ICI was first formed in 1927, the word 'Nobel' was simply replaced by "ICI".

For many years this trade mark was referred to in the company as 'The Circle and Wavy Lines Device". This rather lengthy title was

replaced by the more snappy 'roundel'.

ICI has embarked upon a policy of 'global marketing'. Its products can be marketed in many different countries, using the same packaging in different languages. This 'World Class' approach allows ICI to adopt the features from successful marketing campaigns in any market they operate in, while the roundel provides consistency and a recognised mark of quality assurance.

ICI also believes that it can still learn from its world-wide competitors, despite its huge stature in the marketplace. ICI continues to tackle strong competitors 'head-on' with its brand of wholesale, corporate promotion, to good effect. ICI Autocolor has already felt the benefits of this approach - sales doubled in the USA in 1994, even in the face of strong competition.

In recent years ICI has mounted a major drive into Asia, where the largest world chemicals markets will be in the 21st century, and is building major market positions there in paint, polyurethanes and PTA.

BRAND VALUES
ICI is a forward thinking company which sets out to foster talent and ideas to best effect. It sets as one of its core values the inspiration and reward of talented people. Many of ICI's inventions have changed the way we live and work today.

Despite its huge size and enormous spread of interests, ICI remains a formidable single brand entity spanning a variety of differing markets. This has been achieved by successfully taking original ideas to the stage of commercial development and ultimately the marketplace.

In 1996 it launched a Vision and Values statement. It is: To be the industry leader in creating value for customers and shareholders by: market driven innovation in products and services; winning in quality growth markets world-wide; inspiration and reward of talented people; exemplary performance in safety and health; responsible care for the environment; relentless pursuit of operational excellence.

Things you didn't know about ICI

○ In French speaking countries, the name ICI must appear with full stops between the letters, eg: I.C.I, to avoid confusion with the French word 'ici'.

○ Every year ICI makes enough paint to decorate and protect more than 5 million homes.

○ There are over 300 different shades of blue in ICI's range of coloured perspex.

○ ICI spends about £250 million per year on research and technology development.

○ 40% of Chinese fridges are insulated with ICI polyurethanes.

○ ICI paint was chosen for the world's tallest building - the new Petronas Towers in Kuala Lumpur, Malaysia.

THE MARKET

Sending flowers has traditionally been a way of marking a special occasion or simply a nicer, or more romantic way to relay a message. Flower-sellers used to congregate in town-squares and markets lending colour and scent to many a street scene. Florists came into existence offering skilled floral arrangements and a delivery service. With the wider availability of an exotic range of flowers imported from all over the world in recent years and the advances in design techniques, the florist trade has become ever more specialised. The sending of flowers has also become an increasingly efficient process making use of the latest advances in technology.

Each year the British spend an average of £15 per person on cut flowers, however, economic uncertainty in the early 1990s signalled lean years for the florist business. However, 1995 saw the beginning of an upturn in orders which has been maintained into 1996, showing that as the economy picks up so will floristry. One of the best ways to show you care, is and always will be with flowers.

ACHIEVEMENTS

Interflora is unique. There is no other organisation quite like it anywhere in the world. It is not a franchise but a democratically run network of 60,000 independent florists able to deliver flowers almost anywhere in 160 countries world-wide. A heartfelt message can be relayed from Alaska to Russia, or from Dublin to Western Samoa. Interflora can target just about anywhere in only 24 hours. This special service has even stretched to "out" of this world, when the British astronaut Helen Sharman sent a message to Interflora from space, requesting a bouquet to be sent to her mother with the accompanying message:

"Many thanks for supporting me in everything I've done, Love Helen". Interflora can be relied on to "say it with flowers" just about anywhere.

Each member-florist has a terminal in their shop, linked to the main computer which facilitates the processing of orders from one place to another. The system works. Each year, over half a billion orders are sent through the Interflora network world-wide. Valentine's Day is traditionally the single busiest day. In the UK, Interflora florists usually deal with around half a million orders on that one day - mostly for 12 red roses!

Interflora has played an important part in so many of the key occasions in our lives. Interflora marks the moments, from birth, at birthdays, weddings, during illness, any of the triumphs or trials of life and, of course, to funerals. For over 70 years, Interflora has handled sensitive situations on our behalf with tact and sincerity. It has expressed our feelings perfectly when words couldn't quite articulate what we really wanted to say. And so well. Interflora will go to great lengths to meet the needs of its customers. Every measure is taken to guarantee punctuality of delivery. Particularly for the big occasion. Any instructions are closely followed by Interflora florists. They often have to sculpt very complicated designs in flowers, such as motorbikes, footballs, military coats of arms, pieces of furniture, the "Gates of Heaven", the ubiquitous Mum and Dad - you name it, Interflora will do it and always with good grace and with a high degree of professionalism and quality.

HISTORY

In the United States, at the turn of the century, it took four days to send a bouquet from one end of the country to the other. Needless to say, after such a long and arduous journey, the flowers weren't as fresh as could be hoped for on arrival. It took two resourceful florists in 1910 to think up a more

efficient system. Taking advantage of the latest telegraph technology, the businesses linked-up, processing orders to be delivered at the opposite side of the country by the fellow-florist, settling their accounts on trust. Other florists soon followed suit.

The idea was taken up by two British florists in 1920, one in Glasgow, the other in Essex. By 1923 there were 17 so-called "foreign members" of the American Florist's Telegraph Delivery Service. In 1935 the British Unit ceased to be an appendage of the American operation and 11 years later, the British, Americans and the Europeans joined forces to become the International Florists Association. The name changed to Interflora in 1953 and the famous Mercury symbol was adopted.

Since then the Interflora network has grown to enormous proportions enabling the delivery of bouquets to all parts of the world via Interflora's 60,000 member-florists.

THE PRODUCT

The British unit of Interflora is based in the Lincolnshire market town of Sleaford and communicates with its members by means of a hi-tech computerised system which links every Interflora florist with the central database.

In the UK and the Republic of Ireland there are 2,800 member florists. Interflora members meet strict criteria to join the organisation's network, as well as paying a membership fee. Standards set by Interflora are extremely high and professionalism at all times is a must. In this way, customers can always feel assured of a quality service. To ensure tip-top service and prompt delivery, the central computer system is constantly updated at the Interflora headquarters.

Interflora (British Unit) is a non-profit-making organisation. The £2.99 service and transmission charge is used to operate a rigorous quality control programme. When a florist applies for Interflora membership, they are required to conform to certain standards of floristry and service and also agree to subject themselves to an on-spec testing programme using members of the public to receive anonymous orders. These orders are then evaluated by teams of top florists. This testing process is respected as a means of ensuring the network operates to the high standards set by the Association. Any complaints or queries about the service, which can't be handled directly by the member-florist, are addressed to the customer services department based at HQ, which acts as arbitrator. In such a way, the customer is assured of recourse if they feel the service has fallen short of its usual high standards.

Interflora florists are always open to customer requests and are only too willing to please - however whimsical the request may seem.

And if Interflora promises to deliver, by hook or by crook it will do just that - unless they have been given the wrong instructions by the customer. Certain cases have proved to be trickier than others. Deliveries to ships and hospitals are notorious! The "disappearing hospital patient" syndrome can be a tough one, as increasingly, people are discharged from hospital at short notice.

When a delivery is ordered to a ship, details have to be particularly clear. Interflora cites a case where a mother was sending a bouquet to her daughter on board a cruiseliner, but both misnamed the ship and muddled the ship's itinerary. Florists ended up chasing the wrong ship around the Greek Islands. Three separate flower arrangements were made up at three different ports by three different florists before Interflora Greece were able to trace the correct ship.

RECENT DEVELOPMENTS

Keeping up with a tradition for taking advantage of the latest advances in communication technology, Interflora was one of the first services available on the Internet. The service is a "natural" for most shopping mall developments including CompuServe, the international online service. It will shortly even feature on a major international airline's seatback monitors enabling travellers to send orders whilst in-flight, with the possibility of deliveries being made before the plane reaches its own destination!

Sainsbury's, identifying Interflora's personal delivery as a particular strength, has developed Flowers Direct, providing its customers with a freecall service to order floral arrangements designed in consultation with Interflora. Paula Pryke, the Interflora florist who works closely with Delia Smith on her television cookery series, is retained by Sainsbury to style future designs for this flower delivery service.

Fresh Post Bouquets, established in 1994, is Interflora's postal arm providing customers with a low cost alternative to the relay system. Interflora Flowers, a wholesaling operation set up in 1993, is now offering Interflora member florists high quality flowers at competitive prices delivered by Interflora's fleet of vehicles, guaranteeing the correct care from grower to retailer which is so important for the eventual life-span of flowers.

PROMOTION

Interflora supports its network of member-florists with national advertising campaigns. Most memorable is the campaign which coined the slogan, "Say it with flowers", which has become a worthy catchphrase for the Interflora organisation. More recently, Interflora has introduced the slogan, "Delivered by hand, straight to the heart".

Since 1914, the speedy messenger Mercury has featured on Interflora's logo. In 1936 Mercury swapped his traditional staff for a box of flowers and the slogan "Say it with flowers" was added. The logo was further simplified in 1939 to portray Mercury alone, framed by a

gold, circular band. In 1979 the words 'Since 1910' were added.

A recent successful campaign used 48 sheet posters displayed on hoardings all over the UK and Republic of Ireland. Strongly styled flower images ensured impact in major city centres reinforcing Interflora's quality marque which, according to 1995 research, retains its 99% recognition level.

The common root of Interflora's marketing policy is ensuring customers are aware of the range and flexibility of services Interflora has at its disposal. This includes the recently launched freecall service linked to Interflora florists throughout the country, as well as the delivery of additional gifts such as chocolates, balloons and soft toys.

However, Interflora ensures it is present, not only at people's personal special moments, but also at special sporting moments which mean a lot to the nation as a whole. A successful sponsorship programme with British Athletics has guaranteed Interflora a high profile over the last eight years. Future activity is likely to focus on tactical opportunities for sponsorship titles like the 1996 Interflora Valentine Classic in Glasgow, continuing to show the value of flowers for winners which has been so popular with both audiences and athletes like Sally Gunnall and Linford Christie. To illustrate the flexibility of this winning theme, Interflora is just as at home at the Chelsea Flower Show, Crufts Dog Show, the World Ice Skating and the World Canoeing Slalom Championships, although here the flowers and yellow ribbons received rather too much water!

Specially designed bouquets and attractive promotions also serve to link Interflora with other famous names like Nescafé in the Love Over Gold promotion, with Harper Collins featuring Barbara Taylor Bradford's latest title, as well as BT, Cathay Pacific and Diners Club.

BRAND VALUES

Whatever the occasion you'll find Interflora. But the essence of Interflora is not just about sending someone a bunch of flowers. It is the experience that this moment of delivery represents, and the thought that went behind it that really counts. Interflora can be relied on to ensure that this precious moment goes to plan, or in the case of a romance, has the desired effect! Interflora can help us say it with flowers - their message is "Delivered by hand, straight to the heart".

The Interflora service signifies quality and professionalism, and a dedication to meeting the demands of its customers. Interflora is an experience anyone can enjoy. After all, everyone from childhood to death, is a potential customer - or a recipient, at some time during their life.

Things you didn't know about Interflora

❍ The international Interflora network operates in its own currency - the Fleurin. This has been used since 1948 and is loosely tied to the Swiss franc.

❍ Interflora offers customers a twenty four hour seven days a week FreeCall Service (a Mercury free number: 0500 434343 i.e. For Free, For Free, For Free). During shop hours, the number can connect a customer to their nearest Interflora florist. At any other time, the call is connected to a centralised Flowerline based at Interflora headquarters.

❍ Interflora has relayed some "interesting" messages with flowers, such as "Thanks for last night but can I please have the bath-taps back?" and from a soldier in the Gulf War, "I hope these flowers smell better than the camels round here!".

❍ During the Second World War, Interflora set up an agency to provide military personnel with their own dedicated flower delivery ordering service. This extended to the Gulf War, when a special ordering facility was provided for military personnel living under canvas in the desert. When the tornado squadrons returned to base, Interflora provided the homecoming crews with flowers to give to their loved ones in celebration.

❍ In 1996 a Visa Delta card survey confirmed that women value a delivery of flowers above a romantic meal or even a weekend away. What is more, the same survey also revealed that men enjoy receiving flowers too. Contrary to the belief of almost 50% of the women surveyed, 70% of men said they would be flattered and pleased to be sent a bouquet of flowers.

THE MARKET

The UK beer market has never been tougher. With an increasingly discerning and marketing literate consumer and the most challenging trading climate that the UK has ever seen, only brands which offer a relevant consumer proposition will prosper.

Within the UK beer market, the bitter sector commands an estimated annual retail sales value in excess of £5 billion. As with consumer markets in general, the ales sector of the beer market is continuing to polarise around big brands which are well-supported and which provide drinkers with taste and quality.

ACHIEVEMENTS

John Smith's is Britain's number one bitter brand and UK drinkers down more than a million pints of John Smith's every day. The brand has been the clear market leader in the take-home trade since its in-can launch in 1979 and massive growth in sales - in pubs, clubs and off-licences - has enabled John Smith's to topple its rivals and take overall market leadership as Britain's biggest-selling bitter.

The introduction of John Smith's Extra Smooth Bitter in March 1995 has been widely hailed as the industry's most successful draught beer launch ever and is now worth more than £250 million per year.

John Smith's award-winning television advertising campaign featuring comedian Jack Dee has been greeted with acclaim from both consumers and marketing pundits. The ads have won no less than 46 awards since 1992.

John Smith's impressive growth - more than 20% year-on-year - has been spearheaded by a quality product, award-winning advertising and successful brand development. This combination has helped John Smith's become the nation's favourite bitter.

HISTORY

John Smith's Bitter is one of Northern England's most famous ales and has been brewed in Tadcaster, Yorkshire since 1847. That year, young John Smith was just 24 years of age when he purchased a run-down brewhouse in the North Yorkshire town and started a brewing heritage that has spanned a century-and-a half.

John Smith quickly realised the potential of Tadcaster as one of the country's most prominent brewing centres, based on its abundant supplies of hard water which is so necessary for brewing ale. One of John Smith's foremost concerns was the quality of ingredients

and brewing techniques used in the production of his beers, and that concern remains of paramount importance today.

Soon after his arrival in Tadcaster, John Smith started construction on a new brewery. Sadly, he died in 1879 and did not see the finished brewery which was later hailed by the Yorkshire Herald as "... the largest and most complete in Yorkshire".

Since that time, the story of John Smith's Tadcaster Brewery has been one of continuing progressive development in every aspect of the brewing industry. Although the Tadcaster brewery has been greatly expanded and millions of pounds have been invested on the most up-to-date production plant and associated services, the company is extremely proud of the original buildings.

They have been carefully preserved as a reminder of John Smith's belief in the future potential of the brewing business in Tadcaster.

THE PRODUCT

John Smith's Bitter, which has been brewed in Tadcaster since 1847 is Scottish Courage's leading bitter brand and enjoys a massive following amongst beer lovers who appreciate its full-bodied flavour, thick creamy head and 'No-Nonsense' reputation.

1979 saw the introduction of John Smith's Bitter in cans and, since that time, the brand has enjoyed market leadership in the off-licence trade.

The much publicised addition of the now-famous 'widget' for the launch of John Smith's Draught in 1993 drove take-home sales even higher and brought the word 'widget' into everyday use.

In March 1995, John Smith's Extra Smooth Bitter was introduced. Its unique dispense tap and increased levels of nitrogen delivers a smooth tasting pint with a thick creamy head that lasts to the bottom of the glass. John Smith's

you don't need gimmicks". The 'gimmicks' - which included dancing ladybirds and penguins - provided the comic touch and complemented Dee's trademark deadpan delivery.

One of the first ads portrayed Jack Dee reluctantly joining in a song and dance routine with some giant ladybirds - thanks to the incentive of a large bag of money - and, since that time, Dee has remained singularly unimpressed. The antics of a tap-dancing, all-singing troupe of penguins in the "Help Yourself" advertisements for John Smith's Extra Smooth Bitter attracted huge popular interest amongst consumers and the special effects used in the commercial's production were featured on the BBC programme "How Do They Do That?".

The Jack Dee ads for John Smith's were created by BMP and directed by Mandy Fletcher, well-known for the highly popular and critically acclaimed Blackadder comedy series.

On top of its award-winning TV campaign, John Smith's has also benefited from high-profile sports sponsorships including the Great Britain, England and Wales Rugby League Teams and heavyweight consumer and trade promotions.

Extra Smooth, which is also served at a refreshingly cool temperature - similar to that of lagers, is 'Pure Silk in a Glass'.

RECENT DEVELOPMENTS
John Smith's Draught - the one with the 'widget' - has recently undergone a packaging redesign and is adopting the name of its on-trade sister product, John Smith's Extra Smooth Bitter.

The canned product offers the same 'Pure Silk in a Glass' proposition as the on-trade version and, by establishing a common identity in both the on and off-trade sectors, Scottish Courage aims to communicate, more clearly, the product benefits in everyday consumer language.

1996 has also seen the launch of a new advertising campaign which continues to feature comedian Jack Dee.

PROMOTION
John Smith's enjoys a massive £10 million marketing programme each year, and is the most heavily supported ale brand in Britain. The biggest component of the brand's marketing programme over recent years has been its high profile advertising campaigns.

It is difficult to think of John Smith's without the image of the archetypal Yorkshireman Arkwright coming to mind. Gordon Rollings played the much loved character in an advertising campaign which earned numerous awards. When Rollings passed away so the

campaign was laid to rest following a tribute to the cloth-capped hero.

Recent ads focus on the idea that bitter drinkers share comedian Jack Dee's 'No-Nonsense' attitude: "When you've got a widget -

BRAND VALUES
John Smith's is a top quality mainstream ale brand with a distinctive full flavour that delivers taste, quality and the reputation of a brand which drinkers ask for by name.

John Smith's Bitter is summed up by its advertising strapline - No-Nonsense. The brand personality is straightforward and unpretentious with a dry and highly developed sense of humour, as evident in the witty Jack Dee advertising campaign.

While encapsulating the heritage values of a true Yorkshire bitter, the brand has helped extend the market from its traditional Northern heartland to drinkers of all ages, in all regions, of the UK and John Smith's Bitter has succeeded in becoming a truly international brand.

Things you didn't know about John Smith's Bitter

❍ John Smith's is the UK's biggest-selling bitter brand.

❍ More than a million pints of John Smith's are sold every day in the UK.

❍ John Smith's is enjoyed in many parts of the world - including Australia, Africa and the Arab Gulf.

❍ John Smith's has an annual retail sales value in excess of £450 million.

❍ John Smith's has produced some of the best-known TV advertising in Britain. The brand's famous 'No-Nonsense' campaign with Jack Dee has won no less than 46 awards.

❍ John Smith's Bitter has been brewed in Tadcaster since 1847 when a 24 year-old John Smith bought a run-down brewhouse in the North Yorkshire town and began a famous brewing heritage which now spans nearly 150 years.

❍ John Smith's has consistently been Britain's biggest-selling canned bitter since its launch in 1979.

❍ More than 100 million pints of John Smith's Extra Smooth have been sold since the brand was launched in March 1995.

Kellogg's

THE MARKET

Breakfast is viewed by many as the most important meal of the day. Research shows that 93% of the UK population eat or drink 'something' for breakfast, with 44% eating ready-to-eat cereals.

This signifies the change in UK breakfast eating habits over the last 20 years. In 1968, approximately half the population tucked into a cooked breakfast on a regular basis. By 1990, this had dropped to an estimated 10% of the population.

This is often attributed to the increase in working mothers, currently estimated to be around 7.1 million compared to just 2.7 million in 1951, and 3.8 million ten years later. The average working mother doesn't fancy the chore of washing-up in the morning (or indeed when she gets home from a tiring day at work) and increasingly children are preparing their own breakfast. And what could be easier than pouring milk on a bowl of cereal?

However, with ever pressured lifestyles, breakfast is often sacrificed to the exigencies of keeping to a tight timetable. One of the major challenges facing cereal companies today is to persuade consumers that cereals can be enjoyed at any time of the day, not just in the morning. Children are the greatest breakfast eaters, particularly favouring cereals.

In terms of volume, the UK is the largest consumer of cereals in Europe. In 1995, the market was valued (at RSP) at £946 million, representing an increase of 2% on 1994. Per capita consumption has risen by 25% over the last 10 years, and currently stands at 6.4 kilos, with children and the over-55s the greatest consumers.

Branded cereals fare best in the UK market, with private label holding just a 16.7% share.

ACHIEVEMENTS

Kellogg's Corn Flakes is the UK's and Europe's number one breakfast cereal. In 1995 alone, over 105 million packets of Kellogg's Corn Flakes were consumed. Indeed, around half of all UK households are likely to have a packet of Kellogg's Corn Flakes in their home.

Kellogg's Corn Flakes is by far the biggest brand in the UK ready-to-eat cereal market. With sales currently valued at around £114 million in the UK, Kellogg's Corn Flakes holds a 15% volume share of the market. Its closest contender, Weetabix, has just a 9% market share. Within the UK cereal market as a whole, the Kellogg Company has 12 out of the top 20 brands and holds a 52.7% sterling market share.

Of course, Kellogg's enjoys international renown and can be bought in over 160 countries.

HISTORY

The discovery of what was to become Kellogg's Corn Flakes was a quirk of fate. Back in 1884, Dr John Harvey Kellogg, superintendent of the internationally famous Seventh Day Adventist Battle Creek sanitarium, in concert with his business manager brother, Will Keith (WK) Kellogg, was developing a nutritious cereal food for his patients.

However, a freak laboratory accident exposed cooked wheat to the open air for over a day. The Kellogg brothers then processed the wheat through rollers, ensuring an even distribution of moisture - resulting in wheat flakes.

The patients loved this new flaky cereal product, and demanded supplies, even after leaving the sanitarium.

Building upon this opportunity, the Kellogg

brothers formed a company in partnership with The Sanitas Nut Company, with WK Kellogg as general manager.

From wheat flakes to corn flakes was a simple process. WK added malt to his flake product and used only the heart of the corn in manufacture. He was so impressed with his corn flakes, he started up his own company to market them.

However, his business plans were temporarily put on hold when a fire swept through his brother's sanitarium, which WK volunteered to help reconstruct and re-establish. It took until 1906 to kickstart his business activities. The company he formed was called The Battle Creek Toasted Corn Flake Company, but this was soon changed to the simpler Kellogg Company. By now, the sanitarium's success with its flake products had spawned up to 42 imitations from local rivals. To counter this, WK had his name and signature scripted on each individual package of Kellogg's Corn Flakes.

WK quickly realised the benefits of advertising and demand was soon exceeding expectations. By 1909, more than a million cases of Kellogg's Corn Flakes were sold across the US. A variant, Kellogg's Bran Flakes was introduced in 1915, followed by All-Bran in 1916 and Rice Krispies in 1928. Since then,

Coco Pops, Frosties and Special K amongst many others have been added to Kellogg's repertoire.

International expansion became inevitable. Kellogg's Corn Flakes was first introduced into the UK in 1924, and in 1938 a new factory was opened in Trafford Park, Manchester. Manufacturing plants were also built in Canada and Australia. Today, Kellogg's operates plants in 21 countries and employs around 16,000 people, marketing its products in over 160 countries worldwide.

In the UK, Kellogg's operates a manufacturing facility in Wrexham, North Wales. Over 2,000 people are employed, producing around 24 different cereal products.

THE PRODUCT

Research shows that breakfast is one of the most important sources of nutrients and energy in our daily diets. Breakfast literally means "break - fast". After all, by the time we get up in the morning, we may not have eaten for some 12 hours. Studies of US and British school-children have borne out the importance of taking breakfast. Children who ate nothing or very little for breakfast, demonstrated signs of inattentiveness and mental fatigue by the late morning, compared to their breakfast-eating counterparts.

Nutritionists recommend that a good breakfast should supply about one quarter to a third of our daily nutritional needs. Kellogg's breakfast cereals are designed to do just this, providing a well-balanced source of fibre, and essential vitamins and minerals. Kellogg's cereals contain Niacin, Vitamin B6, Riboflavin (B2), Thiamin (B1), Folic Acid, Vitamin D, Vitamin B12 and Iron.

Consistent quality checks and testing ensure Kellogg's cereals are always in tip-top condition. Since 1914, Kellogg's has used a sealed inner liner as well as an outer carton to ensure fresh and high quality products.

RECENT DEVELOPMENTS

The Kellogg Company continues to innovate the cereals market. In August 1995, Kellogg's launched Sustain, backed by a significant promotional spend. Developed in collaboration with the Australian Institute of Sport, this cereal has been specifically formulated to meet the needs of athletes. In just three months after launch, Sustain took a 0.8% volume market share.

Kellogg's major cereal brands fared well during 1995, boosted by on-pack consumer offers, such as Premier League Football stickers on UK packs of Kellogg's Corn Flakes.

Further promotions in 1996 included major sponsorship of the Euro '96 football championships in England. This featured on packages of Kellogg's Corn Flakes, Frosties, Coco Pops and Rice Krispies.

1996 also saw the launch of Kellogg's Hot Krumbly Tropical Fruit into the UK hot cereals market - traditionally the most under-developed sector in the overall cereals market. Where Kellogg's Hot Krumbly Tropical Fruit has differed from its rivals is that it can be prepared in the microwave in under one minute. The product's key message has been "You won't find a better hot breakfast".

PROMOTION

From the outset, WK Kellogg realised that promotion was vital to growing his brand. In 1906, he invested in a full-page ad in The Ladies Home Journal with astounding results. Sales grew from just 33 cases a day to 2,900. Spurred on by this success, WK embarked on a series of sales promotions offering free samples of "The Original and Best" Kellogg's Corn Flakes, including the 'Give the Grocer a Wink' campaign, and a book in 1910, "The Jungleland Funny Moving Pictures". One of Kellogg's early promotions in 1938 was a realistic gliding model aeroplane offered free to Kellogg's customers.

By 1911, Kellogg's had spent $1 million on advertising - a huge sum in those days. This was capped by a 106ft wide and 80ft tall electric sign, bearing a 60ft K, positioned on the roof of the Mecca building in Times Square, New York.

In keeping with his commitment to health and nutrition, WK hired Mary Barber in 1923, to develop in-house recipes using Kellogg cereals. This spearheaded a company tradition, which is upheld to this day, to update consumers on diet and health issues. Detailed package labels continue the practice of ensuring customers always know the nutritional values of the cereal contents.

The Kellogg Company was swift to use TV as a new and exciting advertising medium. In the early 1950s, the Kellogg Company sponsored two of the US' most popular family shows, "Superman" and "Wild Bill Hickock". Then, in 1955, Kellogg's first UK TV advertisement appeared, promoting Ricicles. Since then Kellogg's has invested heavily and consistently in TV advertising.

In 1930, WK gave up a large proportion of his shares in order to set up the WKK Foundation, with the mission to"help people help themselves". Over the years, this foundation has donated money to agricultural, educational and health institutions across the world. Every year, it supports up to 400 projects worldwide and is one of the largest philanthropic organisations in the USA.

BRAND VALUES

Kellogg's Corn Flakes have enjoyed a long history of popularity based on their appetising taste and high nutritional value. The brand has been driven by a belief, first perpetuated by its founder WK Kellogg, that cereals can provide an integral part of our diet, as a high carbohydrate, low fat food. This approach holds special appeal for today's increasingly health-conscious consumer.

Kellogg's Corn Flakes remain popular with all members of the family, offering a top quality, wholesome and nourishing product with a heritage of 'goodness' that can be relied upon.

The Kellogg Company has successfully strived to maintain its status as a socially responsible corporate citizen, with a consideration for the environment in all that it does.

Things you didn't know about Kellogg's

◯ Kellogg's Trafford Park factory was opened in 1938 by a Nottinghamshire housewife, Mrs Florence Millward. She attended all subsequent Kellogg's events.

◯ WK Kellogg, who founded The Kellogg Company, was an interesting character whose destiny appears to have been tied up with the number seven. He was the seventh son of John Preston and Ann Janette Kellogg, born on the seventh day of the month. His father was also a seventh child and the family surname, Kellogg, of course, has seven letters. WK first started work at the age of seven! He spent the rest of his life indulging a superstitious liking for the number - opting for seventh floor hotel rooms with numbers always ending in seven.

◯ The Kellogg Company was the first to print recipes, product information and nutrition messages on the side and back panels of its cereal packages.

◯ Kellogg's do not make cereal for anyone else.

◯ Before developing his famous cereal, WK Kellogg also developed a grain-based coffee substitute, a type of granola and peanut butter.

◯ An early advertising campaign for Kellogg's Corn Flakes coined the slogan "the sweetheart of the corn" to describe the corn grit main ingredient used in the product's manufacture.

THE MARKET

First tailored in California during the 1850s, jeans and denim wear have become ubiquitous items of clothing around the world. Smart, casual, young, old, denim can be fashionable, and yet tough, equally suited to the rigours of physical labour. Worn at work, at home, or out and about, jeans are the most versatile and accepted pieces of clothing, taking pride of place in most people's wardrobes.

In the UK, the 1980s witnessed a downturn in the jeans market as the result of changing fashion trends. However, the relaunch of Levi's 501 jeans injected new life into the market and volume growth has continued steadily ever since.

ACHIEVEMENTS

Levi's jeans are richly deserving of their title - the Originals. Sure enough, they were the first jeans ever to be produced and marketed by Levi Strauss Company, during the 1850s Californian Gold Rush, and since then, they have become fashion icons for every succeeding generation.

The excellent product quality of Levi's jeans, allied with what must be one of the powerful and scintillating advertising campaigns ever created, has thrust Levi Strauss & Co into an enviable position as one of the most famous brands around the world. After all, literally millions of people, from every walk of life in just about every part of the globe, wear, and often love, their Levi's jeans.

The brand's enduring appeal has been achieved through a consistent policy of renewal and diversification, with recent advertising highlighting how the brand has come full circle, with the relaunch of the Original Levi's 501 jeans. These are as relevant for consumers today as for the hardworking gold-diggers, cowboys and pioneers of yesteryear.

The fashionable status of Levi's jeans has succeeded in forging a worldwide brand with quintessential American values. Most famous of all are Levi's 501's, the world's best-selling jeans.

HISTORY

The original Levi Strauss was a Bavarian Jewish émigré who worked as a peddler in New York during the 1850s. Hoping to earn sufficient capital to open his own novelty store, Levi Strauss moved to California with bales of tough brown canvas which he planned to sell to the gold-miners for building tents. He was met with disdain. Miners didn't care how they lived. They wanted gold, and lots of it. That was all that counted. They pointed out that hard-wearing trousers, withstanding the rigours of a sweaty day's work in the mines, would have been a far greater asset.

Willing to please, and recognising an

excellent commercial prospect when it came his way, Levi Strauss obliged, manufacturing tough canvas overalls instead. Levi's jeans, as they were called, were an outstanding success.

In 1856, Levi Strauss opened a store, Levi Strauss & Co, and began marketing a new brand of clothing tailored from a durable dyed indigo cotton fabric from serge de Nimes. This was soon shortened to 'Denim'.

Levi Strauss continued to trade his denim wear in and around California, and was soon producing luxury wear for the city-dwellers as well as the miners, cowboys and railroad workers. Levi Strauss & Co was a family firm which began to enjoy considerable success in other parts of the USA. Even so, manufacturing remained a centralised operation, always under the watchful eye of the company founder, with selling often coordinated by a team of door-to-door salesmen. By 1870, the company was exporting its clothing abroad.

After his death in 1902, the company continued to thrive, masterminded by his four nephews. The San Francisco earthquake in 1906 knocked-out the company's headquarters, but it was soon business as usual from a new base in Oakland. Eventually, the company returned to San Francisco, where it is based today.

Even the depression of the 1930s was kind to Levi Strauss & Co, as jeans were viewed increasingly as affordable casual wear,

popularising jeans as much on the East coast of the USA as the West, the original birthplace of denim wear. The 'romantic' rugged image of the cowboy was used in marketing the Levi Strauss & Co brand. This, alongside the greater freedom of movement across the USA afforded by the advent of the motor-car and railroad, meant that jeans were popularised everywhere, and were soon worn by men and women, both at work and as a fashion statement.

US troops during World War Two introduced Europeans to their first real taste of denim wear, sparking a new trend, with demand soon outstripping supply. Levi's jeans had become a status symbol.

The 1950s witnessed an explosion of American youth culture into many parts of the world. Jeans were tightly bound into the identity of the new young 'teenage' generation. Rock bands and famous actors sported jeans as statements of fashion and increasingly, as a statement against conventional dressing and its matching lifestyle. This extended into the 1960s and 1970s when flared jeans were all the rage at one time, and straight, tapered 'drainpipes' at another. It wasn't a case of if you wore jeans as much as how you wore them - that was what really counted.

Eventually, Levi Strauss & Co turned full circle, relaunching their original 501 jeans during the 1980s. These jeans, based on the original 1850s prototype and named after the warehouse lot number 501 to which the first serge de Nimes fabric was imported, featured the famous button fly, and soon forged an unmistakeable, classic identity. Levi's 501 jeans have continued to grow in popularity, assuming cult status and generating strong worldwide sales.

THE PRODUCT

Levi's jeans were first manufactured from canvas and later from serge de Nimes, imported from Europe. These days, one single factory in the USA manufactures Levi's denim material. The process remains a closely guarded secret. This denim is rigorously tested using machines that can wreak a lifetime's havoc to the denim in a few short hours, plus three washes to test for shrinkage.

Each pair of Levi's 501's is produced from 51 different pieces of fabric and undergoes 35 sewing operations, using six types of thread. All stress points are riveted by copper-plated steel, stamped L.S. & Co. S.F.

In addition to its classic line of Levi's 501 jeans, Levi Strauss & Co produce a range of denim wear and jeans styles. Levi's Red Tab

represents the original denim ranges, with Orange Tab denoting a more varied, modern cut. Throughout the years, accommodating changes in fashion and lifestyle, Levi Strauss & Co has produced coloured jeans and stonewash jeans, all in a variety of shapes and sizes.

RECENT DEVELOPMENTS

In the UK, 1996 saw a number of campaigns built around some of Levi Strauss & Co's most popular lines. The authentic Red Tab range was boosted by a return to dark indigo finishes on a number of denim garments. Dark denim also inspired the "Distress" and "Dark Distress" finishes available in the Levi's 501 jeans style.

Promotion for the all-original Red Tab denim range was based around a series of photographs from Nick Knight and styled by Simon Foxton, featuring 'real' Mid-West models - ranchers, a rodeo star, and the oldest surviving black cowboy in Colorado - all wearing a selection of Levi's Red Tab denim jeans wear.

Levi's jeans for women was also highlighted during 1996 with a range of workwear - from Red Tab and Orange Tab selections - cut specifically for the female form, as well as the Levi's skirt and T-shirts.

New colours and styles were introduced to the White Tab corduroy range, plus a selection of colourful short and long sleeved shirts.

Levi Strauss & Co's stylish TV advertising has continued in a similarly successful vein with new campaigns "Planet", where a stunning alien girl cuts a dash in Smalltown, Planet Galactica in her pair of Levi's 501 jeans for Women, and "Washroom", a darker tale with a cunning twist set in contemporary America, where a glamourous young woman has to change into her Levi's 501 jeans in a men's washroom, under the watchful gaze of a presumably 'blind' man, as suggested by his holding a white stick. However, the audience eventually learns that he is not blind at all, but merely holding the white stick for a genuinely blind man who is in one of the cubicles.

PROMOTION

From the outset, the original Levi Strauss was an astute marketer, building his empire with meticulous judgement and skill. The company he founded has continued to promote the Levi Strauss & Co brand with considerable panache and expertise, culminating with the Levi's 501 jeans campaign - undoubtedly one of the most highly praised and popular campaigns in advertising history.

Coordinated by agency Bartle Bogle Hegarty, the relaunch of original Levi's 501 jeans in 1985 spearheaded a 'retro' mood, reviving the spirit of 1950s America. Already a design classic in their own right, Levi's 501 jeans were already worn as an exclusive symbol of 'taste' by trendsetters. A series of TV commercials, offering witty storylines backed by classic soundtracks, soon re-established Levi's 501 jeans as the world's most popular denim wear. In just 12 months after the official relaunch of Levi's 501 jeans, sales rose by 800%, with sales doubling yet again the year after. The soundtracks also soared in popularity. In one week in 1986, two Levi's 501 jeans soundtracks, Ben E King's "Stand By Me" and Percy Sledge's "When A Man Loves A Woman", were positioned at number one and two in the UK record charts. Subsequent chart successes have included "Spaceman" by Babylon Zoo and "Inside" by rock band Stiltskin.

TV advertising was matched by press advertisements in the fashion and music press and billboard posters. Levi Strauss & Co also became a prominent music sponsor, supporting the likes of Jamiroquai, Northern Uproar and a selection of UK festivals. Other events in the UK to benefit have been the Hammersmith Odeon 60th Anniversary and a fashion gala, the White Heat night, was also staged at London's Cafe Royal to raise funds for Nordoff-Robbins Music Therapy. This event featured the work of twenty famous international designers, from John Galliano to Vivienne Westwood, all briefed to customise a pair of white 501 jeans. The resulting collection was modelled by some star names, including Neneh Cherry, Sidney Youngblood and Amanda de Cadenet. In addition to Levi Strauss & Co headlining TV commercials and poster advertising, Levi's has proved active in ensuring below the line promotional activities, through in store posters, interactive computers and videos, as well as extensive

and acclaimed work on the Internet, continue to build the focused, style-conscious message behind the Levi's brand.

BRAND VALUES

Levi's jeans are the prevailing fashion icon - not just for this generation, but for all generations. Over the last 140 years, denim wear has become ubiquitous, prized for its hard-wearing, comfortable, yet multi-purpose qualities. It suits equally well in the workplace, as casual wear or as a stylish garment.

Over the years, Levi Strauss & Co has have stood more than just the test of time, they have withheld the onslaught of copycat brands and cheaper jeans wear. This is because Levi Strauss & Co is the original symbol of youthful rebellion, as expressed in clothes. It stands for individuality, attitude, style and integrity.

It is a brand definitive in its market: a brand which owns the emotional heartland of its category.

Things you didn't known about Levi's

❍ Despite the mass of imitation button-fly jeans launched by rival companies, Levi's 501 jeans remain the world's top-selling jeans brand.

❍ The name 'Denim' is derived from the original material, serge de Nimes, used to manufacture Levi's jeans.

❍ Levi's 501 jeans have garnered a string of awards, including the Smithsonian Institute award for engineering. Levi 501's are now on permanent display at the Institute.

❍ Levi Strauss & Co's first jeans were made shrink-to-fit. In the early days, gold miners and ranchers simply put on their new jeans, submerged them in a watering trough and left them to dry.

❍ Levi's jeans gained the Red Label identity tag in 1936.

❍ The Levi Strauss & Co trademark leather patch, featured on all Levi's jeans, was added in 1886, and commemorates a pulling contest between two horses and a pair of Levi's.

❍ The double line of orange stitching found on the back pockets of Levi's jeans is known at Levi Strauss & Co as "the arcuate". Legend has it that it symbolises the wings of an American eagle and was first introduced in 1873.

Marlboro

THE MARKET

According to figures from the Tobacco Manufacturer's Association, there are an estimated 16 million smokers in the UK. This represents around 34.5% of the total adult population. In 1994, tobacco sales amounted to almost £11 billion. A total 87 billion cigarettes, 4.3 million kg of handrolling and pipe tobacco and nearly 1.2 billion cigars were sold.

WARNING: PLANT CROSSING.
Welcome to Marlboro Country.

ACHIEVEMENTS

Marlboro is one of the world's most valuable brands. According to Financial World magazine, in 1995 Marlboro was worth around $38 billion. Marlboro is probably one of the most-recognised brands in the world.

Its outstanding success has been based on a quality product and distinctive advertising. Although an archetypal American brand, Marlboro is sold in over 160 countries around the world and is the leading cigarette brand in most markets, a 25% market share in Europe, for example.

HISTORY

Marlboro cigarettes were first launched in the USA by the Philip Morris Company in 1924.

In view of the overt masculinity of the Marlboro brand, it is odd to think that Marlboro was primarily pitched at women. The cigarette was launched under the advertising banner "Mild as May" and smokers could choose between an ivory tip cigarette or what was known as the "Red Beauty Tip", designed to conceal lipstick marks.

Clearly, this targeting exercise failed, as by 1954 sales had dipped to below 0.25% share of the cigarette market. A drastic turnaround of fortunes was called for.

The brand was repositioned across the sexes, and was promoted as a masculine, full flavour cigarette. Philip Morris added a cork-tipped filter to the cigarette and completely redesigned the packaging.

In so doing, Philip Morris led the way in cigarette package design, introducing the first crush-proof flip-top box. The archetypal Marlboro red and white roof-top graphics, depicted on all Marlboro Reds cigarette packets, has remained to this day.

The Marlboro brand soon extended its global reach. In 1957, Philip Morris forged its first licensing agreement in Switzerland and opened an office in Paris two years later.

In 1961, Philip Morris became the first US company to sign a license agreement with the French state-owned tobacco monopoly, SEITA. This was followed by similar agreements with MONITAL, the Italian state-owned tobacco monopoly, and its equivalent, Austria Tabakwerke AG, in Austria. In 1974, a licensing agreement was finalised with the Spanish state tobacco monopoly, Tabacalera. Since then further agreements have been forged with a number of Central and Eastern European companies.

Consumer demand led to the opening of manufacturing plants across Europe, including the opening of Europe's largest cigarette-production plant in the Netherlands and expansion into Berlin, Germany, in 1972, followed by a further plant in Dresden built in 1990.

THE PRODUCT

Philip Morris is fully aware that with all the best marketing intentions in the world, if the product does not match consumer expectations, the brand is a non-starter. The company operates stringent controls to ensure that a consistently quality product, using only the finest tobacco, is produced. This rule applies to all its global operations.

In the UK, there are currently two Marlboro variants; Reds and Lights, available in Hard Pack 10's/20's and Soft Pack. Packs of 100's are also available for both variants.

The Marlboro family of products in the USA has gained further brand extensions over the years. In 1966, a Marlboro Menthol was launched, followed by Marlboro 100's in 1967. A new Marlboro Red King Size 25's convenience pack was launched in the USA in 1985, with Marlboro Menthol Lights rolled-out four years later. More recently, in 1991, Marlboro Medium was launched into the US market.

Around the world, Philip Morris operates a number of brands. Aside from the ubiquitous, top-selling Marlboro brand, Chesterfield, F6, L&M, Merit, Muratti, Multifilter, and simply, Philip Morris, ensure the company enjoys the largest brand share in the global cigarette market.

In Europe, the company's interests are controlled by Philip Morris EEC Region. This division, based in Lausanne, Switzerland, oversees the manufacturing and marketing of Marlboro to Belgium, the UK, France, Germany. Greece, Italy, Portugal, Luxembourg, Spain, Ireland and Israel. All Marlboro products sold in Europe are manufactured from European tobacco leaf, harvested from France, Greece, Italy or Spain.

Philip Morris EEC Region also operates five factories in Europe, in the Netherlands, Germany and Belgium. Philip Morris España operates a factory in the Canary Islands, and specialised production units manufacturing cigarette filters and roll-your-own tobacco, are located in Brussels, Belgium, and Italy.

RECENT DEVELOPMENTS

In July 1995, Marlboro launched a major advertising campaign. Titled "Welcome to Marlboro Country", the campaign features a series of poster advertisements, depicting scenes of American Mid-West countryside. The posters carry a tongue-in-cheek by-line, emblazoned in Marlboro's typical red lettering, which relieves the overall austerity with comic understatement.

For example, a scene of an isolated house, literally in the middle of nowhere, with a tornado looming outside, carries the deadpan by-line "Better get the cat in".

Another poster shows a desert wasteland with a sign saying 'Subject to flooding'. The Marlboro comment is simply "!".

PROMOTION

Once Marlboro had been repositioned as a male-oriented brand in the early 1950s, Philip Morris needed a suitably masculine image to promote it. A series of strong masculine images were employed, including pilots and naval officers.

However, consumer research targeted one particular image, which the public strongly associated with rugged masculinity.

The Marlboro cowboy was born.

Although a distinctly American character, the cowboy was easily assimilated into other cultures as an authentic masculine icon.

In 1964, Philip Morris hired the Leo Burnett advertising agency in Chicago, to devise a universal Marlboro campaign, centred, not just on the Marlboro cowboy, but on the concept of Marlboro Country. The aim was to assert the Marlboro brand identity and reinforce the message that the Marlboro cigarette was rich and full in flavour.

The longevity of the Marlboro Country campaign bears witness to the astounding success of the brand's advertising.

In all aspects of the Marlboro product, a consistent brand image is presented. However, the Philip Morris Company, has also adopted a decentralised, localised approach to its marketing. Regional offices are able to make marketing decisions for their particular market when local conditions are considered most receptive.

The campaign's universal appeal is explicit in the company's sales figures. Marlboro is a top-selling cigarette in more than 160 countries worldwide.

The success of Marlboro's advertising is even more notable when you consider that tobacco advertising is in fact banned - often by voluntary agreement - in many parts of the world.

In the UK, for example, all tobacco advertising and promotion has been controlled by a voluntary agreement made between the tobacco industry and the Government since 1971. This was just updated in 1994. The agreement stipulates that tobacco advertising should not incite people to start smoking, particularly children, but solely aim to persuade existing smokers to switch brands.

Tobacco companies cannot advertise their products on television and all advertising has to be cleared by the UK's Advertising Standards Authority (ASA). Poster advertising is prohibited within a 200 metre radius of any school or playground and cannot feature in publications targeting the under-18s.

Tobacco companies have become leading sponsors of sporting events, ranging from motor-racing, cricket, golf to snooker.

Marlboro is especially well-known for its sports sponsorship activities, particularly in motor-racing.

In 1972, Marlboro formed the Marlboro World Championship Team (MWCT), which aims to provide support to motor-racing operating at all levels, from Formula 3000 to the more high profile Formula 1 Grand Prix racing.

Since 1974, Marlboro has been associated with the Marlboro McLaren Formula 1 team which has enjoyed a string of Grand Prix successes. A number of Marlboro drivers have secured world titles and become popular household names. These have included some of the greatest racing-drivers of all time: Ayrton Senna, James Hunt, Emerson Fittipaldi, Nikki Lauda, Alain Prost, Keke Rosberg and Alan Jones.

The Marlboro-McLaren link is now the longest-standing association between a team and a non-technical sponsor in the history of motor-racing.

Over the years, Marlboro has also been involved with the ISO team in 1973 and 1974, the Marlboro Team Alfa Romeo between 1980 and 1983, and has also been connected to Scuderia Ferrari.

Marlboro has also been chief sponsor for major motor-sports events, such as the Hungarian Formula 1 Grand Prix, The Marlboro Masters in Formula 3 in Holland and the French Formula 3 Championships.

Similarly, Marlboro is actively involved in the World Rally Championships, and has reared a number of successful rally drivers through its MWCT programme.

Marlboro also runs a support programme for motor-cycling, which began with its 1974 sponsorship of Giacomo Agostini, who went on to win the World Championship no less than 15 times, with 311 Grand Prix victories. Eddie Lawson and Barry Sheene are other champions to have benefited from Marlboro's backing. The Marlboro Team Roberts, a motor-cycling team set up in 1990, has already netted the top honours, winning the 125cc, 250cc and 500cc World Championships.

Marlboro's brand strength has led to a range of promotions, featuring merchandise described as 'The Marlboro Country Collection'. The items offered in the collection are described as "the latest and finest authentic American gear" and range from the "classic Zippo to the best denim". These gift products can be exchanged for the appropriate number of pull foils or seals from packs of Marlboro reds or Lights.

Marlboro also publishes ICON - an upbeat magazine, emphasising American culture. This magazine was the ISP and SPCA Creative Award Winner in 1995.

BRAND VALUES

Marlboro has a distinctive brand identity. It exudes masculinity, confidence and independence. Marlboro is unmistakably American in character, representing an authentic, original, pioneering America - as typified so perfectly by the famous Marlboro cowboy.

Things you didn't know about Marlboro

❍ UK cigarette smokers pay more tax than smokers in the rest of the EC. So, for example, in April 1995, a pack of cigarettes costing £2.74 in the UK would have cost about £1.84 in France and £1.48 in Spain.

❍ In 1995, UK smokers contributed around £9 billion to the Treasury in tobacco taxes. This represented about £17,000 every minute.

❍ Marlboro has built a ground-breaking global network of licensing agreements with tobacco companies around the world, often state-owned tobacco monopolies, including in the People's Republic of China.

❍ In 1992, Marlboro sold over 360 billion cigarettes worldwide, amounting to 18 billion packs. If placed end-to-end, these would circle the world 100 times.

❍ The word 'nicotine' is derived from Jean Nicot, the French ambassador to Portugal in 1960. Nicot introduced tobacco to the French court. His name was given to the plant Nicotiana.

❍ The first cigarette-making machine was invented in 1867.

❍ Captain Ralph Lane and Thomas Harriot introduced tobacco to England in 1586. Sir Walter Raleigh popularised smoking in the English court.

THE MARKET

When it comes to sales, the UK savoury spreads market is a veritable feast. The increasing tendency to take a packed lunch to work or school has given rise to the tremendous popularity of the sandwich. One important sector of the savoury spreads and sandwich fillings market is meat and vegetable extract pastes - valued for their healthy goodness and distinctive taste, popular on toast, in sandwiches, as a hot drink or flavoursome additive to stews and soups. UK sales of meat and vegetable extract pastes amount to £34,466,000m on a moving annual total basis. This market is dominated by MARMITE yeast extract (a vegetable extract paste), which took an estimated £23,353,000m share by value on a moving annual total basis, with BOVRIL, a meat extract paste, taking £8,424,000.

ACHIEVEMENTS

With sales topping £23.5 million, MARMITE is one of the UK's most popular savoury spreads, dominating the meat and vegetable extract market.

Heralded for its nutritional content and unique taste, MARMITE is enjoyed by all members of the family. In 1995, household penetration was up 0.4% on 1994 reaching 24.3%.

HISTORY

The basic raw material used in the manufacture of MARMITE is spent brewer's yeast, a substance whose original and only use was to

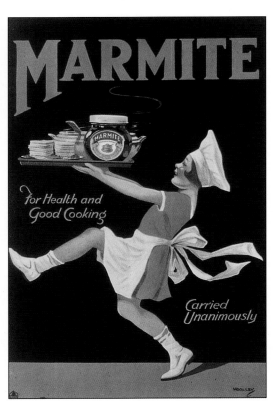

ferment sugars into alcohol. For many years, this by-product of the brewing process was seen as a nuisance rather than a potentially valuable food source. However in 1680, a Dutch scientist, Leouwenhoek, examined this yeast under a microscope and saw that it was composed of tiny spherical and ovoid cells. The French scientist, Louis Pasteur, realised that these cells were in fact living plants. Further investigation by a German chemist, Liebig, found that this yeast could be made into a concentrated food product, which resembled extract of meat in appearance, smell and colour, however was vegetarian.

A number of people tried to manufacture this yeast extract for commercial purposes, but with little success. This changed in 1902, when the Marmite Food Company Limited, later changed to Marmite Limited, was formed. This company was committed to producing a perfected form of yeast extract for popular consumption. They rented a disused malthouse in Burton-on-Trent for the modest sum of £100 a year and set to work.

However, it was found that the yeast they were producing from British beer did not lend itself to the same treatment of continental yeast where methods of fermentation were markedly different. New machinery had to be bought in and a series of changes in the manufacturing

process were implemented before a satisfactory yeast extract product was ready to market.

It took time to bowl over the British public with the distinctive taste of MARMITE. Gradually however, the business expanded. The freehold of the malthouse was purchased and operations were extended to meet growing demand. Eventually, a second site was obtained in London, and the company consolidated production at a new greenfield site at Burton-on-Trent.

The discovery of vitamins in 1912 boosted the popularity of MARMITE, when it was realised that yeast provided a good source of five B vitamins. Its healthy proposition meant that greater quantities of MARMITE were consumed in hospitals, schools and institutions, with tons dispatched to war-torn countries overseas. During both the World Wars, MARMITE was served to soldiers on military duty and was used to combat outbreaks of beri-beri and other diseases. During the Second World War, MARMITE became a valued dietary supplement in prisoner-of-war camps.

Both the MARMITE product and packaging have undergone few changes since the turn of the century. MARMITE stock cubes were launched in a distinctive green tin during the 1920s, but this brand extension was eventually dropped, to concentrate on the increasingly popular paste product.

Since 1924, following the death of the first chairman of the company that produced MARMITE, both the MARMITE and BOVRIL brands have enjoyed a close association, leading to Marmite Ltd becoming a wholly-owned subsidiary of Bovril Limited. Further changes of ownership ensued and in 1990, CPC (United Kingdom) Ltd took over both the BOVRIL and MARMITE brands.

THE PRODUCT

MARMITE is a concentrated yeast extract paste, enjoyed at any time of the day, whether on toast for breakfast, in sandwiches at lunchtime, or as an added ingredient in stews and casseroles.

MARMITE is 100% vegetarian, but unlike some vegetarian meals, MARMITE provides an excellent source of vitamin B12. This vitamin helps to prevent anaemia. It also contains a good source of Riboflavin and Niacin as well as an excellent source of Folic Acid.

MARMITE is good news for the nation's slimmers. It contains virtually no fat or sugar. A single 4g serving amounts to only 8kcal/35kJ typical values. Spread on toast with butter, this comes to 145 kcal (704 kJ), although skipping the butter cuts the calorie count down to 72 kcal (350 kJ).

Although MARMITE has a salty taste, there is more salt in the bread and butter on which the MARMITE is spread than in the MARMITE itself.

MARMITE has a distinctive savoury taste, unlike anything else. It remains a popular food for all the family, loved equally by the toddler of

100% VEGETARIAN.

the family through to the Grandpa. Over the years, other companies have taken the basic raw materials used in producing MARMITE and infused its special taste into other products, resulting in such delights as muffins flavoured with MARMITE yeast extract and cheese flavoured with MARMITE.

RECENT DEVELOPMENTS

Since taking over the brand in 1990, CPC (United Kingdom) Ltd has continued to vigorously support MARMITE - a £4 million promotional budget in 1996 alone, for example - and has looked to extend the brand further. Although formerly abandoned, MARMITE stock cubes are a bright idea from the past which have made a come-back. In addition to its more common role as a nutritional, savoury spread, MARMITE is being positioned as a cooking ingredient.

PROMOTION

Early advertising emphasised the nutritional value of MARMITE. Poster advertisements used the 'Good for You' slogan. The product's versatility, as a savoury spread, cooking ingredient and even a drink, has also been highlighted in promotions.

More recently, advertising has focused on the intrinsic family values of MARMITE as a good source of five B vitamins with a great taste. The current advertising slogan reads: 'Nothing tastes quite like "MY MATE MARMITE"'.

Advertising targets mothers with babies over six months of age (who are particularly partial to MARMITE as a weaning food) and adults aged 20 - 44 years old.

Pregnant women are also an important market. Through a combination of TV and press advertising, editorial, sampling and education leaflets, the makers of MARMITE drive home the message that MARMITE contains vitamins such as Riboflavin, Niacin and Folic Acid, which helps prevent spina bifida in unborn babies. In fact, four slices of bread and MARMITE a day provide a pregnant woman with all the Folic Acid she needs.

BRAND VALUES

The chief proposition of MARMITE is that it is a nutritious, tasty savoury spread, enjoyable on toast or bread or even as a cooking ingredient. Being 100% vegetarian and containing useful vitamins, MARMITE is valued for its goodness, as a reliable part of the everyday family diet. In troubled times, when a decent, well-balanced meal is hard to come by, MARMITE has been viewed as an essential food supplement.

It could even be said that Britain has been weaned on MARMITE. Mothers recognise the nutritional qualities of MARMITE yeast extract, and babies love it! With a health-giving legacy and delicious flavour, MARMITE really is "MY MATE MARMITE".

MARMITE and MY MATE MARMITE are registered trademarks of CPC International Inc.

THE MARKET

The British love their 'tea-break' - a hot cup of tea (or coffee) and a biscuit. In fact 70% of all biscuits consumed in the UK are served with a hot drink. Given the amount of tea consumed, biscuits are big business. In the UK the biscuit market is worth over £1.6 billion - four times the size of the tea market and twice the size of the wrapped bread market. The average spend per head per week on biscuits has risen from 85p in 1985 to £1.40 in 1995, and the market has grown over 60% in value and 9% in volume in this period. Even in 1991, when the recession was hitting hard, £130 million was added to the value of the biscuit market, indicating a year on year growth of around 10% - largely attributed to 'snacking', estimated to account for 44% of all biscuit sales.

The overall biscuit market can be divided into sectors, reflecting the different occasions when we enjoy a biscuit.

The largest sector is 'countline' biscuits, wrapped chocolate bars often found in lunch-boxes. Typical brands are McVitie's Penguin and Nestlé's Kit-Kat. In 1995, this market was valued at some £477 million.

The second largest sector is the 'biscuit barrel' home-consumption sector, which features the most popular and well-known brands such as McVitie's Digestive and McVitie's Rich Tea. This market was worth £447 million in 1995, and accounted for 27% of all biscuit sales.

Biscuits are also viewed as everyday treats, for example chocolate brands, such as McVitie's Jaffa cakes or Hob-Nobs. The public certainly enjoy 'spoiling' themselves with a quality biscuit, as shown by the value of this market - it is worth £342 million, and represents 21% of all biscuit sales. It was the fastest-growing sector in 1995, adding +8.5% in value.

The seasonal biscuit selection grew 15% in value from 1990 to 1994, and not surprisingly peaks at Christmas, with 80% of sales from October to December. It is now worth £184 million.

Savoury biscuits can be divided into two sectors. Plain and savoury biscuits, usually eaten with cheese or spreads, were worth £115 million in 1995. Savoury snack biscuits,

typically McVitie's Mini Cheddars, recorded a growth of 70% volume from 1990 to 1994, and is now the second fastest growing sector.

ACHIEVEMENTS

McVitie's is the clear leader of the UK biscuit market. Five out of the top seven biscuit brands are McVitie's, giving the company a 42% share of the whole market (including own label).

Famous McVities brands include Homewheat, Digestive, Penguin, Rich Tea and Jaffa Cakes among the top ten biscuit brands in the country.

McVitie's dominates the biscuit-barrel sector of the market, with its two most famous brands, Digestive and Rich Tea ranking first and second respectively, and another old favourite, Ginger Nuts, in third position. McVitie's flagship brand, McVitie's Digestive, is now over a hundred years old and is still Britain's favourite Digestive with just over six million digestives eaten every day. That's about 70 digestives being munched per second.

McVitie's enjoys a similar position in the chocolate biscuit market, where Homewheat and Jaffa Cakes are the two most popular brands, with Chocolate Hob-Nobs in fourth place.

McVitie's was responsible for pioneering the savoury snack biscuit sector with the launch of Mini Cheddars in 1985. Mini Cheddars are still the most popular brand in this market.

HISTORY

McVitie's was founded by Robert McVitie, a Scottish baker, who set up shop in Edinburgh in 1830. McVitie's bakery became firmly established as a quality retail outlet with several branches dotted across Edinburgh. Robert McVitie Junior expanded the family business throughout Scotland and eventually into England. McVitie's soon specialised in biscuits as they were easier than bread to preserve over long periods of time and could be baked in Scotland, then carted to England for sale.

In 1888, company salesman Charles Price was made a partner in the company, which then became McVitie and Price. Then, in 1892, a fellow-baker, one Alexander Grant, stormed into the McVitie's shop claiming that he could make better scones than those posted in the window. A bemused Robert McVitie suggested he try - which Grant did, with stupendous results, one of which was the famous McVitie's Digestive.

The peculiar origins and consequent success of the Digestive merits closer attention. The aforementioned Alexander Grant adopted the recipe for the Digestive from a concept cooked up by two Scottish doctors who developed the first Digestive biscuit in 1839 with nothing more than the relief of flatulence in mind. The original recipe had a high content of baking soda, known to aid digestion ... hence the Digestive name. This recipe has neither changed nor been divulged in the ensuing century since it was first baked by McVitie's and has remained a closely-guarded secret ever since.

The Digestive is viewed as the pride of McVitie's. It has become synonymous with all that is traditionally British. It is exported to over 90 countries world-wide and is a best-seller in Scandinavia and Hong Kong. One of its more unorthodox introductions to foreign climes was in 1939 when the explorer Commander Reginald Smith was travelling in the Amazonian jungle. However, he was unfortunate enough to cross the path of hostile natives who were set on executing his doctor. Smith thought this a timely moment to introduce their captors to the wonders of the Digestive biscuit with incredible results. Smith managed to secure the release of himself and his doctor in exchange for several tins!

McVitie's has since grown from strength to strength and is now a £630 million turnover business with 8,000 employees and over 55 brands. Its brand share stands at 25.5% over 2½ times that of its nearest competitor. In 1995 alone McVitie's launched 36 new product innovations and line extensions.

THE FINEST OF ALL WHEATMEAL BISCUITS

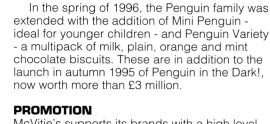

THE PRODUCT

McVitie's core brands are sold in each sector of the total biscuit market. Digestive is probably the best-known McVitie's brand. It is the brand leader of the 'biscuit barrel' market, and is the nation's favourite snack, and tea-break biscuit achieving sales in excess of £40 million per year. In May 1996 the brand was revitalised with improved ingredients and a unique re-sealable tab - a first in the biscuit market - as part of a £9 million marketing investment. McVitie's now emphasises that McVitie's Digestive has been a "Natural part of life since 1892".

McVitie's Homewheat is the company's leading brand, achieving annual sales in excess of £55 million. The biscuit was developed in the early 1900s and was named because the wheat in the recipe was sourced from the home market, while competitors used imported ingredients.

McVitie's Rich Tea achieves annual sales in excess of £20 million and has benefited from the launch of milk chocolate and plain chocolate versions. The brand has been made famous with the advertising tag-line, "A drink's too wet without one".

Penguin is McVitie's most popular chocolate biscuit bar, with sales of over £30 million in 1995. Penguin has benefited from an increasing need to eat satisfying, tasty snacks 'on-the-hoof', or as part of a packed lunch. The durability of this brand - Penguin is 64 years old - has been strengthened by the classic 'p...p...p...pick up a Penguin' advertising campaign.

Best known for the 'smashing orangey bit in the middle', and the combination of dark chocolate and light sponge, Jaffa Cakes remain one of the leading brands in the biscuit market, whose success has spawned Mini Jaffa Cakes, a bite-sized version of the popular original. First launched in late 1994, these proved an instant hit, generating £8 million in just 12 months.

Other well-known McVitie's biscuits include Ginger Nuts, Boasters and Riva.

RECENT DEVELOPMENTS

In the last few years, McVitie's has successfully launched a series of modern brands which provide a perfect complement to the heritage brands for which the company is renowned. McVitie's always has a biscuit for every occasion, be it as an accompaniment to a hot drink, a snack, a light meal, something to pop into the lunchbox or something to give as a gift or share with friends.

In 1996, McVitie's has continued its relentless drive to stimulate the biscuit market through innovation. In February McVitie's ACE 'countline' biscuit bars were launched with an "incredibly thick chocolate" proposition, supported by a dynamic, animated TV campaign from the award-winning makers of the Wallace and Gromit characters.

The hard-hitting campaign created a first within the biscuit market through a direct response television (DRTV) campaign breaking in May.

In the spring of 1996, the Penguin family was extended with the addition of Mini Penguin - ideal for younger children - and Penguin Variety - a multipack of milk, plain, orange and mint chocolate biscuits. These are in addition to the launch in autumn 1995 of Penguin in the Dark!, now worth more than £3 million.

PROMOTION

McVitie's supports its brands with a high level of marketing activity and invests heavily in television advertising, which is seen as the most effective method of communicating core brand values to a peckish and impulsive public. Actress and accomplished cook Jane Asher has been the corporate campaign spokeswoman for two years, extolling the benefits of the McVitie's range.

Promotions have always been viewed as a vital marketing tool in the biscuit market. Value packs offering extra bars have proved popular, particularly for the lunch box 'countline' market, and intelligent merchandising on the shop floor has been encouraged to appeal to the impulse shopper. In order to catch the casual shopper's eye, bright and attractive packaging is a priority. The brand has also benefited from major publicity initiatives including sponsorship via McVitie's ScotSplash headed by the Olympic medalist, swimmer Sharon Davies. The art of biscuit dunking has also been recognised by McVitie's National Dunking Day, taking place on November 19, 1996.

BRAND VALUES

McVitie's is a quintessential British brand. It is traditional, part of our heritage. It inspires trust and warmth. We expect a wide range of excellent quality, delicious biscuits which will appeal to all members of the family. Consumers know they can rely on McVitie's. This is largely due to the longevity of the brand and the "honest pleasure" experienced by Digestive-devotees and Homewheat-lovers over the years. Moreover, in a highly competitive environment, McVitie's also manages to stay ahead, introducing new brands and line extensions that the British public love.

McVitie's successfully marries its remarkable brand heritage with current consumer trends to drive the biscuit market forward by continually launching top quality, delicious biscuits.

Things you didn't know about McVitie's

○ McVitie's have been baking since 1830.

○ The McVitie's Digestive brand is now 104 years old.

○ Over 70 Digestives are eaten every second.

○ The Digestive biscuit was originally intended to be a food that aided digestion due to its high content of baking soda. This is how the name 'Digestive' was formed.

○ Over the course of a year McVitie's biscuits are bought by shoppers in 92% of UK households.

○ If all the McVitie's Homewheat biscuits eaten in a year were put end to end, they would span the length of the Channel Tunnel 176 times.

○ 70% of all biscuits are consumed with a hot drink - that's 90 million biscuits a day.

MICHELIN

THE MARKET

The wheel is an ancient device, but it has only been during the twentieth century that our lives have been changed beyond recognition by the advent of modern transport - cars, trucks, airplanes, trains, subway systems. Hand in hand with this development has been the monumental growth of the world tyre industry - now valued at $60 billion.

However, recent years have been comparatively leaner times for the industry, although 1995 showed signs of a healthy renaissance, as the increase in prices of raw materials - chiefly rubber - began to stabilise and the companies at the head of the industry improved their efficiency. The three market leaders are Michelin (France), Bridgestone (Japan) and Goodyear (US). Other contenders include Continental, Sumitomo and Pirelli.

ACHIEVEMENTS

The Michelin Company is the world leader in the tyre market with almost a 20% share and a consolidated turnover of FF 63.3 billion. Michelin is based at Clermont-Ferrand in France but operates 69 manufacturing plants in 15 countries, five rubber plantations in Africa and South America, five testing facilities and five research and development centres in France, Japan and the US. The company operates a comprehensive sales network throughout some 170 countries.

According to the Global Tyre Report 1995/96, Michelin topped the league of tyre manufacturers in both sales and brand value. Michelin has consistently pursued an effective marketing strategy, catapulting its 'Bibendum' Michelin Man corporate symbol into the ranks of the great icons of brand history.

Michelin has consolidated its status through pioneering acclaimed tyre products which set standards for the entire industry.

HISTORY

Until 1889, the Michelin factory at Clermont-Ferrand, France, produced mainly rubber products such as hoses and general farming implements. But then, a beleaguered cyclist - both tyres of his bicycle punctured - arrived at the Michelin factory in an ox cart. Andre and Edouard Michelin, the brothers who controlled Michelin, spent many hours repairing the tyres but they soon punctured again. This was because tyres were then attached to a wooden wheel. Waiting for glue to harden while repairing something as simple as a puncture, could take up to ten hours.

This situation puzzled Edouard Michelin to the extent that he spent some time devising a solution - a detachable pneumatic tyre, which could be removed and repaired in just fifteen minutes. This development was to revolutionise the worldwide transport industry.

Having patented their detachable pneumatic tyre, the Michelin brothers sponsored an unknown cyclist, Charles Terront, to enter a bicycle race from Paris to Brest, using their tyres. Terront went on to win the race by a full

eight hours, because he found it easier than his competitors to repair his punctures.

To prove their point, Michelin organised a bicycle race from Paris to Clermont-Ferrand, secretly depositing nail booby-traps en route to cause punctures. They then had 240 opportunities to prove how easy it was to repair a puncture. A year later,

over 10,000 cyclists were riding on Michelin tyres.

Michelin then decided to develop tyres for carriages and persuaded Paris cabs to try them out. By 1903, there were 6,000 Paris cabs using Michelin tyres.

But Michelin's great breakthrough came with the car. The first cars used solid tyres. To demonstrate how a car could be fitted with their pneumatic air-filled tyres, the Michelin brothers entered a race from Paris to Bordeaux. Driving an automobile nicknamed L'Eclair (lightning) - due to its zig-zag steering mechanism rather than its speed - after a series of trials and tribulations, breakdowns and even a fire, the Michelin brothers finished ninth out of 210 competitors.

The conception of the famous corporate logo, the Michelin Man known as Bibendum, in 1898, spearheaded Michelin's marketing thrust and its evolution from a notable French company to a multinational corporation.

By 1905, a trading house had been set up in London and a manufacturing facility in Italy the following year. Building on the company's successes in car races around the world, the Michelin company bought a US rubber company and started manufacturing tyres in the USA in 1908.

When the First World War broke out, Michelin

turned its hand to airplane manufacture and made 1,884 planes for the French war effort.

After the war, Michelin developed tyres for passenger rail-cars on the railroads. Further key developments in tyre-making were succeeded by a wave of international expansion, which included the opening of Michelin plants in the UK.

However, the Second World War brought great personal tragedy to the Michelin family. Edouard died in 1940 (Andre had died nine years previously), and family members were killed in action - one died in a German concentration camp. The company refused to collaborate with the occupying German forces who took control of many of their manufacturing plants.

However, under the guidance of Robert Puiseux, Edouard's son-in-law, Michelin managed to skirt around the hard times which affected industry after the war. He was eventually succeeded by Francois Michelin, in 1955, the current head of the company.

In 1946, Michelin registered the world's first radial tyre - known as the Michelin 'X' - the prototype of the broad-based pneumatic tyre we use today. This was truly a momentous moment for the tyre industry. Michelin was soon kick-started into massive expansion to meet demand.

This entailed a move into the US market in 1950 with the incorporation of the Michelin Tire Corporation, based in New York. Progressive development in tyres for all types of vehicle led to the opening of ever more factories around the world. In 1966, Michelin made its ultimate breakthrough in the US market when the car company Ford decided to launch its new model, the 1968 Lincoln Continental III passenger car complete with Michelin's radial tyres.

Throughout the 1960s, the radial model had begun to dominate the tyre market. During the 1970s, Michelin underwent explosive growth - 23 new plants to manufacture just radial tyres, and in the USA, still regarded as the prize market for passenger transport, Michelin was by then the foremost supplier of tyre equipment.

Michelin managed to stave off the worst effects of the ensuing worldwide recession with aggressive expansion plans, particularly in the

Far East. By the end of the 1980s, with the acquisition of the Uniroyal Goodrich Tire Company, Michelin was the world's leading tyre manufacturer.

THE PRODUCT
Michelin produces over 3,500 types of tyre for virtually all types of vehicle, including bicycles, motorcycles, cars, trucks, trains, airplanes and even the NASA space shuttle.

The company has pioneered the tyre industry since 1889 when it developed the first detachable pneumatic tyre. Other firsts have included: the tread pattern (1905); the twinned wheel used for buses and heavy goods vehicles (1908); rail-tyres "Michelines" (1929); the radial tyre, developed in secret during the Second World War and now the standard broad-based tyre design used for most motor-vehicles (1946); aircraft tyres, Boeing 777, for example (1980s); and tyres used for tube-trains, first used in Montreal in 1951. Michelin has also developed the tyres for rallying and racing cars and helped Ferrari win the Formula One World Championship in 1977.

A particularly successful off-shoot of Michelin's core tyre-making activity has been Michelin road maps and guides. The logic behind the maps was to get more people onto the roads. Andre Michelin, an ex-official at the French Ministry of the Interior Map Department, supervised the publication of the first Michelin Guide in 1900. Up to this point, there had been minimal road-mapping, but Michelin ensured a constant stream of updated guides for years to come.

RECENT DEVELOPMENTS
Michelin has made great in-roads into ensuring tyres afford greater safety, as well as durability and speed. In 1990, the company announced the 'Green Tyre', responding to public environmental concerns. This tyre ensures rolling resistance with the road is reduced, thus saving on fuel, and, of course, helping to reduce pollution. A range of "Green X" energy-saving tyres, branded Energy, has been produced for cars, and in 1995, an Energy truck tyre range was developed, promising a 20% reduction in rolling resistance, equalling up to 6% fuel saving.

In addition to developing new technologies, Michelin has also sought partners and investments in the flourishing Pacific Rim, and undergone a complete corporate overhaul to ensure greater efficiency. In doing so, Michelin has weathered the storm of the recession, and guaranteed its lead of the tyre-making market.

Between 1960 and 1990, on average, Michelin was opening a new factory every nine months. However, after its acquisition of US-based Uniroyal Goodrich in 1989, Michelin appears to have halted its aggressive expansion and consolidated its current interests to best effect. It now plans to boost its US manufacturing facilities by $900 million. Last year, the company also announced a majority shareholding in a Polish tyre-making concern and a joint venture in China.

PROMOTION
Michelin secured a strong marketing presence with its familiar symbol Bibendum, The Michelin

Man. This congenial figure built out of tyres, has been used in all Michelin's poster/TV advertising, corporate literature, and features on all Michelin road-maps. He has even been converted into key-rings, inflatable Bibendum balloons, desktop ornaments and toys, to name but a few of his multiple uses. Bibendum is now one of the oldest and best-loved corporate logos in the world with a history dating back to the end of the last century.

He was conceived by Edouard Michelin at an exhibition in Lyon in 1898, when a stack of tyres struck him as almost lifelike. His brother Andre, with the artist O'Galop, conceived the Michelin Man, in a now-famous poster of a rotund 'bon vivant' wine drinker, made of tyres, raising a glass of road debris (overcome by Michelin tyres of course), with a sign overhead reading "Nunc est bibendum" - Now is the time to drink. The name Bibendum was coined by a famous race-driver, Thery.

Early posters depicted Bibendum in various roles. An early O'Galop poster showed him as a wrestler, flippantly kicking the dangers of the road into touch; a contemporary artist, Grand Aigle, had Bibendum as a Tyrolean, while Rene Vincent portrayed Bibendum as the rescuer of a car with a puncture.

Bibendum has taken on many guises during his long life, - a film star, a mime artist, a politician, a sailor - and continues to evolve with changing times. He doesn't smoke anymore, his body consists of less, but fatter tyres, reflecting modern standards, although he is now a little sleeker than before, for fashion's sake. After all, one of Bibendum's recent feats was to run the London Marathon.

In addition to its high-profile TV and press advertising campaigns, Michelin also publishes Michelin Sport, highlighting the tyre company's strong associations with rallying, touring car and motorcycle racing. Michelin's notable Formula One Grand Prix successes have been with Renault and Ferrari - particularly during the 1978 Grand Prix series. Michelin's involvement with motor-racing stems from the company's earliest days when Michelin tyres showed their superiority over the competition in road-racing.

BRAND VALUES
Michelin is a truly international brand with an incredible heritage. It is renowned for its pioneering, ground-breaking achievements in the tyre industry. These feats have been achieved through a full understanding and anticipation of customers' needs, combined with an open-minded approach - learning from past experiences, but consistently looking beyond the here and now to something even better.

We have come to expect consistent high quality and reliability from the tyre company which works to ensure we travel in safety and with ease and to guide us with its road maps. Michelin is always prepared to "Take a great tread forward".

Microsoft®

WHERE DO YOU WANT TO GO TODAY?™

THE MARKET

According to research from GfK, around 3.3 million UK households own a PC; combining a CD-ROM and Internet access capability on the increase. Forecasts show that around 7 million UK households may own a multimedia PC by 1998. The PC market is growing at an extraordinary rate and shows no signs of slowing down. This rise in penetration is partly attributed to the strength of consumer interest in the Internet and online service. It is estimated that around 30 million people may already be using the Internet worldwide - paving the way for a new information age.

ACHIEVEMENTS

Since its founding in 1975 by Bill Gates and Paul Allen, Microsoft has steered itself into an extremely strong position as the world's leading software manufacturer for personal computers (PCs) and increasingly, for the Internet. The $5 billion company now employs more than 15,000 people across the USA and at its 49 subsidiaries worldwide. Added to this, Financial World magazine ranked Microsoft the world's best-managed brand in 1994, and with an estimated brand value of $11,740 billion, the company was ranked the world's sixth most valuable brand.

Microsoft has risen to become one of the most influential companies in the emerging technology markets and will play a key role in defining this category into the next century. The brand has achieved remarkable levels of recognition and trust among PC users worldwide. As awareness of Microsoft has risen, so has the consumer's understanding that the quality of their software products determines the quality of their experience with a PC. This awareness has positioned the brand positively against some other more well-established IT brands such as IBM and telecommunications companies such as AT&T in the United States.

What distinguishes Microsoft as one of the most powerful brands in the world must surely be its vision of a future where new technologies become an integral, commonplace asset in our lives. This is what Microsoft is working towards and it believes that the launch of Windows 95 has firmly established the brand as the only well known software vendors that can deliver the promise of the new world of information technology.

HISTORY

Bill Gates, the founding chairman and chief executive officer of Microsoft, was already programming computers at the age of 13. In those days, computers were large, cumbersome and had comparatively minuscule processing power compared to today but Gates still managed to teach his computer to play noughts and crosses.

Together with Paul Allen, a school friend of Gates, he pursued his interest in programming when he went to college. Gates and Allen decided to set up in business, writing the first ever computer language programme for a PC, called BASIC. From the outset, Microsoft made a conscious decision to focus on computer software products at a time when the industry was almost entirely hardware-oriented. Then, in 1980, the computer giant IBM hired the fledgling Microsoft to develop an 8-bit operating system for its new personal computers. Microsoft didn't actually have a suitable system to offer IBM, but they soon found one called DOS and bought the rights from the developers, Seattle Computer. Microsoft licensed the MS-DOS operating system, as it was known, to IBM and the rest is history. MS-DOS became the industry standard with nine out of ten of all the world's 140 million computers using it. MS-DOS was followed by the user-friendly icon-based Windows, the world's best-known PC interface. Good marketing and factory installation of Windows on to personal computers ensures a positive outlook.

The UK subsidiary of Microsoft Corporation, Microsoft Ltd, is based in Winnersh, Berkshire and has grown from a company of only five employees in 1980 to become an organisation employing 500 people in the UK in 1996.

THE PRODUCT

Microsoft designs, markets and supports a wide range of personal computer systems, applications, development tools, computer languages, hardware peripherals, books and multimedia applications. These products are available in 28 languages and are sold in 275 countries. Each Microsoft product is designed to make it easier for people at work and at home to take advantage of the full potential of personal computing.

The product development involves a high level of customer consultation, with a significant part of the development process involving customer testing of Microsoft's products for 'usability', ensuring that the features of Microsoft products are exceptionally easy to use in practice. The widespread popularity of Microsoft products means that virtually every personal computer in the world runs Microsoft software, over 120 million people are using MS-DOS and 60 million using Windows. This is being added to at a rate of 1.5 million new users every month.

Realising the potential of network computing, Microsoft also produces the Windows NT Server and a variety of related applications. For the home, Microsoft has developed a plethora of CD-ROM products, including Microsoft Encarta Encyclopedia and Flight Simulator, as well as Microsoft Money, a complete package to handle personal finances. A series of 'fun' titles have also been developed for the Windows operating system, in line with Microsoft's aim to be the first choice for playing games, educational and entertaining software.

In keeping with growing consumer interest in the Internet and online services, Microsoft has also developed a wide range of Internet products and operates its own Internet-based online service, the Microsoft Network (MSN).

RECENT DEVELOPMENTS

With the launch of Windows 95 and the speed with which the company has responded to the challenge of the emerging market for developing Internet-based applications, Microsoft has become a multifaceted business competing in the arena of the Internet, productivity software, networking and multimedia. This is a far cry from the days of MS-DOS and early versions of their Excel spreadsheet.

Microsoft's suite of Internet software products includes the Internet Explorer, a World Wide Web browser; and Internet Studio, a package of Web-authoring tools to enable companies and consumers to design and build their own Web-pages.

In August 1995, Microsoft launched the Microsoft Network (MSN), an online service with a network extending to 35 countries with content relayed in 20 different languages. This service changed in 1996 from a proprietary online network - which consumers subscribed to from their Windows 95 operating system - to a subscription-based service accessed via the World Wide Web, potentially available on any platform.

At the end of 1995, Microsoft carved a deal with US broadcaster, NBC, to develop MSNBC - a 24 hour news channel, available simultaneously on cable and satellite TV, and as an MSN news and information service. Microsoft has also forged alliances with leading players in the games and entertainment industry, including Japanese games giant Sega and Hollywood studio DreamWorks SKG, which plans to produce films, TV shows, interactive stories, CD-Rom games and multimedia software.

PROMOTION

Microsoft invests heavily in advertising. In the UK, Microsoft's total media spend during 1994 and 1995 was second only to IBM, in the information technology market. The majority of

Start organising   Start managing   Start learning   Start Windows 95

Microsoft's advertising expenditure in 1994 and 1995 was largely directed towards TV commercials. Microsoft's global advertising strategy is co-ordinated by Weiden Kennedy, with UK advertising directed by Euro RSCG. In the UK, Microsoft's advertising build-up for the launch of Windows 95 in August 1995 included a high profile splash in The Times, negotiated by Mediastar, the media agency of Euro RSCG.

Microsoft's recent global advertising has been embodied by the tagline "Where do you want to go today?", and is focused on the notion of integrating personal computing into every aspect of an individual's life, work, home, education and entertainment. Feedback from the campaign has shown a significant increase in brand awareness amongst the public, in particular current PC-users and information technology managers in the workplace.

BRAND VALUES

Microsoft attributes its success since 1975 to the company's dynamic vision of computing in the 1990s and beyond. This vision is built on the principle that in the future there should be a PC on every desk and in every home - empowering individuals and organisations by making information increasingly easy to find and utilise.

The company bases its success in the microcomputer business on its focus on this long-term vision and its attention to two key areas: producing powerful and easy to use products that help people do their jobs quicker and more effectively; and making it easier for people to get the most out of their software by providing a range of services that recognise the needs of the individual and corporation.

Microsoft is a brand that has always responded to the challenge of bringing the world of information to the fingertips of the PC user. The Microsoft brand represents the ability of the consumer to access the benefits of technology here and now at an achievable cost. The brand is a "consumer brand" in that key innovations represent the best application of software technology to the developing needs, desires and experiences of the consumer. Extensive user testing and product design enhancement have established Microsoft's leadership with the consumer.

Things you didn't know about Microsoft

○ In 1980 when IBM was scouting around for a company to produce the operating system for its PC, the computer company's first port of call was Digital Research. Luckily for Microsoft, the company chairman, Gary Kildall, claims that he was out fishing when IBM called. IBM's second call was to Microsoft, who obviously realised they'd just caught the biggest fish imaginable.

○ One of the keys to the success of Microsoft is the management of the company. From the earliest years, Bill Gates has used stock options to motivate employees and foster a highly competitive entrepreneurial atmosphere within the company.

○ Life and work at Microsoft's Redmond-based campus, near Seattle, has been fictionalised in a novel by Douglas Coupland called 'Microserfs'.

○ Bill Gates has published a book called "The Road Ahead" outlining his vision for the future.

MINI

THE MARKET

In the UK, the small car market is booming. The small car market grew from 420,000 sales in 1991 to 550,000 sales during 1995, ensuring that small cars remain a popular fixture on our roads. Car manufacturers are eager to meet the demand. Indeed, customers have never been faced with such a dizzying array of product choices.

The competition is fierce. A wide range of small car competitors vie for customer's attentions and market share, with a barrage of new products, advertising and special offers.

ACHIEVEMENTS

The Mini has become an icon of our times. It enjoys an illustrious brand heritage and reputation as a stylish, quality car, occupying its own particular niche in the market.

Since its introduction, over 36 years ago, 5.3 million Minis have been produced, with 500,000 Minis currently in everyday use in the UK alone. Today, the Mini is still in production and is now sold in over 20 countries, with more than three-quarters of the production going to export markets. Many feel that the Mini continues to outclass its rivals in the small car market, in the face of strong competition.

HISTORY

When the Mini started out life 36 years ago, its creator, Sir Alec Issigonis, intended it to be a practical alternative to a motor-cycle and side-car and to provide an answer to the raft of bubble-cars which were finding favour amongst the British public during the 1950s.

The Mini was designed from the inside out, aiming to provide the family man with an astonishing amount of interior and luggage space in a car that was only 10 foot long.

The resulting transverse engine and front wheel drive layout was quite revolutionary and has had a powerful influence on the car industry as a whole ever since.

The Mini's minimal front and rear overhangs and diminutive size gave the car phenomenal manoeuvrability and handling. The car's incredible handling characteristics meant that it quickly drew the attention of the motorsports industry, in particular the Formula One racing car constructor John Cooper.

The Mini's size and shape meant it was ideal for taking corners at speed. The racing version, the Mini Cooper, quickly became a natural for racing and rallying. Before long, it had become a racing

legend, as a three times winner of the prestigious Monte Carlo rally during the 1960s, bagging its first victory in 1964. Amongst its other accolades, the Mini won the 1960 Geneva Rally.

Popular enthusiasm for the Mini Cooper has never dwindled, and the famous rallying car is still available.

Since its golden racing days, the Mini has gone from strength to strength, incorporating new designs and engine improvements along the way.

Yet the fundamental design of the Mini, masterminded by Alec Issigonis, has remained unchanged. In today's environment of congestion, pollution, impossible parking, Autocar magazine says this: "Most remarkable of all, the 36-year-old Mini deals

with today's motoring problems better than designs a quarter of its age ... economical, reliable, desirable". For its pioneering design and its powerful influence on not only the automotive industry but on society as a whole, the Mini can be considered as one of the greatest cars of all time.

THE PRODUCT

The classic Mini design has undergone some revisions over the years. After all, the early sporting Minis had engines of just 850cc. Today, the current product line-up includes the Mini and Mayfair, powered by a 53PS fuel injected engine, and the Mini Cooper whose 63PS engine, continues to power the Cooper to a class-leading performance. Thirty years since the first Mini Coopers were winning races, John Cooper has again helped develop the current Mini Cooper 1.3i, which uses the same engine as its forebears, but now includes fuel injection and a catalyst in its impressive design specs.

John Cooper himself, still sells Minis from his dealership in Ferring, Worthing.

When the Mini was first introduced, Issigonis omitted space for a radio, believing that music would interfere with the main business of driving. Of course, this has all changed. Minis can accommodate a car stereo, as well as a heater - formerly an extra accessory. The suave Mini Mayfair model boasts traditional chrome bumpers and a radio-cassette security device offers a detachable key pad and is security-coded.

Of course, the Mini is not just a car, but a personal belonging. A large number of Mini-devotees like to customise their Mini, and a variety of accessories - chrome plated brass valve caps with Cooper branding, for example - have been made available. A wide range of attractive new colours and options, ensure that customisation is simple.

Mini Special Editions are always popular and Limited Editions such as the Mini Cooper Monte Carlo are treated as much sought-after collectors items.

All Mini's feature burr walnut veneer in the interior and use independent rubber-cone suspension, to ensure the Mini retains its industry-leading handling characteristics.

RECENT DEVELOPMENTS

In recent years, continued development has led to a number of refinements in the Mini's design, including the addition of fuel injection and

catalytic converters to meet emission requirements, and improvements to the interior of the car to increase comfort levels.

As popular now as ever before, in November 1995, Autocar magazine voted the Mini "Car of the Century".

Furthermore, a panel of experts on Classic and Sportscar Magazine voted the Mini Cooper as the All Time No.1 Classic Car.

PROMOTION

When Mini first went on the roads, its owners were proud to sport stickers in their rear windows, proclaiming "You've just been Mini'd!" as they whizzed past larger, more cumbersome cars, in traffic. This inadvertent advertising has been typical of the Mini's star quality which won it a leading role in the famous 1968 film, "The Italian Job," in which three Minis were used as getaways after an audacious robbery. The film featured breath-taking driving stunts from Remy Julienne.

Undoubtedly, the Mini is a unique car and appeals to a particular segment in the market. Rover therefore targets these customers very closely, using effective direct mail, targeted black & white and colour press campaigns, as well as events sponsorship (such as Mini Seven racing and the "Italian Job" charity run - in commemoration of the film).

BRAND VALUES

The Mini has proved to be a timeless classic. Nothing looks like, or drives like a Mini. It is unique, enjoying a particular Britishness and heritage, which has earned it an iconoclastic status.

The Mini also has a personality all of its own. Cheeky, mischievous, energetic, fun and nippy - the Mini is a car to be enjoyed by drivers from all strata of society.

ONLY £12,040 A PAIR.

The new Designer edition Mini Rio. In exotic Polynesian turquoise, romantic Caribbean blue or simple classic black. Available separately at £6,020 each including delivery, number plates, tax and a smile. For more information about the alternative fashion accessory give us a ring on 0800 545 545.

MINI rio

perrier

THE MARKET

The UK market for bottled water is growing more quickly today than any other sector of the soft drink industry. In 1995 over 600 million litres of bottled water were consumed and it is estimated that by the year 2000 this figure will have grown to over 1300 million. Although 1995 was an exceptionally hot summer there were other more important factors that influenced the growth of this market, one of which was the radical change in the social and environmental climate. The benefits of a healthy lifestyle are now more widely recognised than ever before and the most natural drink for the health and fitness conscious is natural mineral water. They prefer to drink a water that is wholesome and drinkable in its natural state rather than tap water and other waters that are treated with chemicals to make them safe to drink. Now worth over £350 million the market has attracted more brands, more and many different kinds of retail outlets and, in-store, a great deal more shelf space.

ACHIEVEMENTS

Perrier is the number one sparkling mineral water in the world. The famous green bottle, instantly recognisable, has changed little since it was first produced nearly 100 years ago.

Perrier, which according to research, is the adult soft drink most often asked for by name, leads the UK market. Its influence is enormous: it stands alone, separated from all competitors by its style, its wit, and most importantly, by its quality. As the advertising says, "Perrier. Everything else isn't".

There are certain brands on the market that have an identity that is so strong and so lasting that they have become 'classics'. Perrier is one of them. What other water in one year could organise (for the 16th year) one of the greatest comedy events in the UK - the Perrier Pick of the Fringe, be appointed the official mineral water to London's International Fashion Week, become a star in the new, breathtaking James Bond film Goldeneye and make Sunday Lunch with Perrier (featured on Classic FM, the radio station) a popular national pastime?

Despite a fiercely competitive market Perrier remains a dominant force. It sells twice as much sparkling mineral water (bottles) than any other brand through grocers and enjoys the largest distribution in restaurants, pubs, clubs and hotels of any bottled water brand.

The UK natural mineral water market was built, almost singlehandedly, by Perrier. It has invested more in the market than any other brand and it is the best known bottled water in the world. It is currently exported to over 120 countries.

HISTORY

In 1994 Perrier celebrated its 90th birthday. But in fact it has been around a lot longer - as long ago as 218BC when Hannibal (he of the elephants), discovered an effervescent spring in the Vistrenque Plain at Vergeze in what was to become France. The spring was conveniently situated just 200 yards from a road built by the Romans for traversing between Spain and Italy and it was at this time in the first century AD, that the spring's reputation began to spread.

The spring was known as Les Bouillens - "the bubbling waters" and the Roman baths built alongside it steadily gained in popularity.

However, the fall of the Roman Empire ultimately led to a fall in popularity for the bubbling waters, and the spring's fame soon dimmed into obscurity. Only local villagers continued to visit the site regularly believing the water to have health-giving properties.

The bubbling water was first bottled under the charge of Napoleon III in 1863 as he decreed that it should be bottled "for the good of France". The nearby town Vergeze was developed into a spa resort. Yet another set-back occurred in 1869 when the site was gutted by fire and Perrier may well have eluded us altogether had it not been for an Englishman, St John Harmsworth, who went to Vergeze to recuperate after a motor car accident in 1903. His doctor guided him round the site and Harmsworth was intrigued to see bubbling water gurgling in the ground. The villagers told him of its vitalising qualities. He drank the water, and instantly recognised its commercial possibilities.

Harmsworth bought the spring with the intention of bottling and selling the water. But it needed a name and a striking bottle if it had any hope of selling. So he decided to name the water in honour of the man who had introduced it to him in the first place - one Dr Perrier. The famous green bottle was based on the Indian clubs Harmsworth used for exercising.

Harmsworth was truly a man of vision. He instantly saw a tremendous marketing opportunity open to him in the form of the expatriate community posted abroad, whether it be in a military or civil service capacity. Throughout the British Empire of the time were a variety of far-off places where the English community viewed the local water as contaminated (it often was) and in short supply. Perrier provided an ideal alternative and, of great importance, a marvellous mixer with whisky. The British loved it. The brand was even favoured by royalty, receiving two Royal Warrants from Edward VII and George V respectively.

Harmsworth's marketing ploy proved successful. Perrier became "the champagne of table waters"

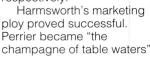

and could be found in high-class establishments across the world. But strangely enough, not in its country of origin. It was easier to find a Perrier in Singapore than in Paris. But this didn't have too much of an adverse effect on sales. By 1922, six million bottles of Perrier were being produced every year, and by 1933, when Harmsworth died, this figure had risen to 18 million.

Perrier returned to French hands in the later 1940s when a French company, calling itself Societe Source Perrier, bought the brand. A new bottling plant was built, producing over 130 million bottles annually, although the product became increasingly Franco-centric with only 20% exported abroad. Until the 1970s, there was little marketing of Perrier in the UK and in 1972 only half a million bottles were sold. But it soon made a comeback when a subsidiary company Aqualac (Spring Waters) was opened in London. The British rediscovered it with a gusto only matched by the impact of Perrier's advertising, and by 1986, over 77 million bottles a year were being sold and the Aqualac company was renamed Perrier (UK). In 1996, following its acquisition by Nestlé, the parent company was renamed Perrier Vittel SA reflecting its expertise in both sparkling and still waters. The company markets its waters in all five continents and owns 55 bottled water brands. However, Perrier remains the flagship and the most international of any brand with its unique quality and style.

THE PRODUCT

Perrier is one of the few naturally bubbly waters in the world. It springs from a source in the Vistrenque Plain near Vergeze in Southern France, where a volcanic eruption beneath the spring thousands of years ago resulted in this unique water with natural bubbles. The water is also of a very high quality. It is a refreshing, enjoyable drink and it is an excellent mixer. Particularly popular amongst the clubbing/pubbing youngsters of today is Perrier with a Twist, the first flavoured mineral water of its kind - a refreshing blend of Perrier with a dash of lemon, lime and orange.

SLEAU LUNCH

IN VEAUGUE

ZEREAU DEGREES

SEAU PURE

'swirlingly' successful. Appearing in national newspapers and strategically placed on 48 sheet poster sites, such themes as Sleau Lunch (Perrier Snail), In Veaugue (Perrier Hat), Seau Pure (Perrier Cherub), Zereau Degrees (Perrier Penguin) have left people of all ages waiting for more.

Although the advertising is based on the famous 'Eau' theme, the new advertising takes the brand years forward, right into the 21st century. It expresses the enormously confident stature of the brand and is so obviously the advertising of a Superbrand.

Perrier is youthful, fresh, sparkling and brimming with vitality. It is also innovative and very active in the market place. Bottle Art is a subject that it is pursuing with a great deal of imagination and fun. Having dressed itself up for Christmas in 1992 and 1993 it celebrated its 90th birthday in 1994 by inviting leading artist Brian Grimwood to create three anniversary bottle sleeves. Consumers loved them and very quickly they became collectors items. For the launch of the new James Bond film Goldeneye in December 1995 Perrier bottles appeared in Eau Eau 7 garb. Collectors of Perrier Art bottles went searching for their 'prey' joined by thousands of James Bond fans.

Interest in Bottle Art is growing and Perrier is leading the way. Special edition bottles during 1996 have included Perrier Jazz (coinciding with the London Jazz Festival), and Perrier Lemon Girl.

RECENT DEVELOPMENTS
Perrier has always led the UK bottled water market setting standards and instigating trends. It was the first brand to introduce its sparkling mineral water in 330ml cans and the first brand to launch a flavoured water - the well established Perrier with a Twist.

Perrier has adopted a very powerful marketing strategy against which every proposed activity is assessed. It has a very strong presence in all retail sectors and in hotels, restaurants, clubs and pubs. As would be expected of the number one sparkling natural mineral water in the world, its presence is felt at all the famous social and sporting occasions in the UK calendar. Perrier has long been established as an enjoyable drink in its own right. It is drunk at parties and it is taken to parties instead of wine. As one journalist wrote: 'When the Perrier runs out the party's over'.

PROMOTION
A flash of green, a hint of yellow, an eau so subtle wit and an intuitive grasp of what the 1990s is all about. This is the new advertising campaign Perrier launched in 1995. It is seductive and very stylish and the unmistakable qualities of the brand are communicated with great subtlety. Created by Publicis, the advertising agency, the campaign is 'head-

BRAND VALUES
Perrier is a classic. It has enormous style and it offers consumers a totally natural, enjoyable and fashionable drink. Marketed with great skill and distinction it achieved and has maintained star status with clear-cut brand values. It has a name and a package that are both instantly recognisable. It attracts enormous goodwill and commands universal respect. It plays a natural part in the environment of the day. And it is the natural choice of all those who determine fashion in its widest sense.

Things you didn't know about Perrier

○ The Eau-so French brand was first marketed by an Englishman.

○ Perrier was the first mineral water to create its own comedy awards. Nowadays, "The Perrier Pick of the Fringe" awards are described as the Oscars of alternative comedy.

○ Perrier was the first mineral water to be mass-marketed in cans.

○ Perrier has its own jazz band and its own Café Quartet.

○ Witty slogans featured in Perrier poster advertisements have included 'Eau La La,' 'H2Eau,' and 'Anything else is Pseaudeau'. When London telephone code numbers were changed, Perrier announced it to the world - 'Eau71 Eau81'.

○ In 1994, Perrier was the official sponsor of the V&A's (Victoria and Albert museum) Street Style Exhibition, charting the history of fashion since 1940.

Persil

THE MARKET

The UK soap and detergents markets is one of the most competitive in all Europe. It can be split neatly into two main areas: low suds, for use in washing machines, and high suds products, suitable for hand washing, twin tub and some top loading machines but not front loading washing machines.

The low suds market, however, is continuously growing in line with the profusion of new product launches and relaunches traditional to this sector. This dynamism is spurred by the competitive nature of this market, hence the need to take advantage of new technology in order to stimulate consumer interest.

The machine wash detergent market can be split into powders and liquids, concentrated and conventional products. Powders account for 75% of the total market and liquids hold a 25% share.

According to research company Datamonitor, in 1995 the washing detergents market was worth around £1.14 billion. Lever Brothers had a 32.1% share of this market with its Persil, Radion and Surf brands. Meanwhile Procter & Gamble held a 50.9% share with its Ariel, Bold and Daz brands.

ACHIEVEMENTS

Washing detergents are big business for Unilever, accounting for £6 billion in sales worldwide. This represents a 22% share of the company's total sales.

Persil is the flagship brand of Lever Brothers, a wholly owned subsidiary of Unilever plc. In the 86 years since Persil was first launched it has remained a staunch front-runner in the UK detergents market.

Throughout its history, Persil has always been at the forefront of new technology, and is consequently seen as simultaneously reliable

(by virtue of its heritage and product performance) and innovative.

HISTORY

Persil was originally launched in 1909 as the 'Amazing Oxygen Washer'. The product was originally developed by two Stuttgart professors - Professor Hermann Giessler and Docteur Hermann Bauer. Persil was first owned by Crosfield, until it was acquired by Lever Brothers in 1919.

At the time of its launch, bar soaps were used for washing clothes. The new Persil was a soap based powder which was combined with an oxygen bleaching agent to remove staining in the wash. Persil functioned rather differently to the traditional bar common at the time, in that it had to be stirred into a paste before being added to water. The conservative housewife was initially a little reluctant to desert her traditional cleaning methods, but gradually responded, and was ultimately convinced by the genuine "whitening" Persil could offer. This, added to the convenience of using Persil. The brand was advertised as 'soap powder that would do away with the dolly rub and washboard and the labour of rubbing clothes'. Nothing could be easier. Clothes washed with Persil needed only 'soaking, boiling and rinsing'.

Up to the Second World War, when housewives started to spend their soap coupons on soap powder as well as soap, clothes washing methods remained largely the same. However, it was all change in the 1950s when the first reasonably priced washing machine was introduced into Britain. As a result washing habits changed quite dramatically. By the late 1960s, as machines became more sophisticated, there was a need for a low lather washing powder so as to prevent excess foam interfering with the spin drying and rinsing process, or even overflowing. Mainly white fabrics were gradually being replaced by coloureds, natural fibres by synthetic and before long high temperature washing was superseded by the low temperature wash. Responding to these changes, Persil had a continual programme of product innovation and improvement.

In 1968, once the early twin tub machines had given way to the automatic front loading drum machines which were technically advanced in contrast to their predecessors, Persil launched Persil Automatic - a name that identified the newly created detergent technology with the new machine technology.

The years since have seen enormous changes in the detergent industry. First Persil made its detergents biodegradable, well ahead of legislation. Then during the 1970s Persil developed a new manufacturing process which enabled its soap powder to be reformulated and improved in both colour and solubility. Throughout this period, Persil spearheaded a series of advances in stain removal. The 1980s saw the introduction of energy efficient ingredients like enzymes as well as the launch of detergent liquids, which offered greater product convenience. The introduction of a non-ionic polymeric soap dispensing agent to improve solubility in 1981 and the launch in

1983 of New System Persil Automatic with low temperature bleach (TAED) and proteolytic enzymes, mirrored the technological development in machines, the changing washing load and increasing concerns about the environment. As did the launch of concentrated detergents. Their benefits were essentially two-fold. They offered greater convenience and were more environmentally acceptable since concentrated detergent packs are smaller, using less packaging materials, and are easier to store. Concentrated detergents require less product dose per wash than conventional detergents.

THE PRODUCT

The name Persil is derived from two ingredients Perborate and silicate, both registered in 1906. Persil prides itself on being able to meet the consumer's washing needs whatever they may be. There is always a type of Persil to suit, be it conventional or concentrated; powder or liquid; non-biological or biological action; specially formulated for coloured fabrics or for use with a twin-tub, top-loading or front-loading washing machine.

The main difference between biological and non-biological detergents is that biological varieties contain various enzymes which break down stains derived from protein, starch and grease at low temperatures, around 40 to 60 degrees centigrade. Often, people with sensitive skin opt for non-biological detergents.

Persil is able to produce both super-concentrated powder and concentrated liquid products. These products are dispersed using a 'dosing ball' and are therefore more economical as there is less product wastage than when using the detergent drawer of the machine. In fact, the manufacturing process for the superconcentrated powders uses only 20% of the energy expended by conventional powder manufacturing methods and the process generates no emissions into the atmosphere.

Persil's first liquid detergent was launched in 1988. Liquid detergents do not contain bleaching agents in their formulation and are therefore perceived as being gentle on fabrics. The other major advantage with liquids is that they dissolve easily and quickly, getting to work right away. This also makes them well-suited to hand washing.

More recent additions to the Persil range have been Persil Colour in both powder and liquid formats. These were specifically introduced to maintain the appearance of coloured fabrics for as long as possible through repeated washing. They do not contain bleach or optical brighteners which can, eventually, lead to a fading of dark colours or paling of pastel shades.

RECENT DEVELOPMENTS

The wide range of Persil products on offer today ensures that today's shopper can identify the ideal detergent for each specific wash.

The early 1990s signalled a time of wider consumer choice due to the segmentation of the market. The launch of Persil Micro Liquid in 1991 was a major step for the Persil brand in that it was the first branded concentrated liquid

Persil whites by Mrs Degas

Mrs Van Gogh's washing by Persil

detergent in the UK. This was developed in response to consumer demand for even greater convenience and smaller packs. Liquid detergents have consequently secured a reasonable share of the market, although sales of powder formats still outstrip liquids. Consumer awareness also led to the introduction of the Persil Eco-bag refill and permanent storage tin in 1993. These proved particularly successful. The market for carton refills has also grown considerably.

A major innovation has been the introduction of Persil Colour powder and liquid in 1992 and 1993 respectively. The changes in make-up of washload with more coloured items than ever before, led to further innovation. Persil Colour proved that some consumers were using more than one product to aid them to deal with their specific washing problems. In 1994 Persil Colour was introduced in super-concentrated powder form.

Lever has recently pioneered a revolutionary new production process which takes only dry ingredients - no water - and blends only the purest of raw materials into the most concentrated powder ever produced. This brings major improvement in environmental benefits using 20% less energy than before and generates no emissions into the atmosphere.

The process is less restrictive allowing Lever to include new ingredients. Every component of the powder was therefore improved: a new active system; a new builder; a more effective enzyme system; a new perfume and a new bleaching system.

New Generation Persil and Persil Finesse were both launched in 1995. Persil Finesse was the first light duty detergent from a mainstream brand. It is non-biological, pH neutral and does not contain bleach or optical brighteners. This unique product has a rich lather which cares for machine washable delicates such as silks and wools, cushioning them and gently

cleaning them in the machine removing the hassle and inconvenience of hand washing.

Persil Power was the first powder based on a new production process, featuring a patented catalyst called the Accelerator (TM). However, negative publicity generated by rival claims resulted in this product being finally replaced by New Generation Persil.

In spite of this setback, Persil has steered itself back on track, boosted by a restructuring at Lever UK and a £24 million advertising budget for 1995 alone.

PROMOTION

All Persil packs carry the distinctive Persil logo and design. Persil aims to project itself as a heritage brand which has cared for the family's wash for almost 100 years. The brand's cleaning and care credentials are communicated to consumers via advertising, direct mail, and through a freephone Careline, set up in 1993 to provide a facility for Persil consumers to seek expert advice and make comments or suggestions.

The Persil Roadshow was launched in 1994. This set out to entertain, inform and involve consumers through demonstrations and sampling. In addition, Persil Funfit coordinates a reward scheme through schools for progress in physical education for children.

During the Second World War, Persil emphasised the whitening benefit of Persil with the slogan "Persil washes whiter". Persil's whiteness, in advertising campaigns, was often compared with 'inferior' brands. This style of advertising was perpetuated into the TV age. It certainly worked. The consistency of message, together with the familiar packaging , built a huge brand loyalty that has been sustained over the years.

For so many years the key 'washing' figure in many households was the Mum, as demonstrated by the slogan "Someone's Mum isn't using Persil" and the "What matters to a

mum" campaign , which successfully combined balanced emotion with an informative and rational approach.

Convenience became the key message towards the end of the 1960s as more and more women returned to work. Persil's main advertising theme centred around the theme "A winning team - you, your automatic and Persil Automatic".

In the 1990s, the main ingredients of Persil's advertising have been humour combined with information. In 1990, one of Persil's most famous advertising campaigns, "The Artists Campaign" was rolled-out, which proved a radical departure from traditional detergent advertising. The award-winning poster advertisements featured clothes hanging from a washing-line, illustrated in the fashion of a well-known artist, such as Van Gogh and Degas.

BRAND VALUES

Persil is a clean-cut family brand. It has always projected itself as caring and responsible, supported by its consistent and effective programme of research and new product development, which has introduced products suited to each and every washing need. Through the Persil Careline set up in 1993, consumers have direct access to Persil Advisors. As a result, Persil has been able to listen even more effectively to what consumers want from their detergent. It is therefore bright and innovative, uniting its dependable heritage with a modern, progressive approach. As a result, the Persil brand has inspired brand loyalty over many years.

Things you didn't know about Persil

○ Launched in 1909, Persil is the longest-established brand in the UK.

○ 40% of all UK households have a pack of Persil.

○ Persil was the first detergent in the UK to offer a free Careline service where a team of specially trained advisers are available to help with queries about washing and stain removal.

○ There are nearly 6 million washes done every year in the UK - of these, nearly a quarter are done with Persil.

○ Persil was the first detergent to be advertised in the press (in 1910).

○ Persil was the first washing product to be advertised on television (in 1955).

○ Persil was the first washing powder to show a man doing the washing in a television advertisement.

Brooke Bond PG Tips

THE MARKET

Tea to Britain, is like wine to France. The British love it. They simply can't get enough. In fact, they love it so much, they drink some 180 million cups of tea every day. This means that the average daily consumption per person levels out at about 3.46 cups each.

With tea accounting for more than four out of every ten cups of liquid drunk in the UK, it's no wonder that tea outstrips its nearest rival, coffee, in the overall hot beverages market. Annual tea sales amount to £65 billion, which is twice that of coffee. This marks out tea as a very important sector in the UK grocery trade. The UK tea market is currently valued at £530 million (Nielsen MAT, September 1995).

ACHIEVEMENTS

Brooke Bond is the UK's number one tea company, with its flagship tea brand, Brooke Bond PG Tips, an enduring market leader. For the last 40 years, Brooke Bond PG Tips has been the UK's favourite tea brand and currently holds a volume market share of 20.2% (Nielsen MAT January 1996). Looking at one particular sector of the tea market, packet tea, Brooke Bond PG Tips is way out in front with a convincing 26% volume share (Nielsen MAT, December 1995).

Founded over 125 years ago, Brooke Bond has had a long time to market its top tea brand. Awareness of the Brooke Bond PG Tips brand amongst the British public is extremely high, and even more so since the Brooke Bond PG Tips chimps took to our screens in 1956, in what has become the longest running and one of the most successful TV advertising campaigns of all time.

HISTORY

Now a major UK company, Brooke Bond had humble beginnings as a small High Street shop in Manchester. Arthur Brooke opened his shop, selling tea, coffee and sugar, in 1869, with just £400. Breaking from the usual custom of the day, Arthur Brooke didn't accept credit, and only received hard cash for his goods. With an eye to developing a name for himself, Arthur mixed his own teas, formulating specialised Quality blends, selling them in half pound and 1lb paper bags. His teas became a sensation, pulling in the punters and attracting attention from rival grocers besides. They asked if they could buy his tea at wholesale rates and sell it from their shops too.

Arthur needed to brand his teas and settled on the name Brooke, Bond & Co, which was the name of his business. Oddly, there never was a Mr Bond. Just a Mr Brooke. But the name had a certain ring to it ....

Brooke, Bond & Co was soon printed in his own copperplate script on all of the bags he sold on to customers and increasingly to other shops. Before long, customers were associating his Brooke, Bond & Co logo with a top quality tea that could be relied upon.

Such was his success, Arthur Brooke was soon able to open more shops and started advertising the teas which had made his name. His tea, however, eventually earned

itself a brand-name all of its own, and was first known as Pre-Gestee, meaning to aid digestion. However, a change in the law outlawed the describing of tea as medicinal, and the name was changed to PG Tips, after the top two leaves and a bud known as tips, on the shoots of tea plants which provide the finest tea.

Brooke Bond has continued to place high value on the qualities that boosted Arthur Brooke's tea to the forefront of the market. Skilful marketing is the mainstay of the Brooke Bond PG Tips brand. Great pains are taken to ensure that the quality of teas used, and the blending process behind Brooke Bond PG Tips, remain of a high standard.

THE PRODUCT

Nowadays, all Brooke Bond's tea is blended and packed at the company's high-tech factory at Trafford Park, Manchester. The tea comes from plantations in South East Asia, India and Africa, either direct from tea gardens or from auctions. The Brooke Bond blending plant is computer-controlled, and was built as part of a £20 million investment programme. It is one of the most advanced of its kind in Europe. The plant was first built in 1921 to produce tea for Scotland and North England. It now has the capacity to serve the whole of the UK as well as Brooke Bond's overseas market, and is producing around seven billion tea bags a year.

Brooke Bond PG Tips itself is a blend of 28 teas. It is available in tea bags, the most popular form of tea accounting for 90% of all tea sold today, or loose. Originally, all tea was bought loose in packets or caddies. But in the 1950s, tea bags swooped onto the UK market. At first, it took some time for them to catch on, but technical developments, such as a special paper bag which wouldn't break up in boiling water, soon encouraged a flow of custom.

Further innovations in the tea market have included single-serve tea bags, enabling a quick, easy brew made in the cup, first brought onto the market during the 1980s. Brooke Bond PG Tips One Cup was the first single serve tea bag to add a tag and string to the bag for easier handling, and a twin pouch for faster infusion.

An even quicker brew is possible with granulated instant tea - a market which Brooke Bond PG Tips Pure Tea Granules pioneered, using Brooke Bond's innovative freeze-dried granules production technique.

Launched in 1990, Brooke Bond PG Tips Low Caffeine, with half tea's normal caffeine content, appeals to the 'health-conscious' tea-drinker of today.

RECENT DEVELOPMENTS

After four years in the making, in 1996, Brooke Bond PG Tips unveiled their next generation of tea bag. Pyramid (tetrahedral) tea bags were a major development in tea bag technology, promising a brew closer in flavour and quality to loose-leaf tea, than ever before.

Also in 1996, Brooke Bond celebrated the 40th anniversary of the PG Tips chimps advertising campaign. As an appropriate fanfare for the Tipps family and fellow chimp stars who have characterised Brooke Bond PG Tips' famous advertising, a trip down memory lane was in order. A new TV advertisement featured a compilation of key moments from the chimps' campaign, starting from its earliest black and white days when the chimps were drinking packet tea through to the modern day.

The brand also ran its most intensive programme of on-pack offers to date as a reward to consumers who have remained loyal to the brand and kept it in the leading position consistently since the 1950s. A record £25 million was invested in advertising and promotional activity during the anniversary year.

PROMOTION

The hot beverages market is a highly competitive business. To keep ahead of its competitors, Brooke Bond PG Tips has relied on a top quality product and memorable advertising.

The idea for a family of chimps to endorse the taste of Brooke Bond PG Tips tea was brilliantly-conceived in 1956, shortly after the launch of commercial television. The campaign was inspired by news at the time of chimps' tea parties at London's Regents Park Zoo.

The first advert showed the chimps enjoying a party in an elegant country mansion, drinking their tea from silver tea-pots and bone china tea-cups. The commercial was a huge success. It sparked some 100 TV commercials, whose popularity has never waned. In 1992, the Tipps family was introduced, headed by Geoff and Shirley Tipps with their children Samantha and Kevin. The scenes of everyday life depicted in these commercials have generated increased popularity for Brooke Bond PG Tips.

Others have depicted the chimps in unusual situations: as workmen digging the Channel Tunnel; cyclists in the Tour de France race; as racing car drivers and mechanics. The common thread running through all the adverts is the final reward of a cup of Brooke Bond PG Tips following a particularly difficult chore, or as a consolation or calmer after a crisis.

Many of the phrases used in the commercials have become famous, such as "Avez vous un cuppa?" and "It's the taste". Celebrity voices support the cast of chimps. These have included Cilla Black, Bruce Forsyth, Peter Sellers, Stanley Baxter, Kenneth Connor, Pat Coombs, Arthur Lowe, Irene Handl, Bob Monkhouse, and Kenneth Williams.

Despite the roaring success of the classic chimps' campaign, Brooke Bond is never complacent. Running side by side with the TV commercials has been a picture card campaign. Since 1954, Brooke Bond PG Tips has become famous for inserting picture cards into its packs, spawning generations of collectors. Titles of recent series include 'The Sea Our Other World', 'Vanishing Wildlife', 'Discovering Our Coast', and 'A Journey Downstream'.

Brooke Bond PG Tips has also contributed to high profile charity campaigns, including Comic Relief, where almost £1 million was raised. Another popular charity with whom Brooke Bond PG Tips has enjoyed a long-standing association is the World Wide Fund for Nature (WWF UK). Brooke Bond PG Tips has featured WWF on-pack promotions, and has pledged to contribute at least £400,000 towards WWF conservation projects by the end of 1997.

Strong packaging design has also played an important role in Brooke Bond PG Tips' marketing strategy, establishing a recognisable brand identity. Brooke Bond PG Tips packs are well-known for their familiar red, green and white livery and the tea-picker logo. Brooke Bond PG Tips tea bags also bear a watermark motif, depicting a tea leaf overlain by the PG logo.

BRAND VALUES

Brooke Bond PG Tips enjoys a strong brand heritage and reputation for top quality tea. Research has shown that the British public associate Brooke Bond PG Tips with a sense of security, comfort and continuity - everything we long for in a cuppa. Some of its advertising's most recognisable punchlines say it all: "Britain's best-loved tea," "The unbeatable taste of PG," "everything we love in a cup of tea," and of course, "it's the taste".

A cup of tea offers warmth, comfort, a moment of relief or a pick me up. Brooke Bond PG Tips embodies these qualities, and more. Its heritage and gently humorous advertising have won the British people's trust and assured Brooke Bond PG Tips' of its market leading position for many years.

Things you didn't know about Brooke Bond PG Tips

- ❍ With over 2,000 screenings, Brooke Bond PG Tips' 'Mr Shifter' commercial showing the chimps moving a piano downstairs ("Do you know the piano's on my foot?"), has entered the Guinness Book of Records as the most-shown advertisement on British television.

- ❍ Tea-tasting is a more complicated business than you may think. Teas can be biscuity, bright, coppery, creamy or round. These are universal 'tea-tasting' terms used to describe tea.

- ❍ Tea-tasters always test samples of tea twice their normal strength.

- ❍ When Brooke Bond is choosing what tea to buy, their buyers often sample up to 3,000 different teas in a single week.

- ❍ When tea-samples are weighed out for testing, tradition dictates that the quantity is always the equivalent of an old shilling coin.

- ❍ Tea used to be sold in chemist's shops because it was believed to have medicinal properties. However, laws were introduced which soon put a stop to these claims being made.

Philishave®

THE MARKET

The market for men's electric shavers in the UK is worth around £55 million a year. This figure accounts for sales of over 1.4 million models - battery, mains and rechargeables. Although the number of shavers sold each year has not changed significantly in the past few years, the type of model sold has changed.

As in other electrical personal care product markets, users like to 'trade up' to new and better models as they are introduced. In the case of shavers, this means highly sophisticated rechargeable models with many interesting features. Whereas sales of battery and mains models were down in 1995, sales of mains/rechargeable models were up nearly 7%. Almost one in two of all men's electric shavers sold in the UK is a Philishave.

ACHIEVEMENTS

For over 50 years Philishave has been the number one name in the world for men's electric shavers. Throughout that time Philips has invested continually in the brand to ensure its performance as a world-beater is maintained. From the moment that the first Philishave was unveiled to the public in 1939 at a huge Exhibition in Utrecht, the brand has regularly attracted the sort of attention usually associated with a superstar. 1996 has been no exception. The introduction of the new Philishave 5000 series marks another milestone in the history of the brand.

HISTORY

The introduction of the first single-head rotary Philishave on the eve of the Second World War could have seen the end of the brand before it even began, but in fact it was quite the contrary. It was an instant success and even the German occupation of Holland didn't prove too great an obstacle. Philips persuaded the Germans that the continued production of dry shavers was essential as soap was in short supply.

Immediately after the war, a shaver development programme was started and two years later one of the world's most famous designers, Raymond Loewy, created the 'egg' look on which all subsequent designs have been based. As early as 1951 new designs incorporated two rotary shaving heads and a few years later the triple-head rotary shaving models were introduced which are so well known today. Every year over 10 million Philishave models are manufactured at the impressive modern factory in Drachten, Holland. They are marketed in over 145 countries throughout the world with a substantial number sold in the UK.

THE PRODUCT

Philishave is undoubtedly one of the most important products in the Philips Electronics portfolio. Its name is a combination of the manufacturer's name 'Philips' and 'shave'.

Over the last 55 years, in the region of 120 different models have been produced, all based on the rotary shaving system which is unique to the product.

In 1994 the sophisticated Philishave HS990 was launched. It included 'green' Nickel Metal Hydride batteries, a highly sophisticated electronic charge monitoring programme, which among other things, displayed permanently the number of shaving minutes left to the individual user. It also featured micro-groove rotary shaving heads with Double Action 'lift and cut' to give the closest possible shave.

In 1995 the 300 millionth shaver was produced.

The company's research and development team did not rest on its laurels. It continued to look at ways of improving the performance of the Philishave and 1996 has seen another landmark for the brand.

RECENT DEVELOPMENTS

The new landmark is the introduction of the Philishave 5000 series based on a unique Reflex Action shaving system which breaks completely new ground. As with so many innovative ideas, once they have been introduced, everyone wonders why nobody had thought of them before. The three Philishave rotary shaving heads now move in a three dimensional way - convex or concave according to where the shaver is used on the neck or chin. The result is an outstandingly close and comfortable shave.

A three year multi-million pound development programme has resulted in this revolutionary new shaving system which moves the development of the Philishave a quantum leap forward. Philips claims that, just as a top sports car hugs the road at speed, the new Philishave 'hugs' the contours of the neck and face. The Reflex Action shaving system is a perceivable technological breakthrough which speaks for itself. It is the first three dimensional, contour following dry shaving system to be developed and Philips is confident that it will have the same huge impact on the market as the introduction of the first Philishave over 50 years ago.

The research and development team thought well beyond the Reflex Action shaving system. Every aspect of the Philishave was minutely examined and a number of other very important changes have been introduced. There are nine personal comfort settings from which to choose. Now men with the most sensitive skin can achieve a close, comfortable shave by using the shaver with the convex setting.

Improved cutters have been designed for the floating shaving heads and the shape of the shaver has been completely re-thought. Highly sophisticated electronic features on the top-of-the-range HQ5890 can actually calculate each user's average shaving times. Before the shaver is used, the electronic display shows an average of 23 shaves. As the owner shaves, the computer calculates and "learns" his personal shaving time and adjusts the number of remaining shaves accordingly when the shaver is recharged. The shavers are fully charged in an hour to give on average over 23 days (70 minutes) of cordless shaving time.

Extensive consumer research has been conducted by Philips which confirms the company's view that the shavers are something very special. In the two key areas of shaving performance and shaving convenience the new Philishave 5000 HQ5890 consistently out-performed its main rivals on the market. Included under the heading of 'shaving performance' were essentials of shaving closeness, shaving comfort, minimal skin irritation and shaving time. Included under 'shaving convenience' were noise, vibration, comfort in the hand and ease of use. Judged on a rating of 1 to 10 the Philishave was seen to be conspicuously ahead of its rivals in all categories.

Judged in the context of a pleasant experience, shaving with the new Philishave also researched exceptionally well, beating the competition on all points.

In developing the new Philishave 5000

series, Philips left nothing to chance. Four world-renowned specialists were involved in the final decisions as to colour, style and textures. The shape of the shavers is more rounded than before, in line with modern trends, with inset 'waisted' rubber side panels which make them comfortable in the hand.

But perhaps it is where colour is concerned that the design is so different. Gone are the staid blacks and greys of former years. Now the 5000 range introduces strong, eye-catching colours which set the shavers apart from the crowd. They vary from sophisticated silvery purple and metallic racing green to two sporty models - the first in bright spicy orange and yellow, the second in Caribbean blue with orange. Once again, research results showed a positive reaction to the new styling and colours, particularly with young men in the 15 - 35 age group.

PROMOTION

Two major factors have contributed to the long-term success of Philishave. First is the fact that it is a top quality product which, supported by massive investment, has been consistently refined and developed to give a closer and closer shave. The second is the company's long-term commitment to back the brand with high profile advertising and promotional campaigns. Last year here in the UK, for instance, Philishave was supported above and below the line for 48 weeks out of the 52. The

product was seen on TV, in the press and at point-of-sale. A hard-hitting pre-Christmas national newspaper campaign highlighted the flagship HS990 model and a close-up of a man's chin with the slogan 'Close to Perfection'.

Public relations activity included a high profile sponsorship of the British Army Parachute Team. Its colourful Philishave canopies were seen dropping in to major sporting events around the country. The team's tough, efficient, perfectionist's approach links precisely with the ability of Philishave to perform reliably and effectively under the most difficult conditions.

BRAND VALUES

The Philishave is the result of precision engineering and strong marketing. The company has never lost sight of the need for innovation to keep ahead of the race and a perfect example of this has been the 1996 launch of the revolutionary Philishave 5000 series. The combinations of a breakthrough in shaving performance and new, innovative design ensures that the Philishave brand is fighting fit for the millenium ahead.

Things you didn't know about Philishave

❍ The unique Philishave rotary shaving system was invented by Professor Alexandre Horowitz in his spare time.

❍ When Philishave was launched in France in the late 1940s, attractive young ladies demonstrated the shaver on the beaches. Within four years it was the best selling shaver on the market. In Spain, helicopters flew in Philishave promotional teams to the main beaches.

❍ Early success for Philishave in Holland was orchestrated by 'Mr Steel Beard,' a cartoon character with a large head and protruding chin who would make 'live' appearances at football matches and selected retail outlets.

❍ A special 'Moonshaver' was developed in America for the first manned journey to the moon. It had a miniature vacuum cleaner built-in and spark free motor.

❍ One of Philishave's most famous models was known as the "Telephone Hand-Set look".

❍ The concept for the Philishave was produced out of the experience gained from the manufacture of the bicycle dynamo and the material "Philite" originally intended for radio cabinets.

❍ The Philishave has starred in the movies. Anthony Quinn, in the film "The Long Wait", made an entire scene shaving with the "egg" shaver. In another film, a Western, a cowboy used the battery shaver to good effect. It greatly impressed his leading lady.

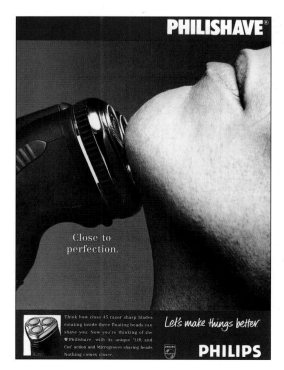

PHILISHAVE®

Close to perfection.

Think how close 45 razor sharp blades rotating inside three floating heads can shave you. Now you're thinking of the Philishave, with its unique 'Lift and Cut' action and Microgroove shaving heads. Nothing comes closer.

Let's make things better.

PHILIPS

Ray-Ban®

Sunglasses by Bausch & Lomb

THE MARKET

Wearing sunglasses has become a fashionable activity. Sunglasses can look cool, ... mean, or simply stylish. They also perform an essential function on bright, sunny days, when the sun can be blinding and cause headaches and nausea. Equally important as fashion and comfort is safety. Scientific research has gone a long way in recent years to prove that our eyes are extremely sensitive to unseen ultra violet rays. Excess exposure can cause cataracts in later years. A study conducted by M/E/Marketing & Research investigated the main reasons people bought sunglasses. Protection was the foremost factor agreed by 91% of the respondents. Durability and comfort were seen as vital factors in choosing sunglasses by 90% and 89% of respondents respectively. The visual appeal was rated next important, and value trailed last. This goes some way to prove that sunglasses are viewed by most as a worthwhile investment. Not only are they a crucial fashion accessory to flaunt, but the protection they offer from potentially harmful ultraviolet rays is a primary consideration.

ACHIEVEMENTS

Bausch & Lomb's Ray-Ban is the most stylish and trusted sunglasses brand in the world. In the UK premium sunglass market, for example, Bausch & Lomb's unit and dollar volume is greater than the next four competitors combined. Ray-Ban is an essential component of what can be loosely termed 'image', hence the fierce brand loyalty the brand incites. Research shows that 82% of Ray-Ban purchasers would buy Ray-Ban sunglasses again. In fact, 72% plan their Ray-Ban sunglass purchase in advance. Buying Ray-Ban therefore becomes a strictly conscious decision as opposed to an impulse purchase, which indicates the quality of the product to be more than satisfactory. But aside from this, Ray-Ban is one of the "coolest" fashion accessories, which is surely why 70% of Ray-Ban purchasers would go elsewhere if they could not buy Ray-Ban sunglasses at the retail outlet they visited.

Bausch & Lomb has built its brand from humble origins in 1853, starting as a small optical shop, to become a world leader in the manufacture of vision care products. This means that Bausch & Lomb has been a leader in the design and manufacture of quality optical frames and lenses for over 100 years. Of all Bausch & Lomb's sunglass lines, Ray-Ban has been the premium quality line for well over 50 years. In the premium sunglass market, Ray-Ban is three times larger than the next largest competitor.

Ray-Ban has earned itself a fine reputation in fashion for the quality of its design. In 1985 Ray-Ban received the prestigious Council of Fashion Designers of America award for its outstanding contribution to fashion. This was followed in 1989 by the Wool Bureau awarding Ray-Ban a special Woolmark award for its continued influence on men's fashion in the United States.

HISTORY

From its beginnings in a small optical shop in 1853, Bausch & Lomb has grown to a sizeable organisation with direct sales and service operations in 29 countries and 24 manufacturing plants in the United States in addition to overseas facilities. The company is based at headquarters in Rochester, New York.

Bausch & Lomb's reputation for manufacturing excellent sunglasses was sparked by the rigorous requirements of a US Army Air Corps lieutenant, John MacCready, who asked Bausch & Lomb to manufacture an absorptive glass for use in flier's goggles.

MacCready had enjoyed brief fame for flying non-stop across the Atlantic six years prior to Charles Lindbergh's historic flight. This experience and his regular flying exercises undoubtedly proved to him the need for more protective goggles to stave off the bright glare found above the clouds which caused severe headaches and nausea for countless army airmen.

Bausch & Lomb devoted time and energy into researching the ideal goggles and came up with the first Ray-Ban green glass. Goggle lenses now had a dual function. Not only did they cut glare but they checked ultraviolet and infra-red rays, thereby proving themselves more than adequate for the army's requirements. In 1936, Bausch & Lomb introduced these anti-glare lenses as sunglasses onto the market, but at a premium price which at first provoked criticism. However, any doubts were swept away by a fine sales performance which assured Bausch & Lomb to proceed further in marketing these highly protective sunglasses. Knowing that Anti-Glare could never be protected as a trademark, the company registered a new name in 1937. In such a way, Ray-Ban first entered the market.

In 1956 Bausch & Lomb responded to consumer preference for sunglasses as a fashion accessory in addition to their primary role as protective eye-wear. Bausch & Lomb expanded the Ray-Ban line with new styles for frames which were a leap away from the standard prescription models used up to that point. The next major change occurred in 1974 when new lens types were added to the Ray-Ban range thereby satisfying the requirements of the fashion market for colour coordinated combinations and the sports market for special performance lenses. There were 16 different lens options on the market by 1986.

One particular Ray-Ban collection, Wayfarer, shot to fame as the sunglasses sported by the Blues Brothers in the cult movie of the same name. The Ray-Ban was lauded in 'Mademoiselle' and 'Gentlemen's Quarterly'. Further glamourous exposure was assured by Tom Cruise wearing Ray-Ban Wayfarers in the film "Risky Business" and Ray-Ban Aviators also took a starring role in yet another Tom Cruise film "Top Gun". Don Johnson in Miami

Vice was a regular fan of Ray-Ban and consequently won the brand further publicity. The "trend" value of Wayfarer pushed sales up to a phenomenal level. Sales in 1986 were fifty times greater than in 1981.

THE PRODUCT

All Ray-Ban products are constructed from top quality materials and engineered precisely to ensure high standards are maintained. Bausch & Lomb intends to create the world's finest lenses at all times. The scientific study of sunglass lenses was largely initiated by Bausch & Lomb in an attempt to ensure their lenses provided optimum protection from ultraviolet rays. Ray-Ban lenses also reduce infra-red transmission and balance light absorption. A range of green, grey, brown and amber brown lenses ensure clear vision at all times.

In terms of style and comfort, Ray-Ban always aims to please. However, durability is a prominent factor when a sunglass consumer is choosing a sunglass brand. Bausch & Lomb takes this very seriously. As a consequence, all Ray-Ban lenses are constructed from the highest grade optical quality glass. Scratch resistance is further enhanced by a multi-stage tempering process which gives lenses extra durability. Frame quality is controlled by hand crafting every component of the Classic Metal Ray-Ban products. Ray-Ban frames are shaped for full eye coverage with self-adjusting nose pads for comfortable weight distribution. As a vital finishing touch, all frame joints are precisely fitted and the lenses are secured properly into the frame, to ensure there are no irritating accidents with lenses dropping out and frames snapping at the hinges.

As the ultimate maintenance of quality assurance, each pair of Ray-Ban sunglasses is inspected twenty times during manufacture. Each Ray-Ban sunglass is then covered by warranty against manufacturer defects. To be a true Ray-Ban, the sunglass must pass a series of tests to ensure product longevity, absorb or reflect at least 65% of all visible light, meet the American National Standards Institute's colour recognition tests to ensure safe driving for example, and, most importantly, provide 100% ultraviolet protection.

RECENT DEVELOPMENTS

Every year Ray-Ban conducts extensive market research and analysis of the sunglass market. In doing so, Ray-Ban identifies the main opportunities for new products, styles and lenses open to the brand.

The 1996 collection therefore reflects various needs and preferences of the Ray-Ban consumer.

The new Ray-Ban Orbs collection was developed for those consumers at the cutting edge of fashion who are looking to stand out from the crowd.

The new Ray-Ban Side Street collection was targeted at the young with a strong street fashion focus and at a price they can afford.

In response to the Ray-Ban commitment to sport, the new Xrays collection of serious sports sunglasses has been developed. And as part of Ray-Ban's sponsorship of the Olympic Games in Atlanta in 1996, Xrays will form part of the British and Irish Olympic Team uniform.

PROMOTION

Ray-Ban was first advertised in 1937. However, Ray-Ban point-of-sale displays have always played a prominent part in promoting the brand. Ray-Ban advises retailers on the best possible way to lay out display stands, frame boards and organise spacing between displays so as to ensure maximum shelf impact and entice the customer to purchase Ray-Ban. The information concerning the potential harm caused by ultraviolet rays should be placed in an area of high visibility, Ray-Ban claims - the idea being that an informed customer is a satisfied customer. For sheer attractive appeal of display units, Ray-Ban advises sunglasses are grouped by colour and separating plastic from metal frames . The sunglass bearing the brightest colour, it is suggested should be placed central to the display as a starting and

ending point for the customer to review the styles on show. All products should be changed frequently, and accessories which could highlight a particular function or setting for the sunglasses should also be moved around on a regular basis.

Ray-Ban has become something of a "cult" in the world of fashion. Its glamourous image has been promoted through fashion journals and propagated by celebrities choosing Ray-Ban as the fashion accessory to be seen in. Ray-Ban has starred in Hollywood movies and been associated with major international sporting events such as the Olympics. Enjoying such cult status, the Ray-Ban brand hardly needs advertising on its style-factor. Ray-Ban, however, is undertaking in 1996 an extensive advertising and public relations campaign to educate the consumer about the new collections and styles in the Ray-Ban range. Ray-Ban is also concerned with educating the public on the need to block ultraviolet rays, and this is a primary function of Ray-Ban sunglasses. Therefore, ensuring the sunglass purchaser understands this, has become a vital component of Ray-Ban promotion.

BRAND VALUES

Ray-Ban sunglasses live up to their own high standards. They are premium quality, scientifically-tested to ensure optimum vision and efficient at checking the dangers posed by ultraviolet light on the eyes. They are durable and through being so hard-wearing, are also good value. On top of that, they are stylish, fashionable and totally cool. Bausch & Lomb set out to be the world's leading manufacturer of the finest possible sunglasses and has more than achieved its aim. Ray-Ban is constantly testing new methods of ensuring it produces even better lenses with higher protection whilst retaining the sunglasses' classic, stylish image. Quality and innovation is the key to the brand's success. Ray-Ban can be both trusted to both protect and impress.

Things you didn't know about Ray-Ban

○ Ray-Ban sunglasses undergo a series of stringent tests before going onto the market. One test involves dropping a 5/8" steel ball from fifty inches onto each lens; The Flex Test bends the temples of each frame past their normal position over 1,000 times; An environmental test bombards the frames with corrosive, polluted atmospheres.

○ All Ray-Ban plastic frames spend three to ten days tumbling in a mixture of wooden "shoe pegs" and polishing compounds to ensure a satin smooth finish.

○ During the Second World War Ray-Ban lenses were standard government issue to the US Air Force to protect pilots' eyes from glare once flying above cloud-level.

○ Ray-Ban sunglasses actually 'exceed' speciality sunglass standards to provide 100% protection from the harm of ultraviolet rays under any conditions.

○ Ray-Ban has introduced a sunglass style called 'The General' which faithfully reproduces the gold-framed sunglasses made famous by Douglas MacArthur as commander-in-chief of Allied forces in the Pacific during the Second World War.

ROYAL DOULTON

THE MARKET

Ceramic tableware is an essential part of any home. Indeed, archaeologists rely on 'shards' or pottery fragments to establish the level of sophistication of past civilisations. For pottery and ceramics reflect the art and lifestyle of the age. Over the past decade casual tableware has become increasingly popular as the traditional family meals are replaced by TV dinners, increased eating out, convenience foods and a generally hectic lifestyle. It is indicative of Royal Doulton's predominance in the marketplace that the company both absorbs and meets the changing lifestyles in their many markets competing successfully for the consumers' spend against foreign holidays, electronic goods, clothes, consumer goods and a vast array of leisure activities. Royal Doulton's sales of casualware rose by 30% last year and its formal tableware remains both a desirable 'special' purchase and an heirloom.

Ceramic giftware has enjoyed considerable growth - gift-giving, home decoration and investment being the main motivations. Despite the introduction of many alternative forms of gifts the ceramic form is sought after as offering true qualities of heritage, traditional craftsmanship and real long lasting value for money.

The key markets worldwide for premium ceramic tableware and giftware are the UK and Continental Europe, North America, Asia Pacific and Australasia. In total, the global market is estimated to be worth around £1.5 billion.

ACHIEVEMENTS

Royal Doulton plc is the world's largest manufacturer and distributor in the premium ceramic tableware and giftware market. Its illustrious brand names include Royal Crown Derby, Minton, Royal Albert, and of course, Royal Doulton itself.

With almost 200 years of heritage, Royal Doulton is a thriving global organisation, with over £200 million annual turnover, employing some 7,000 people, both at its 10 UK factories and numerous distribution operations worldwide. Half of all Royal Doulton's sales are from overseas.

Royal Doulton enjoys a leading position in the ceramics and chinaware markets, around 40% of all English bone china is produced by Royal Doulton and almost half of all the UK's ceramic sculptures.

The company's Hotel and Airline division is also the world's largest supplier of bone china to the international airlines industry.

In total, Royal Doulton produces a range of

30,000 different items in 170 product groups. As well as providing cadres of Royal Doulton devotees with their treasured collection-pieces, the Royal Albert design 'Old Country Roses' has become the world's most popular design with over one hundred million pieces having been sold since its introduction in 1962.

HISTORY

Royal Doulton has been producing ceramics and tableware for almost 200 years. As far back as 1815, the company founder, John Doulton, began producing practical and decorative stoneware from a small pottery in Lambeth, London.

His son, Henry Doulton, built up the business, moving it some 60 years later to Stoke-on-Trent.

By 1901, the quality of the Doulton's tableware had caught the eye of no less than the King of England, Edward VII, who permitted Doulton to prefix the company name with "Royal" and awarded it the Royal Warrant.

Now, as Royal Doulton, the company expanded its production facilities and by the 1930s was involved in the manufacture of figurines and giftware.

Royal Doulton was awarded The Queen's Award for Technological Achievement in 1966, for its contribution to china-manufacture. It was the first china manufacturer to be honoured with this award.

During the 1960s and 1970s, Royal Doulton discarded its drain pipe production interests and went on a spending spree, acquiring Minton, which had begun china production in 1793, and Webb Corbett, a manufacturer of crystal.

Then, in 1972, Royal Doulton was bought by Pearson and merged with Allied English Potteries. This move introduced a number of key brands, noted for their excellence and heritage, into the Royal Doulton family.

Royal Crown Derby was the oldest china brand, tracing its origins back to 1748. George III had granted Derby permission to incorporate the crown as a backstamp in all its wares, with Queen Victoria adding the 'Royal' to the name. Royal Albert, another famous china brand, and the Lawley's retail chain of china and glass shops were also merged into Royal Doulton.

In 1993, Royal Doulton was demerged from Pearson and became an independent listed company.

THE PRODUCT

Each of Royal Doulton's four principal brands - Royal Doulton, Royal Albert, Royal Crown Derby and Minton - enjoys a long association of Royal patronage and holds at least one Royal warrant. All four brands are registered as trademarks.

Due to the company's reputation as a manufacturer of excellent quality, and producer of distinctive, appealing designs, Royal Doulton has secured a high degree of customer loyalty.

When drawing up a new product design, Royal Doulton designers study the market, analyse consumer research and often refer to their own museum and private archives for inspiration.

Royal Doulton provides a broad range of domestic tableware, manufactured in fine bone china and fine china. The Royal Doulton brand is also featured on an extensive range of crystal stemware and giftware.

Royal Doulton produces its famous giftware range, character jugs, china flowers and an array of collectable figurines, often known as the Royal Doulton "pretty ladies". Some pretty ladies are inspired by the history-books, as in Henry VIII's six wives. Targeting the junior members of the household, Royal Doulton also produces nurseryware. Its most popular collection is 'Bunnykins'. Based on well-known book characters, 'Brambly Hedge' giftware and 'The Winnie the Pooh' collection, have also excited interest.

Royal Doulton also provides the chinaware for hotel and airline customers such as the Savoy Group, the Four Seasons chain and British Airways, through its specially-dedicated Hotel and Airline division.

Royal Albert, which traces its origins back to 1896, has become an internationally-recognised brand, offering domestic tableware and gift items - not forgetting its range of children's ware based on Beatrix Potter characters.

Royal Crown Derby is Royal Doulton's oldest brand, dating from 1748. The brand is most famous for its 'Imari' patterns, combining bold reds with cobalt blue and gold and the Royal Crown Derby range of paperweights have become highly prized collector's items.

Equally famous, and sharing a similar heritage since its inception in 1793, is Minton, featuring its most popular design "Haddon Hall," which is particularly favoured in Japan. Minton is also famous for its intricate gold designs where one plate can cost five thousand pounds. The company also undertakes special commissions.

Royal Doulton has a manufacturing capacity of around 750,000 pieces a week in the UK. Its tableware production factories are considered amongst the most advanced in the world industry - a tribute to the research and development department based at Baddeley Green. In addition, the laboratory runs over 3,000 tests per week, to ensure that the highest possible quality of manufacture is maintained. Royal Doulton is noted for its working practices and technology as being among the most advanced and professional in the entire international china industry.

Royal Doulton expects to sell half of its products overseas, so an extensive distribution chain is required to oversee sales and marketing around the world. The company currently operates in over 60 different markets and has distribution companies in the USA, Canada, Australia, The Netherlands, Hong Kong and Japan.

RECENT DEVELOPMENTS

To ensure its potential for growth in the flourishing Asia-Pacific region, in 1994, Royal Doulton bought out Inchcape's half of Royal Doulton Dodwell KK, its Japanese venture. Royal Doulton then assumed complete control of both its Japanese operation and its subsidiary in Hong Kong, renaming them Royal Doulton Japan and Royal Doulton Asia Pacific, respectively. Another venture, again in Asia, was formed with ceramics manufacturer and distributor The Multifortuna Group in Indonesia, where a Royal Doulton factory, producing everyday and casual tableware particularly for the USA and Asia Pacific markets, has been built.

Of course, Royal Doulton has continued to do what it does best - produce top quality chinaware collections. Registering the change in modern eating patterns, Royal Doulton produced a range of casual dining ware in 1995 under the Doulton Everyday brand, offering distinctive designs for practical tableware items, suited to a broad sweep of household applications - dishwashers, microwaves, ovens and freezers.

A new pottery technique using reactive glazes signalled a new departure for Royal Doulton. The method fuses colours during firing in a wholly new, and subtler way, ensuring each piece is completely unique.

Children's giftware was highlighted in 1995 with the introduction of Winnie the Pooh giftware, based on the well-loved characters from AA Milne's stories and poems, written especially for his son Christopher Robin. The giftware set is decorated with scenes from the Winnie the Pooh and House at Pooh Corner books illustrated by E H Shepard.

WINNIE THE POOH
WALL PLATE
by Royal Doulton

IT'S ALWAYS TIME FOR HUNNY

GIFTS THAT SAY IT ALL

PROMOTION

Marketing the Royal Doulton brand employs a variety of promotional techniques, ranging from seasonal magazine and television advertising, to trade fairs, to in-store promotions and selected press advertising - supplements in Bridal magazines, for example.

There is also a strong and effective public relations programme, for example, Michael Doulton, a descendant of the Doulton founders, acts as an ambassador for the brand, travelling to overseas markets, visiting trade fairs and retail outlets, and presenting Royal Doulton's latest wares in infomercials (advertorial TV programmes) on the US home shopping cable channel - QVC.

A new visitor centre was opened at the Royal Doulton factory in Nile Street, Burslem in May 1996. Open 7 days a week it features the world's largest collection of Royal Doulton figures - over 1,500. Visitors are able to tour the factory during the week, bookings need to be made in advance, or see the production processes on a video at weekends. Factory tours are offered also at the Royal Doulton crystal in Stourbridge, the John Beswick studio of Royal Doulton, and the Royal Crown Derby factory in Derby. At Derby, incidentally, there is a superb museum showing the growth of the brand since the 1750's.

As the acknowledged leader in tableware, Royal Doulton is working to maintain its unique position at the cutting edge of product development. Through building on its investments in areas such as Indonesia, Royal Doulton can maintain close control of its marketing throughout the world, making the most of its high brand recognition.

Incremental growth will be created by entering completely new markets such as resin. This will enable Royal Doulton to compete in the rapidly growing novelty and wildlife sectors, both in the UK and abroad.

BRAND VALUES

Throughout the world, Royal Doulton is valued for its sense of heritage and its quintessential Englishness. As one of the oldest and best-recognised chinaware brands in the world, Royal Doulton has earned itself a reputation for excellence, quality and distinctiveness of design. Beloved by collectors the world over, Royal Doulton has an international reach which belies its English roots and product. To maintain this leading position, Royal Doulton continues to invest in its overseas marketing operations and has established high-tech production facilities. Royal Doulton combines the best in artistic design with flawless production skills to produce something both beautiful and practical too.

Things you didn't know about Royal Doulton

○ A single Minton plate can cost over £5,000 and will take one man three whole weeks to complete the raised paste decoration.

○ The largest and most expensive figure made by Royal Doulton takes more than 160 hours to hand-paint and costs over £12,500.

○ Royal Doulton's best-selling nurseryware range, 'Bunnykins,' was designed by a nun and has been in production for 60 years.

○ Royal Doulton was the first china to enter space. China plates were carried on the inaugural flight of the space shuttle 'Discovery' in 1984.

○ There are Royal Doulton ceramics in a time capsule inserted into the base of Cleopatra's Needle, on the Thames embankment, in London.

SAINSBURY'S

THE MARKET

In recent years, the UK grocery retail market has undergone a series of sweeping changes. The advent of large out of town supermarkets signalled the decline of smaller town centre outlets. During the 1980s, it was vital for the large supermarket multiples to pick optimum locations.

Discount stores have invaded Britain from the continent, bringing the likes of Aldi and Netto to our shores.

With the flux in the UK grocery retailing sector, competition has been fiercer than ever, with the market dominated by four key players: Tesco, Sainsbury's, Asda, and Argyll's Safeway and Somerfield. Between them, these multiples hold a 45% share of the market within which they operate.

In addition to the age-old tenets of value for money and product quality, customer care and loyalty schemes have become increasingly important to capture new customers and retain existing ones.

ACHIEVEMENTS

With group sales in 1995/6 topping £13.5 billion and profits standing at £764 million, Sainsbury's is currently the second largest, and most profitable, grocery retail multiple in the UK. It controls the widest spread of operations with DIY and gardening chains, Homebase and Texas, Savacentre hypermarkets and a supermarket retailing chain in the US, Shaw's.

Renowned for its high quality own brand products and best-located sites, Sainsbury's has capitalised on its successful track record with a series of innovative promotions, loyalty schemes, and a reputation for excellent customer service. For example, £10 million has been spent on improving the in-store queueing system alone.

Lower cost own brand items were formerly associated with basic food and household items. Sainsbury's has taken own label to a higher, more sophisticated level, with a vast range of quality goods and strong branding. Sainsbury's has kept its lead in this field by ensuring that all its own brand goods are excellent quality for the price. Recent research has shown that over 73% of Sainsbury's customers considered their own brand products to be as good, or better than a named brand - a whole 11% higher than that achieved by its nearest competitor.

Through its sub-branding, Sainsbury's has scored some spectacular marketing successes in markets previously resistant to own brand development. Overall, 50% of all shelf space in a Sainsbury's outlet is often own brand.

Other recent achievements have included the award for the Supermarket Wine Merchant of the Year in Wine Magazine's International Wine Challenge. Sainsbury's was also the first large UK retailer to open an off-licence in Calais, at the Mammouth hypermarket in April 1994.

HISTORY

The history of the Sainsbury's chain began in 1869, when John James and Mary Ann Sainsbury opened their first shop, a small dairy, in Drury Lane, London. The name and

reputation of the shops was built throughout its early history by offering high quality products at best value prices.

By the turn of the century, the success of the business could be measured by the 48 shops throughout London and the South-East. The range of foodstuff sold had also grown to include bacon, game and cooked meats, as well as the range of dairy products. By this time, Sainsbury's had made a distinctive name for itself, many of its goods were already being sold under its now famous brand name.

Early Sainsbury's stores were distinctive and were identified by their long, narrow shape with a long service-counter, and the decorative style, with patterned wall tiles, mosaic floors, and mahogany fittings. The early style shops

lasted until the 1980s when the last shop, at Rye Lane, Peckham, was closed in 1982.

Sainsbury's was a family business until the public flotation in 1973. The Sainsbury family and its charitable trusts remain major shareholders, with the current chairman, David Sainsbury, a great-grandson of the founders.

THE PRODUCT

In addition to its supermarket shops, Sainsbury's also owns the Savacentre hypermarkets chain, the only specialist hypermarket company in the UK. These stores sell a wide variety of goods, including the Lifestyle clothing range and household items.

Sainsbury's also owns the Homebase chain of House and Garden stores, and the Texas chain, giving the Sainsbury's group a more comprehensive national coverage.

On an international level, Sainsbury's has interests in the US, with ownership of Shaw's supermarkets, and investment in the Giant Food Inc. company.

Sainsbury's range of own brand products are considered to be as good or better than many of the mainstream brands.

The introduction of Sainsbury's Classic Cola is a recent example of how its own brand has made inroads into a market previously considered beyond the fringe for the common run-of-the-mill retail brand. Classic Cola's success can be attributed to the high quality of the product offered at a relatively cheap price and very successful marketing from merchandising through to TV advertising. Such innovation has ensured Sainsbury's is the leading own brand producer in the grocery retail market, with an unrivalled reputation for quality and good value.

RECENT DEVELOPMENTS

Sainsbury's has always regarded good customer service as an integral part of its overall appeal. However, the features that Sainsbury's had introduced as a matter of course, were made the focus of rival's advertising campaigns.

Sainsbury's decided that it was time to start shouting a little more loudly about the services and facilities it was already offering. It undertook a research campaign to find out what the customers really wanted. Its results confirmed that Sainsbury's was renowned for its quality, although its rivals were considered by many respondents to be 'friendlier'.

As a result, Sainsbury's initiated one of the largest staff training programmes ever undertaken by the group. All 110,000 store staff were trained in customer care, and tutored in the key principles of the 'Sainsbury's shopping experience'.

Other measures were also introduced, such as the expansion of disabled parking areas, and the creation of better facilities for mother and baby, including the provision of baby food in Sainsbury's coffee shops.

Sainsbury's also places a high value on providing its customers with clear and useful information about the products, with both the free recipe cards and the on-pack information for the Healthy Eating range, advising customers on the number of calories and amount of fat per serving.

The company has recently introduced its own satellite TV channel, to beam company information into its 363 stores. The project, which has cost around £1m, will initially be for Sainsbury's 110,000 UK staff only, but could be extended to offer long-term communication of promotional opportunities to Sainsbury's eight million customers per week.

Sainsbury's is also exploring the potential of new technology, and now sells wine, flowers and chocolate via the Internet.

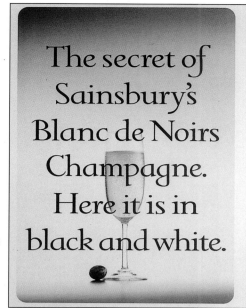

The secret of Sainsbury's Blanc de Noirs Champagne. Here it is in black and white.

Sainsbury's. Everyone's favourite ingredient.

Behold. A miracle cure from Sainsbury's.

SAINSBURY'S Where good food costs less.

PROMOTION

Through the 'Recipe advertising' campaign, Sainsbury's produced a series of highly effective and striking TV advertisements. Each of these advertisements featured a celebrity, such as Shirley Bassey, Julie Walters or Selina Scott, describing their favourite recipes, made from ingredients available in Sainsbury's.

The advertisements featured the line 'Sainsbury's - Everyone's Favourite Ingredient', which was to become the catchword for the whole campaign, and came to be known within Sainsbury's as the 'EFI' advertising campaign.

The campaign proved to be a great success. Its simplicity, and the use of household names, made the adverts stand out. They also provided a set of useful ideas, which anyone could try out, and above all the customer knew where to get the ingredients from. The campaign was well received, and research showed that two-thirds of people who saw the advertisements agreed that they stood out for being different.

This advertising campaign marked a change of emphasis, and took Sainsbury's to a new level of advertising. The celebrity recipe commercials had, in effect, given Sainsbury's the monopoly over this format, and through its success, Sainsbury's took control of a major sector in the battle to be associated with quality and good value; the 'moral high ground' for food.

Sainsbury's competitors did not stand still though, and the result of Sainsbury's success was a change of focus from its competitors. In conceding that Sainsbury's had won the battle

of quality and good value, other supermarket rivals 'moved the goalposts,' and focused on customer care.

Sainsbury's shifted its campaign to include 'service' as an ingredient crucial to Sainsbury's stores as it was felt that the service was indeed an intrinsic 'ingredient' of the whole shopping experience.

BRAND VALUES

Shopping is not just a necessity. It is about lifestyle. Where we choose to shop is a social statement, and says as much about us as the car we drive, or the house we live in.

Sainsbury's has positioned itself firmly in the quality end of the grocery retail market. It has traditionally enjoyed a loyal set of shoppers who identify with the quality and good value offered by Sainsbury's.

All retailers are aware of the importance of retaining a loyal base of shoppers, and of building an affinity with consumers which extends to their choosing own brand products ahead of the main brands.

Sainsbury's has achieved just that. Through creating a strong, clear set of brand values based on quality, value and aspiration, Sainsbury's can compete with the mainstream brands and still retain the advantage in price. Sainsbury's has recently moved successfully into product areas previously dominated by powerful proprietary brands. Its own brand products now account for 65% of sales.

Cost effectiveness, high quality and ensuring a shopping trip is easy and enjoyable, remain at the heart of Sainsbury's marketing strategy.

Things you didn't know about Sainsbury's

❍ Sainsbury's has distributed over 73 million free recipe cards, for the recipes featured in the series of advertisements.

❍ In 1994/95 Sainsbury's opened 20 new stores, and added 617,000 sq feet of sales area.

❍ A typical large Sainsbury's store now stocks over 20,000 products, an increase of 3,500 in the last three years.

❍ Sainsbury's Classic Cola now accounts for 60% of cola sales in-store, and has gained a market share of 13% in the total UK grocer's cola market.

❍ Homebase is the country's leader supplier of real Christmas trees, selling 86,000 last year.

❍ Sainsbury's now has over 10,000 products in its own brand range.

Save the Children

THE MARKET

Wars, civil conflict, famine, poverty and natural disasters continue to throw people's lives into turmoil. We have all witnessed on our television screens the suffering of peoples in former Yugoslavia and Rwanda.

Of course, charities are there during the much-publicised emergencies but - as importantly - many stay after the cameras have gone, investing in long-term development programmes. Short-term measures are not solutions anymore.

Problems are not confined to the developing world - right here in the UK approximately one in three children live in conditions akin to poverty.

ACHIEVEMENTS

One of Britain's favourite charities is Save the Children. Its determination since 1919 to improve the quality of life (or even save the lives) of children everywhere has won it many supporters, elevating it to the ranks of one of Britain's best-loved and well-known charities.

It is difficult to sum up the achievements of an organisation like Save the Children. A headcount of those who have benefited from the dedication and hard work of the charity would be impossible to achieve.

Save the Children is perhaps best known for its high profile emergency work in Africa. And indeed this forms a major part of its work. But as important is its long-term work, both in Africa and in over 50 countries around the world, including Asia, the Middle East, Latin America and the Caribbean. Lesser known perhaps, but equally important, is its work in the UK, where it runs almost 100 projects.

One of Save the Children's key messages is "Prevention is better than cure - and cheaper". This theme underlies much of its work and has resulted in a multitude of daily improvements to children's lives the world over.

Save the Children works where the needs are greatest in a range of ways - through direct work, and through training and influencing to bring about changes that will have a positive

effect on the greatest number of children.

Save the Children aims to make the most of its expertise by influencing decision makers, both in the UK and around the world, on issues affecting children and their families. With over 75 years of practical involvement and expertise, when Save the Children draws public attention to a particular issue, local, national and international organisations often sit up and listen. In this way, Save the Children is able to extend the benefit of its work to thousands more children around the world.

HISTORY

One of the unsung heroes of the twentieth century must be Eglantyne Jebb, the founder of Save the Children. She launched the charity in 1919 on the following precept: "Save the

Children must work for its own extinction. It must not be contented to save children from the hardships - it must abolish these hardships".

Eglantyne firmly believed - and it cannot be disputed - that the children of the world are our future.

Save the Children has proved a persistent and effective force in trying to eradicate the problems that beset so many of the world's children. It has upheld Eglantyne's philosophy that children's needs have to be met not only in times of crisis, but at all times.

Eglantyne was moved to pioneer Save the Children's first campaign by the appalling plight of starving Austrian children after the First World War, launching Save the Children at the Royal Albert Hall in London in 1919. Its first fundraising branches were run on an informal basis and aid grants were raised and distributed to Austria and Armenia where children had suffered from the Allied blockade.

Since then, Save the Children has worked hard to secure assistance for those affected by persecution and discrimination and develop long-term programmes across the world.

THE PRODUCT

The majority of Save the Children schemes focus on building links within communities in a drive towards self-sufficiency. Long-term development is the key which can be forged through improved training, health education and better infrastructure. Overseas, long-term projects include the provision of clean water, mother and child health schemes, immunisation, agricultural self-sufficiency schemes, and work with disabled children helping to integrate them into their communities. Save the Children often works closely with local governments advising them on policies affecting children and young people. And of course, there is Save the Children's well-known response to emergencies, providing food, health and social support in times of greatest need.

However, Save the Children isn't limited to meeting the needs of children abroad. It also plays a leading role in securing decent community care, training and employment opportunities and nursery education in areas around the UK where there is poverty, bad housing, discrimination and poor job prospects. In the UK, projects cover inner-city family centres; training for mothers; work with disabled children; and work with young offenders. Save the Children also works with particularly discriminated groups such as the children of gypsies, travellers and refugee children and has piloted successful visiting schemes to ensure that children do not lose contact with their mothers when in jail.

Save the Children is well respected for its work in the UK and campaigns effectively on issues affecting children's lives in the UK today.

Save the Children often works closely with the United Nations and other leading organisations. It does this in partnership with the Save the Children Alliance, a body of independent sister organisations from across the world who share the same aims.

Obviously, the main product of a charity is its core values. Save the Children's work is firmly based on the Rights of the Child, first drafted by its founder Eglantyne Jebb in 1923, and outlined below in its original form:

1. The Child must be protected beyond and above all consideration of race, nationality or creed.

2. The Child must be cared for with due respect for the family as an entity.

3. The Child must be given the means requisite for its normal development, materially, morally and spiritually.

4. The Child that is hungry must be fed, the child that is sick must be nursed, the child that is mentally or physically handicapped must be helped, the maladjusted child must be re-educated, the orphan and the waif must be sheltered and succoured.

5. The Child must be the first to receive relief in time of distress.

6. The Child must enjoy the full benefits provided by social welfare and social security schemes, must receive a training which will enable it, at the right time, to earn a livelihood, and must be protected against every form of exploitation.

7. The Child must be brought up in the consciousness that its talents must be devoted to the service of its fellow men.

Save the Children is still governed by these principles. Since it was founded Save the Children has helped children in over 130 countries, irrespective of their race, nationality or creed. It has developed a reputation as an effective, highly professional organisation which never reneges on the core values on which it was founded. Eglantyne Jebb stated: "we all of us deplore child suffering, but few of us realise just how much of this suffering is really unnecessary". Save the Children serves to remind us of this at all times.

RECENT DEVELOPMENTS
In 1991 the UK government ratified the UN Convention of 1989 which adopted the Rights of the Child manifesto espoused originally by Eglantyne Jebb and which forms the backbone of all Save the Children policy.

1994 saw the 75th Birthday of Save the Children. It was a year with more than its fair share of troubles and strife. Save the Children was at the forefront of aid programmes in areas such as Rwanda and Somalia. However, the day-to-day coordination and development of welfare programmes persisted, as usual, in those areas of the world where the cameras chose to stay away.

The Save the Children 75th birthday appeal witnessed a number of fun, memorable fundraising events around the UK, and indeed the world, with fundraising as far afield as Uganda, India and Peru. Fundraising events in the UK ranged from birthday parties, concerts, sponsored walks, including Cadbury's Strollerthon, and gala evenings such as the Coca-Cola Festival of Trees.

Current activities include promotions with Sock Shop, Tie Rack, Early Learning Centre and HMV.

PROMOTION
Save the Children enjoys a high profile amongst the British public with an impressive 96% prompted awareness. Research conducted by Mike Imms via OMNIMAS has shown that 87% of the population believes that Save the Children does very worthwhile work.

The active involvement of its president, HRH The Princess Royal, in addition to its professional fundraising and publicity team and 20,000 volunteers around the country ensures Save the Children maintains a high profile and maximum exposure. The active support of a range of celebrities and companies enhances this profile. For example, the visit of Clive Mantle, Mike Barratt in BBC1's Casualty to Save the Children's health projects in Ghana.

Save the Children maintains its independence and security of income by attracting and receiving funding from a variety of sources: from its network of volunteer fundraisers in branches around the country, from shops and trading, legacies, donations and corporate fundraising. It also receives national and international government support and funding. In recent years, Save the Children has raised over £100 million annually to help improve children's lives. To maintain this level of income requires an experienced and creative team of fundraisers in what is an increasingly competitive environment for funds.

One of the most successful elements of Save the Children's fundraising has been the partnership it has built up with leading industries through its corporate fundrasing department. The department has raised over £30 million from the corporate sector since it was set up in 1987.

The emphasis of Save the Children's relationships with companies is on partnerships for mutual benefit - delivering commercial advantage to the companies with whom it works whilst generating substantial funds for its projects with children.

Save the Children has a professional fundraising team which works closely with companies to help understand and meet their business objectives. There are a range of ways in which a company can work with charity - staff fundraising, promotions, sponsored events - many of which result in public interest and press coverage.

BRAND VALUES
It is hard to define the brand values of an organisation as wide-ranging as Save the Children which works to improve children's lives around the world. Research conducted by Anne Ward, however, showed perceptions of Save the Children as "practical and effective, warm and maternal, while remaining non-political".

Things you didn't know about Save the Children

❍ Save the Children is probably best-known for its work in Africa. What many people don't realise is the extent to which Save the Children is working in the UK to improve the lives of so many children and their families.

❍ The charter on which Save the Children was founded has now been adopted by the United Nations as the basis for the UN Convention on the Rights of the Child.

❍ Of each £1 donated to Save the Children, 90p is spent directly on building a better future for children in the UK and overseas. The remaining 10p goes towards administration, fundraising and publicity.

❍ A mere 10p can buy a sachet of oral rehydration salts which can stop diarrhoea, the chief child-killer in refugee camps. At the other end of the scale, £10,000 can supply a mother and child clinic in Nepal with enough medicines to treat over 20,000 children in one year. With more money the possibilities are endless.

THE MARKET

Most of us associate adhesive tapes with the home and office where products such as Sellotape Original are common place. However, over the last fifty years, the adhesive tapes market has diversified and now encompasses technical applications for the electronics, automotive, printing and building and construction industries. Such are these developments that in today's market, adhesive tapes compete with conventional fixing methods such as rivets and welding. The clear sticky tape market is currently valued at over £30 million per annum.

ACHIEVEMENTS

Sellotape was first launched to the stationery trade in the 1930s. Since then it has become synonymous with clear adhesive tape, and the word 'Sellotape' even has its own entry in the Oxford English Dictionary.

It is the number one adhesive tape brand both in the office and in the retail market. Consumer recognition of the brand is very strong. In fact, around 98% of UK consumers recognise the Sellotape brand name, and in unprompted research, it was placed in the top ten of well-known brands.

In the UK, 60% of sales are for the company's technical products. These can range from applications as diverse as space technology, undersea operations and racing cars. Sellotape products are specified by many well-known organisations including British Aerospace, Ford, Kodak and The Ministry of Defence.

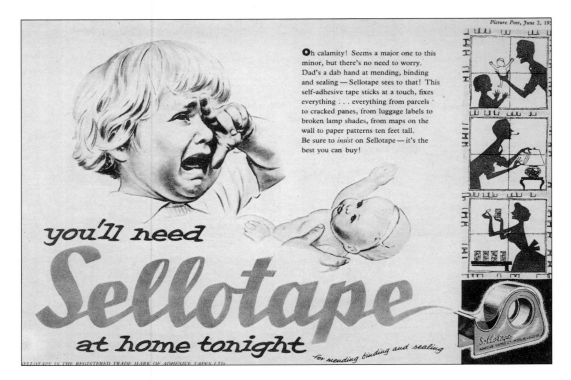

Time and time again, this technical expertise has proved invaluable when developing new and innovative products for the consumer.

HISTORY

The first known use of adhesive sticky tape was in 1600, when it was used to repair lutes. Around two hundred years later, in the midst of the American Civil War, it is known that sticky bandages were put to good use.

Adhesive sticky tape was then used by Henry Ford, renowned US manufacturer of the Ford motor-car. Masking tapes were used in Ford's spray-paint plants, where different coloured cars - aside from the ubiquitous black of the time - were assembled.

In the UK, Sellotape dates back to 1937 when Colin Kininmonth and George Gray coated cellophane film with a natural rubber resin, creating a 'sticky tape' product which had been based on a French patent. They registered their product under the name Sellotape. Manufacturing soon commenced in Acton, West London.

Today Sellotape employs over 750 people in 12 countries worldwide and has an annual turnover in excess of £90 million. While not the biggest company in the self-adhesive industry, Sellotape is certainly one of the most professional and flexible, as its dealings with some of the world's biggest companies demonstrate. Moreover, few of its rivals - let alone other brands from other market sectors - can boast such an ubiquitous and wholly famous brand name.

Sellotape is a truly international brand. It is now sold in 119 countries and operates manufacturing sites in Dunstable and Lymington in the UK, Rorschach in Switzerland and Auckland in New Zealand.

Sellotape consumer products are highly popular in the

commercial stationery market, for use in an office environment for example, as well as being widely stocked in the retail sector where the product is available from stationers, high street shops, supermarkets, independents and DIY stores.

THE PRODUCT

Sellotape Original is Britain's biggest selling clear adhesive tape. The only environmentally friendly, biodegradable tape on the market, Sellotape Original is manufactured from cellulose, a natural wood pulp product. Its natural origins provide a number of intrinsic benefits over rival products. It is stickier than other tapes, static-free for no-tangle handling and easy to tear.

Constant innovation has resulted in extensive development of the consumer product range over the years, beyond the clear sticky tape with which we are all so familiar.

The company has carried out extensive consumer research to design a complete range of over 70 products to suit every 'sticky' need around the home, office, garage and garden with applications as diverse as wrapping a parcel to painting a

window, thus demonstrating there is more to Sellotape than clear sticky tape.

Innovation has been key to the development of the market with the introduction of products such as Sellotape Invisible, for repairing tears, double sided tape for undercover jobs and a range of foam products called Sticky Fixers for fixings around the home and office. And of course, Sellotape is there to help out on any special occasion with its range of decorative products, which are ideal for gift-wrapping.

RECENT DEVELOPMENTS

Sellotape cannot be accused of being a complacent brand leader, as its recent relaunch in December 1995 shows.

The scenario was simple. Sellotape was a household name and wanted to be seen in a fresh light. Even though the company's business had developed over the years to incorporate a portfolio of products specified by industry and used in the home, the success of Sellotape, had placed a constraint on how the company was perceived by the public.

It was seen as the yardstick for clear, sticky tape. However, in the future, a new approach was needed to demonstrate its creativity, focus and innovation.

The introduction of a new identity allowed the company to grow in different directions and extend its product portfolio to new market sectors. In effect, the new identity freed the brands from the brand's old generic image.

Under the new name 'The Sellotape Company', the organisation has masterminded the creation of brands targeted at different market sectors.

The first segment of the multi-million pound business to witness the change was the office and commercial division. New products packaged with upbeat graphics under the 'Sellotape Office' brand name contrasted them with traditional retail products whilst distinguishing them from competitive brands.

The second segment to undergo a change was the retail market, where the most obvious difference was the introduction of new packaging.

The company focused its familiar blue and yellow corporate colours on Sellotape Original while different products received other colour schemes and graphics, enabling shoppers to differentiate between products at a glance.

This approach was pioneered when new packaging was successfully introduced to the company's range of specialist DIY products, including its 'star product', Elephant Tape. Positioned as 'The Toolbox on a Roll', Elephant Tape, a tough multi-purpose cloth tape, is expected to become the DIY equivalent of Sellotape Original.

The company has introduced an exciting new range of adhesive products to be marketed targeting children under the brand name, Stick It!. The range has been launched with Super Snails, tape dispensers moulded into the form of snail characters. An innovative promotional programme is expected to build interest and demand for the range among children and their parents.

PROMOTION

Innovative and creative promotional concepts have become the hallmark of Sellotape's marketing strategy to add value to the Sellotape brand and generate customer demand to pull the product through.

In the retail sector, an outstanding example of this has been the promotional support for Elephant Tape. A nationwide in-store competition offering consumers the chance to win an African safari propelled the product into the forefront of the DIY market.

In the commercial stationery market, the company runs promotional campaigns to support its trade customers, encouraging office staff to specify Sellotape as their preferred office tape. A recent promotion offered purchasers the chance to win The National Lottery which resulted in high profile trade awareness for Sellotape, a dramatic lift in sales, and a Gold Award from the Institute of Sales Promotion for its effectiveness.

This kind of support activity enables Sellotape to sell at premium prices and achieve a good stock turn for its trade customers.

Sellotape once launched a competition, challenging consumers to dream up a brand new innovative use for Sellotape. The company received 35,000 replies, one third of which cited one of Sellotape's most common uses - to remove fluff and animal hairs from our clothes and furnishings.

BRAND VALUES

What could be easier than Sellotape? Above all, it offers simplicity and convenience, where other adhesives, liquid glue for example, can prove messy and difficult to handle. Sellotape attests to the fact that a distinct and honest proposition can enjoy long-term popularity with the consumer and build itself a prestigious, highly valued brand name. Sellotape has now become a compulsory purchase for countless homes and offices throughout the world.

The new strategy, based on market segmentation, puts great emphasis on innovation and builds on the reputation for quality that Sellotape has built up over the last fifty years.

Quality is synonymous with the Sellotape brand name, together with reliability and innovation. These values are founded from the success of Sellotape Original, the original sticky tape.

The same rigorous standards apply at each production location and the sharing of best practice ensures continuous improvement in customer service. All products are manufactured under controlled quality management systems and two of the units are accredited to ISO 9001 and a third to ISO 9002.

Sellotape is a registered trademark. Stick It! is a trademark. Super Snails is a registered trademark. Elephant Tape is a registered trademark.

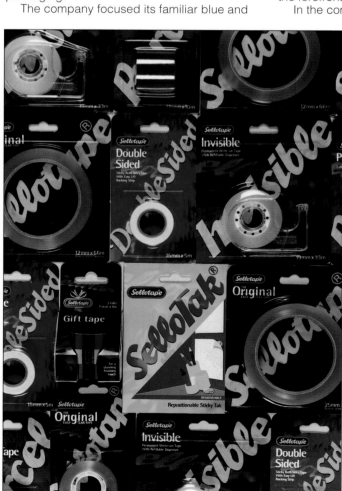

Things you didn't know about Sellotape

❍ On average, we each buy one roll of Sellotape per annum.

❍ A passenger's life was dramatically saved on a flight from Hong Kong to London in May 1995 when a coat hanger, Sellotape and a bottle of brandy were used in an emergency mid-air operation.

❍ Sellotape Original is so popular that if all the rolls of Sellotape sold in one year were joined together they would reach the moon and back.

SONY ®

THE MARKET

Television, video and sophisticated audio equipment have become an integral part of 'lifestyle', rather than a luxury.

However, the world is braced for a revolution, set to blur the divisions between electronics, telecommunications, computers and the entertainment industry. The new media will spotlight the benefits of interactivity, multimedia and online services.

As Nobuyuki Idei, the president of Sony Corporation, told Fortune Magazine in June 1995: "The digital revolution will shake out the total business platform so that brand image and production power and even the best technology won't be enough. We have to recognise that in the future, most of our products will become part of a larger digital network. From now on, Sony's work is to build bridges between electronics and communications and entertainment, not mere boxes".

ACHIEVEMENTS

1996 marked Sony's 50th anniversary. The Japanese consumer electronics giant certainly had a lot to celebrate. Sony has been at the cutting edge of new technological developments since the company's founding by Akio Morita and Masuru Ibuka in 1946. Few companies can claim to have impacted upon youth lifestyle to the extent that Sony has over the last 50 years. And few companies are better-placed to drive the forthcoming digital age into homes and businesses around the world over the next 50 years and beyond.

Just consider the number of consumer electronic products Sony has developed which have now become part of the mainstream.

Sony invented the first magnetic tape and tape recorder in Japan in 1950; the transistor radio in Japan in 1955; the world's first all-transistor television set in 1960; the world's first colour video-cassette recorder in 1971; the Walkman® in 1979, which has now sold almost 150 million units and has come to symbolise a new lifestyle for the young generation; the compact disc; the first 8mm Camcorder; the

MiniDisc in 1992; and with development of the DVD underway, the forging of potentially one of the most exciting eras in multimedia technology.

Sony is not just a leader in the world consumer electronics market, but through research and product development, has made considerable inroads into the world of professional broadcasting, telecommunications, PC technology and now, the Internet.

Unsurprisingly, the Sony name enjoys worldwide recognition, and has been measured as the world's second largest brand name. Its increasingly high profile as an entertainment company through its divisions, Sony Music Entertainment Group and Sony Pictures Entertainment Group, is set to consolidate this ranking further.

Sony is one of the most respected companies worldwide. Its ability to innovate new markets and constant drive for self-improvement earned Sony worldwide sales of $36 billion in 1995. The company now employs nearly 140,000 staff.

What sets Sony apart from so many companies is its ability to never rest on its laurels, basking in the glories of its illustrious past. Instead, here is a company constantly looking forward whose greatest achievements are undoubtedly still to come.

HISTORY

Sony was born out of the chaos reigning in Japan after the close of the Second World War. Fired with a vision for a new future and an abundance of talent and marketing skill - but with a market capitalisation today equating to £850, twenty employees and no machinery to speak of - Akio Morita and Masaru Ibuka founded 'Tokyo Tsushin Kogyo' (Tokyo Telecommunications Engineering Corporation), in 1946. Their aim was to "avoid the problems which befall large corporations while we create and introduce technologies which large corporations cannot match. The reconstruction of Japan depends on the development of dynamic technologies".

Sony has achieved just that. Its leading status as a prime innovator of high-tech electronics products has led to a large-scale expansion of operations outside of Japan, into the United States, Europe, Asia and other regions.

Perhaps Sony's most famous product which pioneered a whole new market, was the Walkman personal stereo. The original Sony Walkman prototype was produced in 1978. At that time, engineers at Sony had been developing a stereo cassette recorder based on the compact Pressman (TCM-10) cassette recorder. This exercise had proved just how difficult it was to install recording and play-back mechanisms in small spaces. Undeterred, Sony set about finding a solution and produced a system equipped with only a play-back mechanism, but with such high quality sound reproduction the product was simply begging to be marketed. Its chief attraction, however, lay in its size. In being so compact it was an ideal vehicle for transporting music to all places at any time when used with a set of lightweight

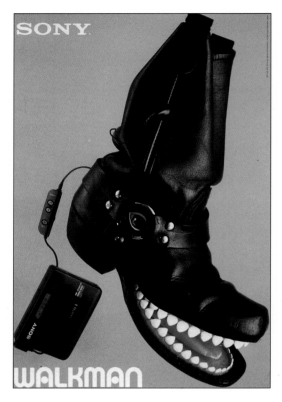

headphones.

The name Walkman was chosen for two main reasons. Firstly, the name reflected the product's debt to the Pressman technology, and secondly, Walkman summed up the essence of mobility which characterised the product.

At first, the Walkman was poorly received by retailers. Eight out of ten Sony dealers were convinced that a cassette player without a recording mechanism had no real future. However, the novelty value of its compact size and excellent sound quality won the day.

During 1980, the Walkman was hailed as one of the most popular new fashion products of the time. The youth of the day soon adopted it as an essential part of their lifestyles. In its first two years on the market, Sony sold 1.5 million Walkman units.

The launch of the Walkman to the rest of the world triggered a sensational response. Fierce competition from rival products however, spurred Sony to research and develop improved products to lead the market. The WM-20 model, often called the "Super Walkman", for example, was engineered to perfection in spite of its tiny proportions, as it was the same size as a cassette-tape case. Since then, Walkman sales have topped 150 million units worldwide and it has become the single best selling consumer electronics product ever produced.

THE PRODUCT

Sony operates in the electronics and entertainment markets. It manufactures video equipment; televisions; audio equipment and CD-Rom drives. Sony has always been involved in the development and production of recording media.

This precipitated Sony's acquisition of CBS Records in 1988, and Columbia Pictures

Entertainment in 1989, to form Sony Music Entertainment and Sony Pictures Entertainment.

Sony Music Entertainment has produced a string of best-selling albums from artists such as Michael Jackson, Mariah Carey, Sade, Pink Floyd, Pearl Jam and Oasis.

The Picture Group has achieved almost a 19% market share in the US box office, propelled by a number of hit films which have included Sleepless in Seattle, Philadelphia, Jumanji and the highly acclaimed Sense and Sensibility.

Sony Pictures Entertainment also holds a stake in STAR TV's music service Channel V and is a partner in the German music channel Viva and the Latin American pay-TV channel HBO Olé and satellite service HBO Asia. The company also operates satellite channels in India and Latin America under the name Sony Entertainment Television.

The fruits of Sony research are not only limited to the enjoyment of the average consumer. Sony's professional product range is used for a variety of applications by broadcast stations, production houses, educational organisations, research facilities, and medical institutions.

RECENT DEVELOPMENTS

Sony continues to be at the helm of new product development.

The Sony MiniDisc, launched in 1992, is pegged to be the replacement for the compact cassette. With a diameter of just 6.4cm, MiniDiscs are available in two formats - pre-recorded and recordable blanks.

Sony has also become a major player in the games industry. Its games software publishing division Sony Interactive Entertainment develops games titles for all games platforms, including the PC.

Sony has also developed its own games console, the Sony PlayStation, with 32-bit processing power, first launched in Japan in 1994 before a worldwide roll-out during 1995. The PlayStation offers real-time 3D graphics to ensure an arcade games-playing experience in the home. To date, an estimated 3 million units have been sold.

Sony has also taken advantage of the PC boom, manufacturing electronic components such as chips and pick-ups, and is also set to market its own Sony branded PC.

In addition to its own company Web sites, Sony has also hooked up with a consortium of leading Japanese enterprises to create a Japanese interactive entertainment network and plans to extend Internet access to 100,000 Japanese customers.

Sony is at the heart of a number of major multimedia ventures forged with the likes of Microsoft, Oracle and even Visa, to develop secure online electronic transactions.

Sony is also a leading player in the developing DVD industry. DVD is being heralded as the next major milestone in the consumer electronics and multimedia industry. DVD is a single layer disc holding 4.7 gigabytes of memory, more than seven times as much information as today's CD and comparable to a full-length feature film. The dual-layer version is expected to offer as much as 8.5 gigabytes of memory. A further option will offer double-sided discs with up to 17 gigabytes of storage space.

Sony appears to be setting the wheels in motion towards fulfilling its president Nobuyuki Idei's strategy of building new products for "Digital Dream Kids", the next generation of consumers in a digital future.

PROMOTION

When it comes to marketing, compared to its main rivals in the consumer electronics market, Sony has not proved to be the biggest spender. The phenomenal strength of the Sony brand worldwide is surely a testament to the company's reputation for producing innovative products of exceptional quality and value. As Idei said in 1995: "Marketing is not just a function within Sony - it is a cornerstone of our business philosophy. We are dedicated to a process of constant technological innovation, and marketing plays a vital role in this process".

Sony's advertising uses a combination of TV advertising, national press and specialist magazines. For example, with the launch of the MiniDisc, editorial features, plus single and double-page spreads appeared in newspapers, youth and lifestyle magazines, as well as the music press. This promotional activity worked in conjunction with an upbeat, youthful TV commercial, shot in New York. Specific youth and music-loving markets were targeted through a Pan-European campaign rolled-out on MTV.

The TV advertisement for Sony's Wide screen televisions featured a man skydiving in his armchair. The stuntman in the starring role later said that this was the most difficult stunt he'd ever done.

However, Sony doesn't just rely on brilliantly executed advertising campaigns to secure public attention.

Back in the 1980s, slick PR strategy ensured the Walkman was launched in a blaze of publicity. Sony was canny in its pre-launch marketing, encouraging famous Japanese singers and young Sony employees to sport Walkmans while out and about, exciting both media attention and curious glances from the general public. By the time the Walkman was officially rolled-out, Japan was in a state of high excitement. Within three months, the entire stock of 30,000 units had been sold. Production couldn't match demand. The Walkman had arrived.

Around the world, this marketing ploy exacted similar results. Photo opportunities with fashion and sporting icons ensured the Walkman enjoyed a high profile.

In the UK, Sony uses large-scale home entertainment and consumer electronics events to give the public a chance to sample Sony products and experience the exciting range of software titles available.

In a world where technology is moving forward quickly, Sony puts its full marketing muscle behind explaining the benefits and range of products available to the public today.

BRAND VALUES

Few companies could claim a commitment to the future, to the same extent as Sony has demonstrated throughout the years. Sony signifies innovation, state of the art technology, superior quality and durability.

Sony pursues a policy of continuous improvement, known in Japanese as 'kaizen'. Its considerable investment in research and development bears witness to this.

Sony continues to strengthen its leading position in the markets in which it operates through consistently strengthening its product range and growing the market through a dedication to research.

'Sony', 'Walkman', 'MiniDisc' are trademarks of the Sony Corporation, Japan.
'PlayStation' is a registered trademark of Sony Computer Entertainment Inc.

Things you didn't know about Sony

❍ In 1986, Walkman was included in the Oxford English Dictionary.

❍ Before the Walkman became a world-wide brand name, it was introduced under a variety of names, which included 'Soundabout' in the United States, 'Stowaway' in the UK and 'Freestyle' in Australia.

❍ Sony created the TC-50 tape recorder used in the historic Apollo 10 space flight.

❍ The Sony Music Foundation fosters the talent of young musicians and promotes amateur music through competitions, festivals and concerts.

❍ Amidst initial concerns that the Walkman would flop because it didn't feature a recording mechanism, Akio Morita had such faith in the product he declared: "If it doesn't sell well, I'll resign as Chairman".

❍ Sony's first product was a rice cooker.

St Michael
FROM
MARKS & SPENCER

THE MARKET

Marks & Spencer has the highest pre-tax profit of any retailer in Europe [Times 1000.1996]. The huge European retail market has been distinguished in recent years by a number of influential factors. Companies, aiming to increase their share in an increasingly dog eat dog market, have plunged into a spate of mergers and acquisitions in an attempt to secure more buying power. The emergence of discount retail operations has begun to take its toll on the traditional retail outlet. As a result, retailers have sought to extend their networks abroad and have undergone major restructuring programmes to increase efficiency and clear away any dead wood which could impede their progress.

ACHIEVEMENTS

The St Michael brand epitomises a quintessential British quality which has spearheaded the march of Marks & Spencer retail stores into high streets across the nation and increasingly throughout the world. In the UK, Marks & Spencer is the archetypal British institution. It is well-loved and frequently visited by the public, and is viewed as wholly reliable at all times. The variety of shortened names associated with Marks & Spencer are part of everyday language: M&S, Marks & Sparks, or simply Marks'. The St Michael brand, which is the only brand sold at Marks & Spencer, is regarded as a classic. Just under 80% of all St Michael merchandise is made in the UK.

Marks & Spencer currently operates a total 711 stores world-wide, which encompass an incredible sales footage of 13.8m square feet.

Marks & Spencer is a highly lucrative business. In 1995, group turnover amounted to £6.8 billion, with pre-tax profit totalling a healthy £924.3 million. Marks & Spencer was in fact the first retailer in the world to be awarded a prestigious AAA credit rating which indicates the stability and strength of the group.

Success has not been restricted to Britain alone. Marks & Spencer is one of Britain's largest exporter of clothing. Marks & Spencer has been awarded the Queen's Award for Export Achievement on four occasions, most recently in 1995. In 1996 Marks & Spencer won a Queen's Award for Technological Achievement for the second time.

Marks & Spencer, and its St Michael brand, is held in high esteem throughout all of Europe,

as borne out by Marks & Spencer being voted 'Europe's most respected company' in 1994 (Financial Times).

HISTORY

Marks & Spencer had humble beginnings. It was founded by a young Russian refugee, one Michael Marks, who arrived in the North East of England in the early 1880s. He first eked a living by selling haberdashery from a tray around the villages close to the industrial centre of Leeds. However, Marks was not content to remain peddling his wares in such a wearisome fashion. He had more permanent plans which required funding. He therefore borrowed £5 from a local wholesaler Isaac Dewhirst to enable him to buy fresh stock and set up a stall in Leeds market. His first advertising slogan

was straight-to-the-point. It stated: "Don't ask the price - it's a penny". This was actually a necessary measure, in view of Michael's poor grasp of the English language!

Despite his 'going up in the world' somewhat, when Michael got married to Hannah Cohen in 1886, he described himself on the marriage certificate as a "licensed hawker". This was soon to change.

Less than ten years on, Michael was operating a chain of stalls strewn across the North East of England. He formed a partnership with the like-minded Tom Spencer, a cashier at the IJ Dewhirst wholesale company, which accelerated the growth of the business.

The Marks' interest in the company was upheld by Michael's eldest and only son Simon Marks, who was named a director in 1911. He was to become chairman during the First World War, at a time when the nation was in flux. During these turbulent years, the Marks & Spencer penny price point disappeared. Simon was joined on the board by his lifelong friend and brother-in-law Israel Sieff, in 1917. Together they were to chart the successful course of Marks & Spencer's history. Both became chairman of the company at some stage, and were later granted peerages in their lifetime.

During the 1920s, the company instigated the revolutionary practice of buying stock direct from manufacturers, thereby forming long-lasting, close relationships with suppliers, many of which have continued into the present day. This decade proved an important one for the company, in that many of the ground-rules, which have been key to the company's success, were initiated at this time by Marks and Sieff. Hugely important was the registering of the St Michael trademark, which

distinguished all Marks & Spencer goods, in 1928. The introduction of retail branding at such an early stage assured the consumer that Marks & Spencer products were marked by a specific quality guarantee. In such a way, the company exercised a foresight which was to pave the way for future success. The company certainly grew at a rapid rate, opening its flagship Marble Arch store in Oxford Street, London, in 1930.

Marks & Spencer always took heed of its staff's requirements, as demonstrated by its setting up of an in-company Welfare Department in the early 1930s. It has since become famous as an employer which earns a high degree of loyalty from its workforce. A period of rapid expansion succeeded the Second World War, during which over a hundred stores had been damaged.

Under the chairmanship of Israel Sieff, Marks & Spencer moved abroad. In 1975 the first store to open in continental Europe was situated on Boulevard Haussmann in Paris.

In the UK, further expansion in the 1980s, led to the opening of the first Marks & Spencer edge-of-town store at the Metro Centre, Gateshead. The establishment of St Michael Financial Services led to the launch of the Marks & Spencer Chargecard in 1985. By 1988, Marks & Spencer Financial Services moved into the black, one year earlier than forecast.

THE PRODUCT

Marks & Spencer has always been famous for the quality of its underwear! It has cornered over 35% of the ladies' lingerie market in Britain, and has an equal share in men's underwear. However, it is also recognised, and tremendously popular, as a retailer of fashionable clothing. This is borne out by the facts. In the womenswear market, one in ten pairs of all shoes is bought at Marks & Spencer, ten million blouses are sold at Marks & Spencer every year and the wool from three-quarters of a million sheep is used in ladies knitwear. Looking at menswear, Marks & Spencer sells four million ties every year and one in four men's suits sold in Britain are from Marks & Spencer. About a million school children are outfitted for school by Marks & Spencer every year.

Marks & Spencer is also famous for its high quality food. It sells over 50% of the chilled ready meal market, making it a market leader. Marks & Spencer is always a popular stop-off to grab a quick bite to eat. The good value represented by its wide range of sandwiches has led to its being the leader in this sector too. Overall, food from Marks & Spencer is generally considered to be of an extremely high

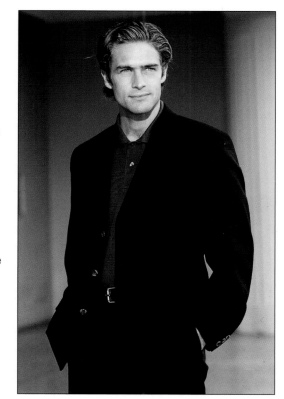

PROMOTION

The St Michael trademark was introduced in 1928 by Simon Marks. He felt that a standard brand applied to all the company's goods would imbue them with a "seal of authority". The idea for St Michael came from the company Corah's 'St Margaret' trademark which Simon liked. He decided to adapt it to his own purposes, changing it to St Michael in respectful memory of his father, and the founder of Marks & Spencer. With Corah's permission, he went ahead and had St Michael registered as the company trademark.

Marks & Spencer has become an integral part of the nation's culture and a prominent feature on high streets up and down the country, although Marks & Spencer has advertised less than most retail brands. Even during the 1950s, when advertising was becoming fashionable, Marks & Spencer was reticent about advertising to increase sales. Turnover soared ahead of its competitors, regardless.

standard.

As well as a variety of goods which include toiletries, gift items and stationery, Marks & Spencer supplies a range of products and furnishings for the home.

Group sales on account cards have risen steadily and at present stand at 23%. In 1995/6, it is expected that total sales on Marks & Spencer Chargecard will have reached £1.8 billion. Along with account cards, Marks & Spencer Financial Services now offers personal loans, unit trusts and PEPs, and a range of life and pension plans.

RECENT DEVELOPMENTS

The last few years have been typified by rapid international expansion. 1988 proved a key year in the company's foreign fortunes, with the acquisition of Brooks Brothers, America's longest established clothing company; the Kings Super Markets 16-strong chain of quality stores based in the United States; and extension into Hong Kong. Further stores were opened across Europe in the early 1990s.

In just one year, 1990, a record half a million square feet of selling space was opened in the UK, mainly in edge-of-town shopping centres.

The steady upward trend maintained by Marks & Spencer can be attributed to its sustaining itself as a quality corporation with a quality brand. Store and product presentation as well as service, have therefore always been of a high calibre. The St Michael guarantee of a refund should the customer be dissatisfied with their purchase, clearly demonstrates Marks & Spencer's commitment to ensuring quality at all times. The slogan 'Quality, Value and Service' has remained at the heart of company policy for many years. Standard-setting and the monitoring of quality control are intrinsic to perpetuating the high level of customer service for which Marks & Spencer is justly famous.

BRAND VALUES

Simon Marks and Israel Sieff expounded six basic principles to guide Marks & Spencer. To offer customers a selective range of high quality goods under the St Michael brand name; to encourage suppliers to make use of the latest technology to ensure goods were as high a quality as possible; to cooperate with suppliers and therefore enforce quality throughout; to expand display space and thereby ensure pleasant, convenient surroundings; to simplify operating procedures and finally, to foster good relations with customers, suppliers and staff.

These tenets form the backbone of Marks & Spencer. As a consequence, the consumer's interests are always held to be of prime importance. Marks & Spencer therefore signifies quality service, and an unfaltering commitment to ensuring its products are the best possible at good value prices. The St Michael brand is a quality guarantee, which projects the image of Marks & Spencer as caring, classy and trustworthy at all times.

IF SOMEONE
HAS JUST GIVEN YOU
A RING WE SUGGEST
YOU GIVE US ONE.

☎ 01925 858502

MARKS & SPENCER
WEDDING LIST SERVICE

AVAILABLE IN OVER 100 STORES

Things you didn't know about St Michael

○ Marks & Sparks, as a slang term for Marks & Spencer, has been entered in the Dictionary of Slang and Unconventional English, published in 1967.

○ Story has it, that a Marks & Spencer employee heading for the washroom, encountered the then chairman Lord Marks in the lift, and promptly scurried away. Lord Marks said, "Come in, you won't catch anything". As the staff member left the lift, Lord Marks added, "Even if you do catch anything, we'll look after you".

○ During the Second World War, Marks & Spencer contributed £5000 towards the national Spitfire fighter fund. The resulting spitfire was named 'The Marksman'.

○ An elderly lady once complained about Marks & Spencer merchandise, saying at her store, "Since St Michael took over your firm I have been unable to find anything that fits me".

○ Marks & Spencer sells over 5000 miles of wallpaper every year.

○ Marks & Spencer sells over 300,000 wedding presents per year.

○ Marks & Spencer sells more store gift vouchers than any other retailer in the UK.

THE MARKET

The alcoholic drinks market is highly competitive, constantly changing and evolving, as brewers fight to increase their share of a relatively fixed volume by introducing new products and categories.

The lager market in the UK has traditionally been divided into two categories, Standard and Premium, based on the difference in price and alcoholic content. The standard lager sector has remained static over the last few years, and has recently shown a slight decline. Premium

ACHIEVEMENTS

Stella Artois is the strongest brand in the UK premium lager market, and the heritage and quality for which Stella Artois has become renowned have become the key determinants of brand value in the sector as a whole.

Throughout a period of unprecedented competition in the premium lager sector, Stella Artois has not only held its position, but over the last 12 months has actually increased its market share.

Stella Artois had been perfected, and was originally brewed as a Christmas beer. The recipe has remained unchanged since then.

Stella Artois was first sold in the UK in bottles in 1937, and in 1976 Whitbread began brewing Stella Artois at its Luton brewery.

THE PRODUCT

Stella Artois is an authentic, distinctive continental style premium lager brewed to 5.2% ABV. Only the finest ingredients are used in the brewing processes, including the

lagers, the market in which Stella Artois competes, is the fastest growing sector and has shown more revenue growth in the 1990s than any other alcoholic category.

The UK lager market is actually a fairly recent creation. With its current popularity, it is easy to forget that lager is not a traditional British drink, and was only introduced to the 'conservative' ale-drinking market as recently as the 1970s. Its phenomenal success in Britain led to the expansion of the market, and the introduction of new products, such as premium lagers, which were first introduced in the 1980s. Within the premium market the emphasis is shifting. When premium lagers were first introduced to the market the focus was on their exclusivity and stylishness. With the rapid growth of this sector, there has been an increasing move by consumers towards product quality and heritage.

Stella Artois has remained the best selling premium lager in the UK for over a decade. It has achieved this status by maintaining a constant public advertising presence in the market. This performance is all the more remarkable given the growth that this sector has experienced recently, and that several of its competitors, such as Budweiser and Holsten have consistently outspent Stella Artois on advertising.

HISTORY

The origins of Stella Artois can be traced back to 1366, and a small brewery called 'Den Horen' (The Horn) in Leuven, Belgium. In 1717 Sebastian Artois bought the brewery, and by 1800 it was the largest brewery in the French-speaking world. In 1892, the Artois brewery began experimenting with bottom fermenting yeast. By 1926 the recipe for

female Saaz hops, rare two row malting barley, and the original Stella Artois yeast. Stella Artois comes in draught form, available in pubs and clubs, in cans from specialist off-licences and supermarkets, and is also available in two sizes of bottle, the 33cl and the continental style 'stubby' 25cl bottles.

RECENT DEVELOPMENTS

Recent times have seen Stella Artois launched in two new formats; non-returnable bottles in 6-packs, and the 25cl 'stubby' bottles, typically enjoyed by continental drinkers.

Stella Artois Dry was launched in 1993, and with its 'strong yet light' flavour was aimed at the more fashionable end of the bottle market. It has enjoyed a strong growth in sales, and has become a major player in its own right in the lager market.

PROMOTION

The 'Reassuringly Expensive' campaign has run for more than two decades and is one of the longest campaigns in UK advertising history.

Throughout the eighties, Stella's advertising agency Lowe Howard-Spink created a series of press ads which were designed to reflect the brand's exclusivity and premium price.

However, at the beginning of the nineties, as premium lager began to enter the mainstream, the campaign was switched to TV in order to reach a broader audience. The result has been a series of four award-winning commercials, the last of which, 'Good Samaritan' was produced in 1995.

'Good Samaritan' was the most expensive commercial ever made for Whitbread. The storyline follows a rustic good samaritan who does various good deeds for everyone he meets, including helping to deliver a calf and carrying an old man across a river. At the end of the day he arrives at the local bar frequented by all the people he helped during the day. He orders himself a Stella Artois, fully expecting the grateful locals to reward his deed by paying for his glass of beer. However no-one is willing to pay for the expensive lager he has ordered, and he is forced to do one final deed, mending the bar's leaking roof, in order to pay for the beer.

The most recent campaign development was the advent of a revised press campaign which kept the 'Reassuringly Expensive' end line, but shifted the spotlight from the brand's value to it's quality credentials. There are five ads in all.

The first in the series, called 'female' portrays a Belgian peasant woman with a rake slung over her shoulder. The caption underneath the photograph begins with 'Ah there's nothing like the aroma of a full bodied female after a day in the field...'. Presumably to the readers relief, the text beneath describes the harvesting of the exclusive female variety of Saaz hop, used in the brewing of Stella Artois. The four following advertisements entitled 'Namur', 'Van Gogh', 'Rankles' and 'Belgian culture' follow the same formula, each one telling the story of one of the quality ingredients used in the making of Stella. The accompanying black and white photographs are of turn of the century rural scenes.

This campaign was run from August 1995 to February 1996, and appeared in the weekend supplement sections of the national press, and in a selection of men's lifestyle magazines.

BRAND VALUES

As the leading premium lager in the UK, Stella Artois has set the tone of exclusivity and stylishness which has characterised this market since the early 1980s. Premium lager has often been viewed as the preserve of the more fashion conscious lager drinker who is prepared to pay that little bit extra for a top quality drink.

From the outset, Stella Artois focused on the idea that it was a brand that not everyone would be able to afford - but for those who could, it was well worth it. The 'Reassuringly Expensive' promotion conveyed this exclusivity to perfection.

To this day, Stella Artois is generally perceived as more expensive than a standard lager, but it is increasingly being seen as good value for money. Recent advertising campaigns have highlighted Stella Artois' Belgian historical roots, and the quality of the ingredients that are used in the brewing process, in a direct move away from the beer's formerly better-known status as hip and fashionable. The 'Reassuringly Expensive' message has not been dropped, neither has the idea that Stella Artois is expensive, but the longer-lasting value of heritage and quality has been instilled into the brand.

TEFAL

THE MARKET

Household and electrical appliances play a huge part in our everyday lives. Kettles, irons, pressure cookers, electric fryers, toasters and non-stick cookware are just some of the modern inventions which ensure we have a more comfortable, convenient lifestyle. It is no wonder then, that in 1995, the UK market for kitchen appliances and irons was valued at £363 million (source: Lek-Trak) and the cookware and bakeware market alone was valued at £320 million (trade estimate).

ACHIEVEMENTS

Tefal is the leading European brand in a wide range of markets, from kitchenware to barbecues, and scales to irons, enjoying current worldwide sales of around £1.2 billion.

In the UK, Tefal is one of the leaders in the small electrical appliances market with an overall share of 13% and the company is strong in a number of sectors, including toasters, irons, kettles and fryers. Without a doubt, one of Tefal's greatest achievements is the invention of non-stick cookware. To this day, Tefal remains synonymous with non-stick cookware and is currently the UK's cookware brand leader with a 25% market share.

Tefal is renowned for its innovation and design of quality, premium products. Over the years, the company has launched many products that have revolutionised their relevant markets and become part of everyday life. It is no surprise then, that, as a brand, Tefal enjoys a staggering 97% unprompted brand awareness.

Moreover, Tefal has been responsible for pioneering a number of 'firsts' onto the market, through a policy of constant improvement and extensive research and development. Tefal currently spends up to 2% of its total turnover on product innovation.

Its notable successes have included: the launch of the first non-stick frying pan in 1956, followed by Durabase, Ultrabase, Resistal and Armatal Cookware, which all brought significant innovative improvements to the market place. Now 72% of all cookware sold is non-stick coated.

1991 saw a major breakthrough in the cookware market when Tefal launched its range of Resistal Cookware. The range was widely acclaimed for its honeycomb textured non-stick inside and heat expansion channels on the outside, both of which made it a more durable product.

Amongst its other key 'firsts' were the electric filter fryer in 1978; the thick 'n' thin toaster in 1982 and the first coolwall model toaster in 1986. Coolwall toasters now account for over 70% of the toasters market.

Although now taken for granted, the first cordless kettle was launched as recently as 1986 by Tefal. Today, cordless kettles represent over 40% of the kettle market. This

was followed by the first high speed kettle in 1992 which reduced boiling time dramatically.

In 1989, Tefal spear-headed an exciting development in iron soleplate technology and introduced the patented Duraglide Soleplate - the smoothest and most durable on the market. Tefal looked at a technology it knew better than anyone - the enamel on the outside of a non-stick pan - and applied it to a standard soleplate. This proved a tremendous success and the Ultraglide Soleplate is now a feature of all Tefal irons, making ironing much easier.

Tefal is also one of the UK leaders in coffee makers. In 1992, Tefal launched the Classic Hi-Speed coffee maker, the first to feature a 'shower head' full flavour system. Tefal's latest innovative coffee maker, the Integra, is set to add to Tefal's impressive record in this market.

As well as being renowned for product and category innovation, Tefal also has an impressive track record of successful design partnerships with British companies such as Seymour Powell. Notable products that have been developed as a result of this fruitful relationship include the first ever cordless kettle and the award winning Classic toaster.

The innovative relationship developed with established clients, like Tefal, has helped Seymour Powell to develop and continue the philosophy of designing products injected with

what is known as the 'X' factor. This is the innate quality which draws a customer to one product over all the others. This desire to design products with outstanding form as well as function has won Seymour Powell acclaim and has helped Tefal to attain a dominant position in the market.

HISTORY

Tefal UK is a subsidiary of the French company, Groupe SEB, one of the world's leaders in the small domestic equipment sector. Groupe SEB is the world brand leader in non-stick cookware, pressure cookers and electric fryers and supplies up to 140 countries.

Tefal's founder was a Parisian aeronautics engineer and fishing enthusiast called Marc Gregoire. In 1952, he developed a means of applying PTFE non-stick to the metal parts of his fishing rod in order to make its operation easier. However, his wife had the canny - and ultimately more useful - idea of applying PTFE coatings to pots and pans, putting an end to the endless job of scouring dirty dishes.

In 1954, Gregoire patented his PTFE application process and two years later began producing non-stick camping utensils. He named his new company Tefal and began operations from a Parisian garage. Gregoire continued to work at improving his non-stick product until in 1958 when Tefal was acquired by Groupe SEB.

Since then, Tefal has pursued Gregoire's philosophy of devotion to product improvement, and is constantly researching ways of improving its non-stick products. Tefal's remit was extended during the 1970s when SEB acquired Calor, a French manufacturer of small appliances and irons.

Today in Europe, Tefal is a leading brand in all the areas it operates in, with a mission to innovate and develop products wherever possible.

THE PRODUCT

Tefal continues to satisfy its customers with its wide range of high quality, longer-lasting products.

Kettles are an essential household purchase, in fact, 98% of all UK households own a kettle and each year, almost one in four households buys a new one. Tefal's most popular kettles are the Gold Element kettle and the stainless steel Eclipse which combine innovative features with faultless design.

Around 2.6 million toasters are sold every year in the UK, of which, coolwall toasters are the most popular. In 1993, Tefal launched the Hi-Speed toaster which reduces average toasting time by 50% and also introduced removable crumb trays.

Estimates suggest that a quarter of all UK households now own a filter coffee maker and Tefal is one of the leaders in this market with their Classic Hi-Speed coffee maker. This compact, easy to use coffee maker makes an 8 cup jug of coffee in under 7 minutes compared to the normal 15 minutes.

10% of total UK kitchen electrical sales are electrical fryers and Tefal predominates with a 36.7% market share. Again, Tefal had many innovations in this market with the launch of charcoal fryer filters, square fryers and was the first to apply coolwall technology.

Tefal is also a leading brand in the iron market. Research shows that when asked if they were "very satisfied" with their Tefal iron, 83% said they were. The market average was 66%.

RECENT DEVELOPMENTS

The launch of the Tefal Steam Generator irons in the UK started a trend which originated in Europe. Although still a fledgling market, consumers are showing an increasing demand for a professional ironing result and, though more expensive, steam generators offer real benefits to the consumer. As a result, the Tefal Steam Generator irons have gained extensive distribution.

1995 saw the launch of a new pressure cooker, bringing pressure cooking up-to-date for the nineties. Consumers still harbour some reservations about the safety of pressure cooking, but Tefal has designed the ultimate pressure cooker to counter these fears.

The Clipso Easylock Pressure Cooker is easier to use than any other pressure cooker on the market. Unlike conventional twist-fit lids, which need careful alignment to fit, the Clipso Easylock has a simple, one-touch action to securely lock or unlock it. Safety is paramount, and the unique safety system makes the lid impossible to open unless the pressure is down to normal.

With the increased popularity of home-baking, Tefal's new non-stick Resistal bakeware has stormed into the UK bakeware market. Unlike most other ranges, this bakeware is made from aluminium, giving it superior heat distribution and retention properties. Most bakeware products are made from tin which is an inferior conductor of heat and provides a more difficult base on which to effectively bond non-stick.

This range was tested by the well-respected Good Housekeeping Institute (GHI). It performed exceptionally well, leading to a highly coveted endorsement from the GHI, which has consequently developed exclusive recipes for the range.

Tefal's latest innovation in the kettles market is its Gold Kettle. One third of all kettles need

replacing due to scale build-up around the element. Scale prevents a kettle from functioning efficiently and eventually leads to its failing completely. The Gold Kettle offers the solution, featuring a 24-carat gold-plated element, rather than the standard nickel-chrome plated element. This extends the life of the kettle by up to three times by preventing scale build-up.

In 1996 Tefal introduced the award winning Integra, the first coffee maker to feature a fully integrated thermal jug, which literally locks in the heat and coffee aroma for up to four hours.

Also Tefal has capitalised upon the healthy eating trend with the launch of the SteamCuisine Express. This follows the successful launch of the original Tefal SteamCuisine in 1994 and the Hi-Speed SteamCuisine in 1995.

All Tefal electric steamers allow you to cook fish, meat, vegetables or rice in a convenient and healthy way. Although a relatively new market, this method of cooking is becoming increasingly popular as it retains all the nutrients that are so often lost when food is boiled.

The Tefal Non-Stick Contact Grill also takes a step in the right direction when it comes to healthy eating. Made from non-stick coated aluminium, the grill has a powerful heating element which evenly heats up the grill plate. The food is quickly sealed by the heat allowing the juices to be retained, keeping the food's natural nutrients and flavour.

The slatted surface gives food chargrilled stripes while allowing fat and cooking juices to drain away. It is designed for use in the kitchen, at the dining table, or even in the garden.

PROMOTION

Tefal has always invested heavily in advertising and strategic marketing. Throughout the years, there have been some memorable TV campaigns from Tefal - the most successful to date is the 'Brains' campaign, which featured scientific 'boffins' with huge, bulbous foreheads. This was designed to raise brand awareness and show that the range of Tefal products is modern, innovative, easy to use and invaluable in the home. Fourteen years later, people still talk about 'Tefal Brains'.

Having now achieved brand awareness, Tefal has changed its strategy for its most recent TV advertising campaign, primarily focusing on product benefits and features although brand awareness remains important.

October and November 1995 saw a new campaign running across Tefal's core products, Gold Kettle, Armatal Cookware,

Ultraglide Filter Scale Iron and Ultima Fryer. The key objective was to communicate product benefits and so the advertisements featured 'morphing' techniques, where concepts and features transmute into the perfect product.

This theme clearly worked. During the campaign, Tefal monitored consumer research which showed that these advertisements raised awareness and improved the image of the Tefal brand resulting in dramatically increased sales.

In other media, Tefal adopts a category marketing approach, where consumers are identified in terms of their lifestyle and lifestage. Tefal then targets these consumers with specific products to suit their needs. For example, information will be sent to healthy eating enthusiasts on products such as Tefal steamers and the Contact Grill with less emphasis being placed on other everyday products such as irons and toasters.

BRAND VALUES

Tefal's key objective is customer satisfaction which encourages loyalty to the Tefal brand, leading to long-term sales. Products need to be safe, unrivalled in quality, pleasing to the eye while simultaneously benefiting the consumer.

As the company which brought us non-stick cookware and a host of other innovations, Tefal stands for expertise. Tefal has the technological know-how and a glowing track record of responding to consumers' needs. The company is driven to grow the market with improved and new premium quality products. Dedication and research are the company's watchwords.

Quite simply - a kitchen isn't complete without Tefal.

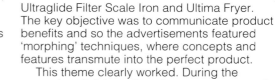

Things you didn't know about Tefal

○ Tefal uses 1,000th of the world's total aluminium supply.

○ At Tefal's headquarters in Rumilly, France, some 4,000 cookware items are manufactured at a rate of up to 200,000 pieces a day. This amounts to 37 million pots and pans being produced per annum.

○ All Tefal cookware is covered by a lifetime guarantee against blistering and peeling of the non-stick.

○ The first patent for Marc Gregoire's invention was registered in 1954. The name was made up by using the first syllables of Teflon and Aluminium.

○ Groupe SEB produces 10.5 million irons each year making them the world's number one iron producer.

○ Tefal's products are sold in 140 countries worldwide.

○ Tefal is the only manufacturer that produces 100% electronic scales making them the most accurate domestic scales.

The Economist

THE MARKET

Demand for specialised information (covering global as well as domestic issues) is growing - particularly amongst the business community.

The Economist is one of the only UK-based weekly publications offering in-depth political and economic information and analysis.

ACHIEVEMENTS

From its beginnings in 1843, as a supporter of the free trade cause, The Economist has become firmly established as one of the world's most influential publications, and is read in more than 180 countries.

Even though the economic recession during the late 1980s and early 1990s hit hard at the publishing industry, and a number of specialist publications were adversely affected, The Economist not only survived the recession, but actually strengthened its position, and increased its circulation - a testament to the marketing and quality of the product.

From 1990 to 1995, The Economist increased its UK circulation by 10% and its worldwide circulation by 34% (source: ABC).

HISTORY

Throughout its history The Economist has supported the principles of the free market and economic liberalism. The celebrated nineteenth century author Walter Bagehot, in his tenure as the editor of The Economist from 1861 to 1877, brought to the publication the values that have set the Economist apart from much of the press and media ever since. The Economist has never been politically aligned, and its independent, radical thinking allied with an emphasis on the freedom of the individual, reflects the same spirit of thinking that was prevalent at the time The Economist was founded. The historical independence of The Economist is guaranteed by the constitution of the company, which since 1929 has prevented any individual or organisation from gaining a controlling shareholding.

The anonymity of the journalists writing for The Economist dates back to 1843, and is intended to ensure that the paper is perceived as a balanced source of informed analysis and opinion.

THE PRODUCT

The Economist is a weekly publication, offering clear reporting and international coverage of world politics, business, finance, science and technology, and also the arts, books and multimedia.

Although it is published in a weekly magazine format, The Economist is called a newspaper, because it is concerned with news, not just analysis, and works to a newspaper deadline. Great care is taken to ensure its topicality, so much of the copy is re-written right up to the moment of 'going to press' simultaneously across Europe, Asia and the USA. Editorially it contains the same copy, with only the advertising varying across the regions.

Despite its positioning as a serious publication, the decision-taking reader has little time to wade through pages of dull looking prose. The editors have lightened up the tone of the paper with striking cartoons, witty headlines, diagrams and photographs.

RECENT DEVELOPMENTS

The Economist's look has undergone changes in recent years. This was first marked by a change in typeface in 1991, and more recently, a new full bleed front cover.

The personnel at the magazine has also changed, with Bill Emmott becoming the 14th editor of The Economist since its foundation in 1843, taking over from Rupert Pennant-Rea in 1993.

"I never read The Economist."

Management trainee. Aged 42.

The Economist

On the edge of a conversation. One of the loneliest places on earth.

The Economist

PROMOTION

Despite the surfeit of titles available to readers and the growth in electronic communications, it became clear through intensive research of its target readership that The Economist offers something extra special - it provided a sense of 'being in the know'. Readers of The Economist felt they had a headstart over non-readers, and it was this emotional response that formed the basis for The Economist's advertising strategy.

The campaign which emerged, was aimed at its target readership of AB class businessmen, in particular those with an international interest. The campaign, based on the brand's distinctive red oblong logo, had intellectual wit and bite. It played heavily on the emotional reasons to read the publication, and so developed a highly competitive, credible and unique positioning. The campaign began in Autumn 1988, and involved advertisements in the quality press and poster sites in London and major UK provincial cities. These advertisements were quite simple in appearance, comprising the familiar 'Economist' red, with the slogan in white. What made the advertisements so eye-catching were the slogans. Aiming at a highly intelligent, business and politically minded reader, they featured slogans and catchphrases which included 'Money talks...but sometimes it needs

an interpreter', 'Insider reading' (not trading!), and an 'election promise' to 'tax nothing but your intelligence'.

The possible consequences of not reading The Economist were featured in two advertisements, one featuring nothing but a white keyhole on a red background, and the other which appears to be advocating not reading the publication with the slogan 'I never read The Economist' until you realise by reading the small print, that the quote is from a 'Management trainee. Aged 42'.

Recent advertising campaigns have followed in The Economist's tradition with the latest addition to the range of intelligent and cryptic slogans introducing the idea of 'being found out' (eg. 'On the edge of a conversation').

BRAND VALUES

As a weekly international publication for business people covering the diverse range of topics that it does, The Economist has to compete not only with the national daily newspapers, but a whole range of different specialist publications.

The Economist has constantly stood above the competition by remaining true to three core values.

Firstly, it speaks with an authoritative expert voice on a wide range of global and far-reaching issues. Its incisive, accurate writing, and lack of partisanship is valued by its readers, many of whom are the world's top political and financial decision makers.

Second, with its readership spanning the world, The Economist can count itself as the only business publication with a truly international perspective, not restricted to documenting events from a wholly British point of view. In fact, over 80% of its circulation is from outside the UK.

Thirdly, The Economist's renowned independence is a highly valuable attribute in the media world. The editor is appointed by trustees, who have no commercial or political influence, and the paper itself is written anonymously, with no by-lines. This ensures that the collective voice of The Economist remains more important than an individual journalist's opinions. This brings about a consistency of view that few other publications can match.

Things you didn't know about The Economist

❑ The longest serving editor of The Economist (so far) has been Edward Johnstone, who held the position from 1883 to 1907, a total of 24 years.

❑ Another famous editor was Sir Alistair Burnet, who edited the publication from 1965 to 1975.

❑ 49% of The Economist's readers hold positions of 'top management', and 25% have a household net worth of over $1 million.
(Source: World Subscriber Survey)

❑ The average reader of The Economist makes seven international air trips each year.
(Source: World Subscriber Survey)

❑ The average time a reader spends with an issue of The Economist is one hour and 47 minutes, and on average he or she will pick it up on four separate occasions every week.
(Source: UK Subscriber Survey)

THE MARKET

Over the past ten years the skin care market has been transformed, driven by the increasing number of women in employment, resulting in a growth in their disposable income. This growth has been coupled by changing attitudes towards personal appearance, personal fitness and healthy eating, reflected in the development of the cosmetic industry, and a need for greater convenience and simplicity.

Having been educated by the press and television, consumers now realise that skin health is more important than merely look and feel. Beauty is seen as an added benefit of healthy skin - market research carried out by Vaseline Intensive Care reveals that 94% of respondents said that healthy skin made them feel more attractive.

The total hand and body care market was worth £111.7 million (RSP) in 1995 and shows steady growth. Four brands: Vaseline Intensive Care, E45, Pond's Body and Nivea dominate the body care market, accounting for over 50% of sales, while private label accounts for about one fifth of the market. These lower price own-label brands are helping to drive overall volume sales.

ACHIEVEMENTS

Vaseline Intensive Care is the number one selling hand and body care brand in the world, with an average 20% volume share of the UK market. Research has shown that 10% of all females use a Vaseline product at least once a week, greater than any other brand usage. Vaseline Intensive Care has been most successful in the hand care market where it dominates sales - one out of every two hand creams sold in the UK is a Vaseline product. Vaseline is also unrivalled in sales of petroleum jelly, with an 80% share. These days, people don't know petroleum jelly as petroleum jelly but by the brand name of Vaseline.

The launch of Vaseline Intensive Care Deodorants was an enormous success with Dry Cream taking an 8% share of the stick/gel market and the roll-on capturing 6% of the roll-on market in 1995. Vaseline Deodorants now account for approximately a quarter of total brand sales.

At the grand age of 125 the Vaseline brand is still well loved by consumers and continues to grow at an astonishing rate, with sales up by a third in 1995. The growth of Hand and Nail Lotion was particularly impressive - sales increased by one fifth in 1995 - because of a strong, clear communications campaign and consumer proposition. It is not just in the UK that Vaseline Intensive Care has been successful. In the US, where other variants are available such as Legs and Feet and Lip Care, the Vaseline Intensive Care family totals in excess of £230 million turnover in sales.

The time and effort that Elida Faberge have put into creating a brand which meets every skincare need has paid off. Many Vaseline products have been endorsed by the consumer press. For example, Overnight Moisture Treatment (OMT) has been awarded Best Body Lotion in the Woman magazine Beauty Awards.

HISTORY

When Robert Augustus Chesebrough first marketed his petroleum jelly over one hundred years ago, little did he know that it would become a highly successful product in its own right and the cornerstone of a successful brand portfolio.

Chesebrough discovered petroleum jelly while working in the oil business. Oil workers would smear their skin with a residue from the drill heads to heal their wounds. Chesebrough refined and purified this residue and made a clear and odourless petroleum jelly. He named it Vaseline and shrewdly registered the name at once. It was first launched in the US in 1859 and proved so successful that the Vaseline Trade Mark was registered in the UK and launched here in 1877.

From Vaseline Petroleum Jelly, the range blossomed, continuing to fulfil Chesebrough's early proposition of healing and

therapy. Over the years Vaseline Research has continued to develop products which provide solutions to specific skin care needs. Vaseline Intensive Care has been established as the leading authority in hand and body care by a wealth of research from a world-wide collaboration of over 2,000 scientists in over 40 countries.

In 1970 the extension of the range began with the launch of a hand and body cream in the US - Vaseline Intensive Care Lotion, launched in the UK one year later.

Chesebrough Pond's was bought by Unilever in 1987, leading to increased investment and a strengthening of the Vaseline brand. The following year, Vaseline Derma Care was launched: a new brand in the therapeutic market which fulfilled the need for a product that cared for problem dry skin. This was succeeded in 1989 by the launch of Vaseline Hand and Nail Lotion, a product specifically designed for the care of hands and strengthening of nails.

In 1991, Vaseline Intensive Care responded to increasing consumer awareness of the dangers posed by ultra-violet rays with the launch of UV Daily Defence Body Lotion. Then, in 1994, Overnight Moisture Treatment (OMT) was launched, the first product designed for use on the skin at night. The skin care range is now sold in standardised packaging and is available in 75ml, 150ml, 200ml and 400ml sizes.

Vaseline Petroleum Jelly is still a firm family favourite. Very few households are without a tub. In the UK, more than five pots of Vaseline are sold every minute and since Vaseline was first launched in the US in 1859, an estimated 250 million pots have been sold all over the world.

THE PRODUCT

Vaseline Petroleum Jelly was initially positioned as therapeutic, recommended for use on severe skin conditions such as eczema and dermatitis. However, Vaseline has always had one hundred and one uses and it is now commonly used in sport; for babies; for cosmetic uses, such as defining the eyebrows and eyelashes, removing eye make up and glossing lips; jobs around the house; car maintenance and the frequently employed trick of using Vaseline Petroleum Jelly on camera lenses, to make photos look atmospheric.

Dry Skin Formula is the highest selling variant of the range, accounting for almost a third of Vaseline Intensive Care sales. It has

been specially formulated with vitamin A and enriched with glycerine to provide long lasting relief for rough, over dry skin caused by everyday wear and tear. While it is essentially a product for care of the whole body, it is favoured by most as a hand cream and is the most popular hand cream in the UK.

Hand & Nail Lotion has a more cosmetic benefit than Dry Skin Formula. Made with liposomes, it conditions hands and nails and stops nails splitting, chipping and breaking. It also contains a keratin complex to make nails at least 30% stronger.

Overnight Moisture Treatment is the newest of the products in the range. A unique, advanced moisturising complex, it works with the skin's natural renewal process whilst you sleep, to help re-balance skin moisture levels.

UV Daily Defence Body Lotion fulfilled a growing demand from consumers for year round protection from the sun, as harmful ultra-violet (UV) rays are nearly as strong in winter as in summer.

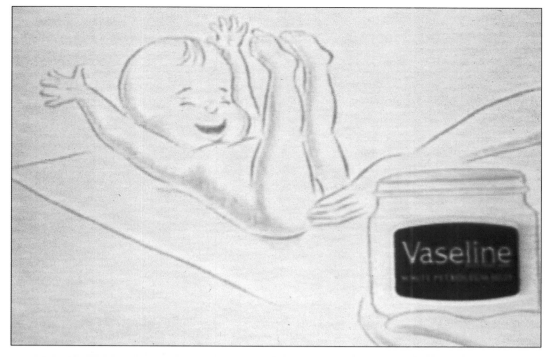

RECENT DEVELOPMENTS
Vaseline Intensive Care continues to reformulate and update original products and constantly develop new ones.

Vaseline Derma Care has been relaunched and is now enriched with lipids, clinically proven to bring effective relief to severe dry skin.

In April 1995 Vaseline Intensive Care spearheaded the launch of skin friendly deodorants in the UK. Both the concept and packaging were innovative. Dry Cream, was one of the first ever deodorants in a cream format to be launched in the UK. It is an effective drying deodorant with a revolutionary mushroom applicator and is one of the mildest formulations on the UK market. The range also includes a larger size roll-on - Big Ball - which is ergonomically designed to fit the underarm, and a high performance spray.

The deodorants build on the Vaseline Intensive Care skin care heritage. They are effective, yet kind to the skin: ultra mild yet ultra protective. The deodorants are dermatologically tested, alcohol free and formulated with a unique blend of ProDerma emollients, a breakthrough skin caring complex which actually helps keep skin healthy. The launch of deodorants was backed by an enormous advertising campaign, totalling a £5.5 million register meal expenditure, the highest advertising spend on a deodorants brand in 1995.

The Vaseline Intensive Care packaging has also recently been revamped and updated. The brand's logo features on all packaging throughout the range. Each product within the range sports its own differentiating colour.

PROMOTION
Since 1993, the message 'From Intensive Research Comes Intensive Care' has backed all Vaseline's promotional work. The Skin Science Update advertising concept was devised to promote the range as scientifically up to date, researched and clinically proven to be effective. The newsreader Pamela Armstrong was used as a spokesperson to add weight to the scientific claims and communicate the idea that Vaseline was making 'news'. Research suggests that the scientific attributes of the brand remain high at approximately 96%.

A great deal of high profile work has surrounded the use of Vaseline Petroleum Jelly, as its inherent qualities represent a heritage of trusted values and protection of this core product is key to the Vaseline range. The sports market was identified as a possible growth area and promotional work began in this market in 1991, with sponsorship of the London Marathon and the Chafford 100 athletes. In 1996 Vaseline

Intensive Care sponsored the British Universities Sports Association. Activities included the organisation of a '100 Championship' across a variety of sports and the establishment of a Vaseline Sports League.

With Vaseline Derma Care, because of its positioning as a product for dry skin, links were made with The National Eczema Society and The Psoriasis Association. Health professionals were targeted through the production of a Royal College of Nurses (RCN) video on treating common skin complaints, a skin care supplement with Midwife, Health Visitor and Community Nurse and attendance at health professional exhibitions. A Derma Care Skin Factfile was launched at the beginning of 1992, produced in conjunction with consultant dermatologist Dr Veronica Kirton.

In 1995 Vaseline took to the road to give Vaseline Intensive Care a human face. Over seven weeks the team travelled to seven shopping centres with skin care consultants, dermatology nurses and manicurists. The tour facilitated trialling and gave away information leaflets and money-off coupons as well as numerous prizes. It was publicised in consumer and trade magazines, in local press and on local radio and in total reached an estimated 7.5 million people around the country, promoting all the products in the range and raising consumer awareness.

Vaseline is a caring brand and this is clearly demonstrated by the work of the Intensive Care Bureau. The Bureau responds personally to all consumer enquiries relating to skin care and skin health and sends out free samples.

BRAND VALUES
The proposition of the Vaseline brand is that it simply and deeply cares for skin's health, in the most effective way - it works with the body, leaving skin feeling naturally comfortable.

Vaseline is a trusted family brand. Its main concern is with providing the very best formulations and so it evolves technically as is necessary. The distinctive core of Vaseline is its depth: of action; of experience; of trust. Vaseline is a strong distinctive brand with deep roots and unquestioned efficacy. It provides stability in a changing world.

Things you didn't know about Vaseline

○ Vaseline has always had the benefit of third party media endorsement. It was first endorsed in 1876 by the leading medical journal 'The Lancet'.

○ In 1882, no less a person than Charles Dickens commented on its value and usefulness in a monthly magazine 'Household Words'.

○ In the thirteenth century the explorer Marco Polo, found that locals in Baku (Kazakhstan) treated diseased camels with petroleum oil.

○ The name Vaseline comes from a combination of the Saxon wasser (water) and the Greek oleon (oil).

○ In the experimental years, Robert Chesebrough inflicted small cuts and burns on himself, in order to test the soothing properties of Vaseline Petroleum Jelly.

virgin atlantic

THE MARKET

The international airline industry is both highly profitable and increasingly competitive. Following a difficult period at the start of the 1990s, the industry is now set for increased growth as new markets, in the Pacific Rim, India and China, open up for business. Even so, transatlantic and European routes are still enormously important markets for airlines to operate in, particularly in the field of business travel. To survive, airline companies have been forced to focus on capturing the market with an improved range of services.

ACHIEVEMENTS

Virgin Atlantic Airways has proved to be one of the most forward-thinking companies of our times, with a strong track record. After all, since its founding in 1984, Virgin Atlantic has achieved no less than becoming Britain's second largest long haul airline. Indeed, over a remarkably short period, the airline has succeeded in breaking British Airways' monopoly on transatlantic routes, gaining a 25% market share.

In the airline industry, Virgin Atlantic has set the standard for excellent customer care. It has introduced a number of unique innovative products to the business, which have become not only the hallmark of Virgin's service values, but of the airline industry as a whole. Virgin Atlantic was the first airline to offer just two flight classes, Economy (a choice of Premium Economy and Economy) and Upper Class, a first class service at a business class fare, abandoning the former three class structure.

Renowned for its consideration of all passenger needs, whether in-flight or at the airline's airport facilities, it is the preferred carrier of frequent fliers, according to TDI research. Furthermore, Virgin's own in-flight surveys have revealed that 91% of passengers in Upper Class would fly with Virgin Atlantic again and even recommend the service to others.

The company is recognised for its achievements through consistent success in winning prestigious awards. It has been voted "Airline of the Year" four times by the readers of Executive Travel, "Best Transatlantic Airline" by Travel Weekly, for seven years running, and was elected as "Brand of the Year - Service" at the ITV Marketing Awards in 1992. Its Upper Class service has been voted "Best Business Class" no less than eight times by Executive Travel and six times by the readers of Business Traveller.

As proof of its endeavours in the field of customer service, Virgin Travel Group has secured financial success, with turnover in 1994/95 of £507 million. In 1995 the airline carried 2.1 million passengers (Source: CAA Annual and Monthly Operating & Traffic Statistics).

HISTORY

At the start of the 1980s, putting the customer first was still a strange concept in the airline industry. Ferrying a passenger from A to B was paramount. Building a reputation for customer care and quality was not considered imperative.

Virgin Atlantic changed this, introducing the tenets of customer care and value for money as customary in the airline business. The company was born in 1984 out of a proposal from an Anglo-US lawyer called Randolph Fields. Incredibly, the airline took just three months to lease its planes and start up its first operation from the UK to New York (Newark).

From the outset, Virgin Atlantic's mission was to provide the highest quality innovative service at excellent value for money for all classes of air travellers.

Before long, the airline's transatlantic routes had mushroomed to take in Miami (1985), Orlando (1986), New York JFK (1989), Los Angeles (1990), and Boston (1991). This was succeeded by flights to Tokyo, Athens, Hong Kong, San Francisco, Dublin and Brussels in alliance with CityJet, followed by the formation of the Asia Pacific Partnership with Malaysia Airlines and Ansett Australia.

More recently, Virgin Atlantic has also launched new routes from Manchester to Orlando, London to Washington and London to Johannesburg.

Throughout its history, Virgin Atlantic has proved foremost in airline service with a string of 'firsts' in customer care. In-flight entertainment has headed the agenda, ensuring passengers enjoy their flights at all times, with individual TV screens provided for all passengers, whether in Upper Class or Economy. Other 'firsts' have included the introduction of onboard automatic defibrillators and staff training to handle passengers with cardiac problems and, constantly aware of safety issues, child safety seats can be supplied on request. Upper Class was also the first business class to offer a sleeper service with flexible meal-options, known as the "Snooze Service".

THE PRODUCT

Virgin Travel Group consists of Virgin Atlantic Airways, Virgin Holidays, which offers 220,000 long-haul holidays every year, and Virgin Aviation Services.

The principal subsidiary, Virgin Atlantic Airways Ltd, is based at Heathrow, Gatwick and Manchester and carries over 2 million passengers a year. Virgin Atlantic operates departure lounges at Heathrow (the flagship, The Clubhouse), Gatwick, New York (JFK and Newark), Boston, Miami, Orlando, Los Angeles, San Francisco, Tokyo, Hong Kong and Washington.

Virgin's revolutionary Upper Class, a first class service at a business class fare, changed the face of business travel. Virgin Atlantic was the first airline to supply a chauffeur driven car to collect passengers at their point of origin and transfer them to their final destination, both on their outbound journey and return. They can also take advantage of a first class baggage

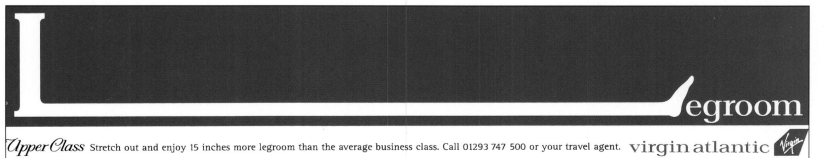

allowance of up to 120kg, separate check-in, and all the amenities of the award-winning Clubhouse at Heathrow to wind down prior to departure. Once onboard, passengers can enjoy 55-60" legroom, a first class sleeper seat, and an onboard bar and lounge to relax in.

Virgin Atlantic also operates one of the most generous frequent flyer programmes available, Virgin Freeway. It was the first programme to offer Freeway miles for travel in all classes. After their first Upper Class round trip, a Freeway member will earn enough miles for 3 return flights between London and Europe. Miles can also be earned with Virgin's partner airlines - SAS, Austrian Airlines, Air New Zealand and British Midland. American Express Cardmembers who are in their Membership Rewards Programme, can transfer their points from the Card to Freeway miles so that they can enjoy the many Virgin Freeway rewards, ranging from flights to a Kenyan safari.

Virgin Atlantic were the first airline to offer full fare paying Economy passengers a special service - Premium Economy. Premium Economy offers facilities and service more comparable to a traditional short-haul business class. Passengers have separate check-in, a separate cabin onboard, and the most comfortable Economy seat in the world with 38" legroom. They also have priority meal service, priority duty free, priority baggage handling, complimentary pre-take-off drinks and newspapers.

Virgin Atlantic's Economy service is the first to provide every passenger with their own seatback TV screen so that they can choose what they want to watch from a selection of up to 24 channels of movies, comedy, news, music and drama, and a Nintendo channel with 10 games. They also receive an amenity kit which includes a headset to keep after the flight, complimentary drinks, and a choice of 3 entrées with meals.

RECENT DEVELOPMENTS

In recent years, Virgin Atlantic has gone from strength to strength, extending its network of routes around the world and capturing market

share from the leading players in the industry. A partnership agreement was signed with Malaysia Airlines in 1995 to ensure a double daily scheduled service was put into operation from London to Kuala Lumpur and a daily service onward to Australia.

Virgin Atlantic also operates a codeshare partnership with Delta Air Lines on all Virgin Atlantic's flights to and from the US.

PROMOTION

The greatest advert for Virgin is probably Richard Branson. Virgin's brand values emanate from him. In many ways, Branson is the consumer's hero, an entrepreneur operating in a style all of his own. In addition to his status as one of Britain's most respected, honourable businessmen, Richard Branson's daredevil antics, such as ballooning across the Atlantic, have guaranteed the Virgin brand its fair share of publicity.

Virgin Atlantic has proved an astute advertiser over the years. The famous logo is highlighted on all its goods and services and is a highly protected property. Virgin Atlantic has implemented an integrated media strategy to promote its brands, including television, newspapers, posters, promotions and direct mail.

Recent TV advertising has secured the endorsement of celebrities, Terence Stamp and Helen Mirren, who had never before appeared in advertising. They were happy to promote Virgin Atlantic because they both fly with the airline and are more

than satisfied with the service on offer.

In addition, a selection of strip advertisements, emphasising Virgin Atlantic's Upper Class services and comfortable facilities, have featured in the UK press, and have won several leading marketing awards.

BRAND VALUES

Virgin Atlantic is famous for providing the best possible service at the best possible value at all times.

It is a distinctive, fun-loving and highly innovative brand which is admired for its qualities of honesty, intelligence and integrity. Judging from the results of a poll conducted by research agency NOP, the public also associates it with friendliness and high quality.

Virgin Atlantic Airways guarantees the passenger is foremost at all times, and this is apparent in all aspects of its service.

Things you didn't known about Virgin Atlantic

❍ Richard Branson's enthusiasm enabled Virgin Atlantic Airways to begin operating only three months after the initial idea.

❍ The first airline to offer "First class service at a business class fare" - revolutionised the industry when the airline was born in June 1984.

❍ The first airline to offer a special "Premium Economy" service to full fare paying Economy passengers. This includes separate check-in, more legroom and a separate cabin on the plane.

❍ Only airline to have an onboard bar and lounge.

❍ Only airline to offer in-flight beauty therapists who offer massage and manicure.

❍ First and only airline on the routes Virgin fly, to offer all passengers their own individual TV screen.

❍ Virgin Atlantic intends to operate the youngest fleet of aircraft in the world, and currently has a fleet with an average age of just under five years old.

NO MORE MR. NICE GUY

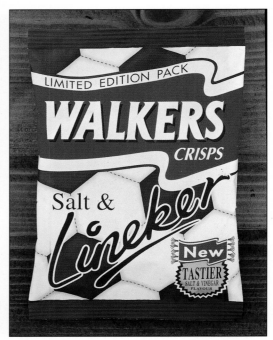

LIMITED EDITION PACK

every bag, every bite.

To ensure that Walkers can maintain this level of quality a team of people are dedicated to ensuring that not only are the crisps golden in colour but the potatoes the right size and the freshness second to none. Every year Walkers invests millions of pounds to ensure the very best keeps getting better - so for example, Walkers were the first brand to move into foil packaging and have just introduced new "Locked in Freshness" technology to ensure that the crisps taste even fresher.

To this excellent product (Walkers consistently beats its nearest competitors 60:40) Walkers then adds great advertising.

The Walkers Gary Lineker Campaign has been an astounding success for the brand. First aired in January 1995 they have proven to be amongst the most memorable ads of recent years.

As a reflection of the brand's success, Walkers Crisps won the ITV/Marketing Week Brand of the Year for 1995.

HISTORY

Crisps were invented in 1853 by a chef at the Moonlake Hotel in Sarasota Springs in the USA. They reached Britain some years later with the first commercial production started by Frank Smith. Frank was a grocery shop manager who in the early 1900s heard about this new way of cooking potatoes and began experimenting with different slice thicknesses and frying times. He opened his first business in 1920 in a north London garage distributing his product in open greased proofed bags by cycling around the neighbourhood. Business boomed and when he discovered that his customers liked salt on their crisps he began adding some in a twist of blue paper to each packet - the start of the famous blue sachet. Crisps had arrived in Britain!

In the 1880s, Henry Walker opened a pork butchery business in Leicester. The firm flourished and still does so today. However the

THE MARKET

Today the savoury snacks market is still dominated by potato crisps (over 50%) with other savoury snacks, nuts, corn products and baked snacks making up the remainder. They are an integral part of everyday life in Britain with an astonishing 1.2 million bags being eaten every hour. And more and more people are developing a savoury tooth with the market growing at an average of 5% per year.

ACHIEVEMENTS

Walkers Snack Foods with brands such as Walkers Crisps, Doritos, Quavers, Monster Munch and French Fries dominates the £2.2 billion pound salty snack market with over 40% share.

Walkers crisps themselves are the UK's favourite food brand and the UK's second favourite FMCG brand, after Coca-Cola. The secret to their success is superior quality -

Second World War brought problems for Henry, and others involved in the food trade. 1940 saw the introduction of rationing due to food shortages, and along with sugar, fats and tea, meat was one of the first items to be rationed.

By 1948, Walkers shops were sold out by 10.00am each day, and Walkers were looking for something else for their workforce to do. The choice was finally narrowed to one option - crisps, which were very popular with the public, and importantly not subject to rationing.

At first potatoes were cut by hand, fried in a small chip shop fryer and then salt sprinkled on. Business boomed, and automation followed in the 1950s.

Today Walkers Crisps are still made in Leicester but rapid growth has meant that further factories were required as far apart as Peterlee in the North East and Swansea in Wales.

THE PRODUCT

Crisps are better for us than we imagine. Research by the Department of Nutrition and Food Services at Kings College London found that crisps are high in carbohydrate and dietary fibre, the vegetable oil is high in polyunsaturates, and there are significant amounts of protein. The fat they contain is all vegetable oil, with no cholesterol and relatively low levels of saturated fat.

Walkers Crisps are available in 10 different flavours on standard crisps and in addition there are

Walkers Crinkles and Walkers Double Crunch (extra crunchy pan cooked crisps). Walkers Snack Foods also makes Quavers, the light potato snack, Monster Munch, Doritos Corn Chips and French Fries.

RECENT DEVELOPMENTS

Walkers has introduced new products and variants to constantly support both its crisp brand and other brands. First crisps: recent development on Walkers Crisps have included the move to foil packaging, new "Locked in Freshness" and the launch of Worcester Sauce, Tomato Ketchup and Pickled Onion varieties. In addition in 1995 a new 50g bag size called Grab Bag was launched - a lot more crisps for a few more pence. But that was only the start of bigger bags - 1996 saw the launch of Family Bags, 175g of Walkers Crisps for only 99p. Other developments have included the launch of Crinkle cut crisps and Pan Cooked Double Crunch.

However, Walkers Snack Foods have not simply concentrated on potatoes. Walkers Doritos were launched in May 1994 and within a year had quadrupled the size of the UK corn snack market. Doritos are growing at a massive rate - over 40% per year with growth coming from all three flavours - Tangy Cheese, Cool Original and Savoury Beef.

PROMOTION

To continue to grow a brand the size of Walkers at its current rapid rate (+20% per year) requires massive investment and continuous innovation. This commitment is clearly demonstrated in the hugely successful Gary Lineker TV advertising campaign. These 'No More Mr Nice Guy' adverts feature the famous football star turned presenter in a new guise. Walkers' choice of Gary Lineker, a son of Leicester and an ex Leicester City player as well as being one of the Britain's favourite celebrities, ties in with Walkers 'favourite brand' status, its Leicester based heritage and its sponsorship of Leicester City Football Club.

Walkers also invests money in the category as a whole, working alongside retailers of all sizes to ensure snacks gain the visibility needed to drive sales. Salty snacks are often an impulse purchase and therefore visibility with good merchandising is very important.

BRAND VALUES

Walkers Crisps are one of the simple things in life everybody enjoys and are Britain's best loved crisps. Whilst producing really fresh good quality crisps is very important, Walkers don't take themselves too seriously - crisps are fun!

Things you didn't know about Walkers

- ○ Crisps were invented by a chef called George Crum.

- ○ Walkers crisps are Britain's most popular food brand.

- ○ 8 million packets of Walkers Crisps are sold everyday.

- ○ Walkers was only launched in Scotland in 1994 and is already brand leader.

- ○ Gary Lineker's favourite flavour is Salt & Vinegar.

WHSmith

THE MARKET

Shopping on the High Street has become a consumer ritual, one that is unlikely to fade in popularity. This is despite the widespread use of catalogues and the advent of home shopping.

High Street shopping is a social, family experience, where customer care remains paramount. Today, the consumer enjoys more choice than ever before.

ACHIEVEMENTS

Despite tough market conditions and disappointing returns in recent years, WH Smith has proved a resilient force on our High Streets. WH Smith Retail is the flagship and frontispiece of the WH Smith Group. It is a familiar feature on all British High Streets, leading the market in a number of product areas. It is the nation's biggest bookseller and is a leader in the music/video, newspaper/magazine, stationery, cards and gifts retail markets. Its 450 outlets stretching throughout the UK, cover some 2.3 million square foot of selling space.

It is no small wonder then, that WH Smith is one of Britain's best-known and trusted brands, enjoying huge brand-recognition amongst the British public - as shown by the estimated 7.5 million customers who shop at WH Smith each week. According to Landor Associates, WH Smith is currently the tenth most powerful brand in Britain.

In recent years, the business has restructured, to highlight its core activities, and to pursue a policy of consistent customer care - anticipating and meeting the needs of the consumer at all times. In 1994, WH Smith's turnover amounted to £2.44 billion, with pre-tax profits pegged at £125 million.

The retail group has made its mark on the community, taking an active role in supporting voluntary organisations and education. Fundraising has been channelled through Link-Up, the WH Smith Group Charitable Trust, set up in 1993. Link-Up is managed by WH Smith's staff, who vote for a charity each year to benefit from 2/3rds of all their fundraising activities.

In 1996, WH Smith has focused on Childline, funding the cost of calls made to Childline, a telephone helpline advising and supporting children, about school related problems.

As the foremost retailer of educational products in the country, WH Smith has proved well-placed to support a series of schools arts projects over the last 25 years, and has cooperated in a business education scheme and placement programmes, for teachers and secondary students to gain work experience.

WH Smith is renowned as one of Britain's top employers and has manifested a serious commitment to the 'Investors in People'

programme, which aims to ensure employee training and development is a top priority. This involves comprehensive management/staff communications, informing staff at all times of the company's 'vision' , and ensuring that every single employee feels an integral part of the overall company structure. Staff training and development programmes are seen as vital to the company's success.

HISTORY

In 1792, Henry Walton Smith and his wife Anna, opened a small newsvendors on Little Grosvenor Street, London. Unfortunately, Henry Smith died a few months later, leaving the entire running of the business to his wife. Anna diversified the business, now called "H&W Smith", trading as a newsagent's and stationer's, until her own death in 1816, when the business passed to her two sons.

The company was renamed WH Smith, in 1828, after William Henry Smith, who had proved the most able businessman. By 1846, his son, another William Henry, commonly known as WH Smith II, entered a partnership with his father, and together the company - now called WH Smith & Son - moved into railway stations, selling books, and inaugurated a

lending library - which actually lasted until 1961.

By 1860, WH Smith I had retired, handing over the reins of power to his son. By now, the company had evolved into the UK's chief newspaper distribution house and had acquired its own printing works.

However, after 1864, WH Smith II changed direction, preferring to concentrate on his political aspirations. The man left in charge was a barrister, William Lethbridge.

He oversaw a number of key changes in the direction of the business, including the opening of the company's first overseas branch in Paris (1903) and the introduction of a superannuation fund for clerical workers (1894) and a pension fund for manual workers (1895).

It was a dispute with the railway authorities, however, which drove WH Smith onto the High Street, where it has maintained such a prominent presence to this day. In 1905, WH Smith lost a number of its 'retail space' contracts with railway stations. The company decided that if its shops couldn't be in the station, it was better to at least be near the station. By 1 January 1906, 150 new WH Smith shops had been opened. In 1913, WH Smith's son, the second Viscount Hambleden, assumed the role of head of the business, guiding the company during the First World War, when its head office - Strand House in Portugal Street, London - was used as the nation's Postal Censor's office.

WH Smith became a private limited company on the death of Viscount Hambleden in 1928, due to the high level of death duties exacted on the business. However, it was a similar situation in 1949, on the death of the third Viscount Hambleden, which necessitated WH Smith becoming a public holding company, with shares held largely by family, staff and the public.

Post Second World War expansion has led to the acquisition of the Our Price Music retail chain and the Waterstones specialist bookshop chain.

In the same year that WH Smith was celebrating its bi-centenary, the WH Smith Group bought 50% of Virgin Retail Ltd in 1992 - including its 14 megastores and 12 computer games centres.

Since then, in 1994, the business of Our Price and Virgin Retail have been merged together.

THE PRODUCT

WH Smith Retail is at the heart of the WH Smith Group's retail and distribution businesses. In the UK, WH Smith operates 450 retail outlets, offering a broad range of family-oriented products, ranging from books - educational and otherwise - stationery, gifts, music, videos and newspapers/magazines. At any given time, WH Smith covers the whole spectrum of leisure interests and hobbies, and is a market leader in the area of special interest videos.

As the UK's leading bookseller, publishers attach a great deal of importance to WH Smith. It can literally make or break a new author. With the ending of the Net Book agreement, WH Smith was instrumental in bringing better reading at better value for money to its customers.

RECENT DEVELOPMENTS

WH Smith has responded to market pressures in recent years by re-asserting its core brand values of trust, knowledge and familiarity, with an added dynamism. Repositioning itself as an increasingly customer-led retailing service, in 1995, WH Smith redesigned its stores and restructured the branch management hierarchy.

WH Smith has been swift to respond to potential changes in the marketplace of the future, realising the growing importance of multimedia as a family purchase, particularly in the field of education. WH Smith now operates over 75 stores with specific multimedia departments, selling up to 500 software titles and multimedia PC units such as the Compaq Presario.

However, despite the emphasis on educational products, WH Smith acknowledges the need for 'enjoyment' with over 100 stores featuring 'Fun Zones', areas dedicated to children aged between 5 - 12 years.

WH Smith has invested in the future efficiency of its retail business with Bookfinder, a computerised ordering service and database featuring 750,000 titles, now available in more than 400 stores. A new till system was introduced in 1995 to speed up the transaction process in its outlets.

Aware that traditional retailing may one day lose out to the easier lifestyle promised by new technologies, WH Smith has been involved in early home shopping trials including the WH Smith Online Bookstore.

PROMOTION

WH Smith positions itself as a family-oriented company, offering a wide range of products aimed at satisfying the needs of every family member.

Encouraging the public to to try new authors, WH Smith has produced a book containing extracts from

Free Winter Collection when you spend £25 at WH Smith. (Compliments of the chef.)

Delia Smith's Winter Collection, normally £9.99, won't cost you a bean when you spend £25 or more at WH Smith on whatever takes your fancy. So hurry while stocks last because there won't be any second helpings.

There's more to interest you at WH SMITH.

Offer subject to availability at WHSmith stores in England and Wales only. Offer exclusive to WHSmith. Excludes the purchase of lottery tickets. Only one redemption per person.

works by new authors - Fresh Talent.

Since 1993, WH Smith has been running The Mind Boggling Books Award, the only major literary award for children, actually judged by children. Only paperbacks are eligible entries as these are thought to probably be the only books the average pocket money allowance can afford. The ten child judges are selected on the strength of a book review they themselves have written.

Special offers and in-store promotions also play an important part in WH Smith's marketing. WH Smith's strong links with education have been reaffirmed with the Back to School campaigns, highlighting the most complete educational product offering on the High Street.

Other recent promotions have included the "For £1" deals, offering hugely popular products such as Batman Forever, Robson and Jerome and Four Weddings and a Funeral for only £1 when customers spend £20 on anything in the store. One of the most successful promotions has been with the BBC, which offered savings on a wide range of books, magazines and videos, and built on the already strong association between the two brands.

A large-scale redesign and refit of all WH Smith stores in 1995 ensured that WH Smith's 'customer first' policy was ever more evident, as store interiors became more spacious and easier to navigate. All items bearing the WH Smith identity, from lorries to notepaper, have also been revamped - a process set to continue into the next century.

BRAND VALUES

WH Smith's product range centres around education, communication, information and entertainment - meeting the wide and varying needs of all the family. The WH Smith brand is strongly associated with quality, trustworthiness, extensive choice of products and good value for money. With a 200 year old history of top-notch customer service, and a solid presence on all our High Streets, WH Smith has become a formidable brand, likely to continue growing its market share as it adapts to rapid changes and innovations in the marketplace.

Things you didn't know about WH Smith

○ WH Smith's major shops stock more than 45,000 product lines, whereas an average food supermarket carries around 10,000 lines.

○ WH Smith has over 450 stores, including station bookstalls and airport shops.

○ WH Smith's high street stores cover over 2.3 million square foot. The largest shop is Birmingham at over 23,000 square foot. The smallest is Radlett at 723 square foot.

○ It would take an entire lifetime to listen to all the CDs WH Smith sells in one week.

○ Each year WH Smith sells enough pens to circle the earth; enough books to fill a library shelf from London to Edinburgh and enough paper to write a letter to everyone in the world.

○ Every minute, WH Smith sells 20 million words.

○ Each year WH Smith sells sufficient cards to send to every home in Britain.

The name on the world's finest blades

THE MARKET

The Wet Shaving market in the UK is currently worth around £165 million, split between replaceable razor blades/disposable razors (£145m) and razors (£20m). Around 520 million blades are used each year by the wet shaving population, which is around 70% of all male shavers.

The last thirty years have seen some fairly dramatic changes in the make-up of the Wet Shaving market. In the early 1960s the market was dominated by carbon steel double blades but these were slowly replaced by stainless steel as the decade wore on. The 1970s saw the first systems products start to take a hold, and also the introduction of disposable razors. The first half of the 1980s was the era of disposables as they became widely available in all forms - single blade/twin blade/ fixed and swivel heads. Double Edge and Systems products suffered under the onslaught, but the 1990s have seen the renaissance of the Systems as the new technology products are now leading the way. Recent years have also seen the growth of a new sector, as the new technologies have been applied to specifically designed products for women.

ACHIEVEMENTS

Throughout its long history, the Wilkinson Sword Company has held a reputation for innovation. Henry Nock, the company's founder, began the tradition in 1772 with his revolutionary gun designs, and this has continued over the last 200 years.

However, one of the greatest innovations was undoubtedly the introduction of stainless steel double edge blades in 1956, at a time when the market was dominated by carbon steel blades. This represented a quantum leap in razor blade technology as up to then it had proved difficult to apply a razor sharp edge to stainless steel, but once achieved, the edge was longer-lasting. The Sword-Edge blade pioneered by Wilkinson Sword has gained significant improvements in the subsequent years. During the 1960s, the stainless steel blade was coated in PTFE, allowing customers a more comfortable shave. Since then, additional coatings have been added, such as chromium and ceramic.

In January 1972 Wilkinson Sword, on their bicentenary, received armorial bearings from the Royal College of Arms, with the motto "SEMPER QUALITAS SUPREMA" - Always the Finest

Quality. Grants of armorial bearings are only very rarely bestowed on commercial concerns, and Wilkinson Sword was therefore greatly honoured.

Wilkinson Sword received their first Royal Appointment, to HM King George III, in 1804, and since that time the company has continuously held Royal Appointments as gun or sword makers to the British Sovereign.

The Wilkinson Sword portfolio of shaving products has grown tremendously over the last 30 years, keeping pace with all the requirements of the modern wet shaver, and today Wilkinson Sword are the only shaving manufacturer to offer a complete range of products in all shaving sectors.

Innovative design

has consistently played a part in Wilkinson Sword's product launches, and the Design Council style awards have been won for no less than five razors.

HISTORY

The history of the Wilkinson Sword company goes back more than 200 years. It was established in 1772, having been founded by Henry Nock - a notable gunmaker of the day - who had premises in Ludgate Street near St Pauls Cathedral in the City of London and workshops nearby. Nock was appointed gunmaker to his Majesty King George III in 1804.

One of Henry Nock's apprentices was a James Wilkinson, who subsequently became his partner and when Nock died in 1805, James Wilkinson inherited the business.

His son, Henry Wilkinson, moved the company to Pall Mall and introduced sword-manufacture as an extension of the company's bayonet-making facilities. By 1877, the company had acquired larger premises in Chelsea and two years later became a private limited company - The Wilkinson Sword Co Ltd.

From 1890 onwards, the company extended its product portfolio to include cut-throat razors, developing the first safety razor in 1898.

At the start of the century, Wilkinson Sword moved to still larger premises in Acton and expanded its activity to provide personal equipment for officers of the Armed Forces. Over 5,000 such items were sold from the Pall Mall showroom.

A military and civil tailoring section was set up. This subsequently led to the development of the famous Flak jacket later used by US Army Air Force personnel in World War Two.

Meanwhile, the onset of World War One ensured the Acton factory was busy producing armaments, including around two and a half million bayonets.

After the war, the company introduced the first garden products (e.g pruning shears) and resumed razor production, leading to the introduction of one of Wilkinson Sword's most famous products - the Empire Razor - in 1929.

But once again, the outbreak of the Second World War meant the Acton factory was soon dedicated to the war effort, producing aircraft fire protection systems, commando knives and armoured clothing. Even when the war was over, renewed razor-production was brought to a halt by a brass shortage, then used in razor-manufacture. So the company extended its activities in the garden tool field with a range of shears and edging knives.

Once full razor-production was restored, Wilkinson Sword was on its way to developing the first stainless steel blade for the double-edge market in 1956 - a turning-point for the company and the market.

Building on this success, Wilkinson Sword continued to develop new products and soon transferred its core razor production facilities to a purpose-built factory at Cramlington near Newcastle-Upon-Tyne.

During the 1970s, new technological developments included the world's first fixed geometry shaving system - Bonded - and the addition of new coatings, chromium and ceramic, to the traditional Wilkinson Sword Double Edge blades.

A string of new product launches has followed, including such famous brand names as Profile, Retractor, Protector, Extra II and the FX Performer.

THE PRODUCT

All Wilkinson Sword razor blades are designed to produce a fine quality tip known as the Gothic Arch section, which is viewed as stronger, more durable, than the more common straight-sided shape used by other razor blade manufacturers. The result is prolonged blade life.

Over the years, the Wilkinson Sword product range has grown considerably as it keeps pace with modern consumer needs. Its first shaving product, the Figaro Razor, was developed in 1890, and was a hollow ground cut-throat razor. This was followed by the Pall Mall, a safety

Punch's Almanack for 1928

razor, in 1898.

One of the most famous blades of all time has been the Wilkinson Empire Safety Razor which first appeared in 1929, and became the basis for a variety of models, including a 7-Day Set offering a different blade for each day of the week. Production continued until 1950, although some Empire razors are still in use.

The leap into modern technology was facilitated by the development of the first double edge blade to be made from stainless steel in 1956, with its significantly increased blade life compared to the ubiquitous carbon steel blades of the time. This was followed by a series of innovations, including new coatings for greater shaving comfort and ease.

The first disposable razor was introduced in 1978. The Wilkinson Sword Close and Easy was a twin blade bonded unit on a plastic handle. A single edge disposable, Wilkinson Sword Handy, arrived in 1980, whilst the first swivelling twin blade disposable, Wilkinson Sword Twin Swivel, was launched in the same year.

The 1980s also saw the introduction of Retractor featuring retractable blades, and the 1990s, the launch of Wilkinson Sword Protector, protecting against cuts and skin irritation while shaving.

RECENT DEVELOPMENTS

Wilkinson Sword first introduced 'comfort strips' in 1986. These strips are now common to most Wilkinson Sword razor systems. A comfort or lubricating strip is normally positioned on the top cap above the blades. The two main strips used are Polyox: containing aloe and/or vitamin E, for added lubrication while shaving, and Aquaglide: a non-water soluble polyvinyl strip which reduces friction between the skin and blade.

As an aid to developing an extremely safe shaving system, the twin blades on the 'Protector' shaving system are wrapped with very fine wire, known as patented microfine wire wraps. This significant step forward in safety has proven to be a successful advancement in the science of shaving.

The FX Performer, the first razor to feature 'flexible blades' was launched in late 1995. Advanced design and special materials allow the blades to flex around the area being shaved, conforming to the unique shape of every face.

Wilkinson Sword was the first manufacturer

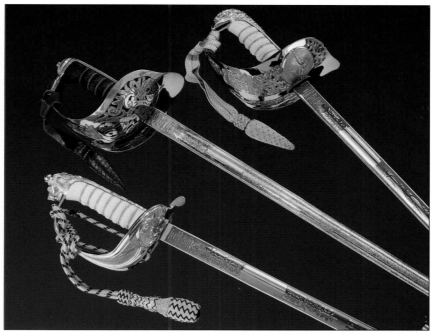

to launch a premium range of female toiletries in 1994 with great success. The 1995 enhancement of the Lady Protector toiletries with added aloe vera and vitamin E will stimulate further growth in this area.

PROMOTION

The Wilkinson Sword portfolio receives widespread support from a comprehensive and innovative marketing support programme encompassing above and below the line activity.

In recent years, Wilkinson Sword has invested heavily in TV advertising across the major brands of FX Performer, Protector and Lady Protector with spend since 1992 in excess of £30 million. The TV presence of the Wilkinson name and its brands has extended to perimeter board advertising at football grounds, sightscreen advertising at cricket grounds and the sponsorship of other leading sports events such as professional European golf.

Within the retail environment it is essential for the consumer to be able to see the Wilkinson Sword portfolio and moreover the leading branded products. The strength of the Protector and the Lady Protector brands was reinforced by novel merchandising units.

Wilkinson Sword has always paid great attention to its advertising. Back in 1961, when the Super Sword Edge blade was developed - a stainless steel double-edged razor blade with a special PTFE coating - it was not allowed to be marketed until it had reached a 100% preference panel testing over existing blades in the market. This was succeeded by an attention-grabbing advertising campaign, known as 'Sword Theme', which enabled the superior qualities of this new blade to rapidly become known. Within a few months, demand had exceeded supply, and the advertising had to be stopped as queues formed in the High Street with customers fighting to buy the new blades.

Humour has also been exploited in advertising. In the 1980s, one TV campaign featured Bob Geldof (not known for his love of shaving) brandishing a razor with the words, ".... would I shave with this? You must be joking".

Wilkinson Sword is the only UK razor blade manufacturer to achieve the BS5750, thus ensuring that production quality standards really do justify the advertising slogan "The Name On the World's Finest Blades," which has been consistently used in advertising since the 1960s.

BRAND VALUES

Above all, the Wilkinson Sword name is associated with quality, reliability, innovation and years of shaving expertise, all personified in the crossed swords logo bearing the slogan "The Name On The World's Finest Blades". This slogan is now instantly associated with Wilkinson Sword.

The company will continue its long tradition of technological innovation, from the stainless steel double edge blade in 1965 to the totally flexible blades of the FX Performer in 1996 and lead the way in shaving, offering "Always The Finest Quality".

Things you didn't know about Wilkinson Sword

○ During the Second World War, Wilkinson Sword were asked to produce reinforced jackets to protect the pilots from anti-aircraft flak due to the high quality of their raw materials.

○ Wilkinson Sword is one of the 100 oldest companies in the UK.

○ In 1905, Wilkinson Sword produced cars, followed by motor-cycles in 1910.

○ Wilkinson Sword continue to produce ceremonial swords for use by military ranks world-wide.

○ The fastest barber on record is Dannie Rowe who shaved 1994 men in one hour using a Wilkinson Sword Retractor razor in 1988.

THE MARKET

Where is the wisdom we have lost in knowledge?
Where is the knowledge we have lost in information?
T.S Eliot, The Rock

If there is a theme to the twentieth century, it is information. From the secrets of DNA, to the infinite breadth of the Internet, it is information that challenges, changes and shapes our life.

As information becomes ever more available, it is even more important to classify it:- to distil it to that which is useful.

Pub and restaurant guides, share price information, train times, cinema guides, houses for sale, company reports, tourist information, sports results, lonely hearts columns - if there is something you need to know, you can guarantee that someone, somewhere is compiling it. It is in this information age that YELLOW PAGES operates as both a provider and distiller. It is here, in whatever new media it appears, that its continued success lies.

Though more recently, YELLOW PAGES has continued to develop into new areas of information dissemination, the brand is best known for being market leader in the UK directories market, recently estimated to be worth around £600 million and still growing. This reflects the dynamic growth in the use of the telephone as a crucial medium for sales and customer service in the 1990s.

ACHIEVEMENTS

From its humble beginnings in 1966, YELLOW PAGES has grown to be far and away the leading directory brand in the UK.

UK households receive a new YELLOW PAGES directory every year - no small feat of distribution with 29,000,000 directories being delivered to homes and businesses across the country, regardless of telephone ownership.

With such a high level of penetration, YELLOW PAGES represents a crucial source of business for companies nationwide. More than 350,000 advertisers place over 650,000 advertisements in YELLOW PAGES to promote their goods and services (Source: YELLOW PAGES Sales Data). And because all companies with a business telephone line are eligible for a discretionary free "line" entry, there are about 2.5 million entries nationwide. Over 50% of adults and 88% of business information seekers refer to YELLOW PAGES every month. Since 1983, usage of the directory has increased by nearly two thirds, meaning that in any one month YELLOW PAGES is now used over 150,000,000 times.

HISTORY

Though directories are closely associated with telephone usage nowadays, they actually pre-date Alexander Graham Bell by a number of years.

In fact, the history of directories can be traced back to Elizabethan times when street directories were published detailing the names and addresses of residential and business addresses in an area. As early as the 1840s, Kelly's London Post Office directories began to emerge.

The onset of the telecommunications era signalled the growth of directories more akin to their present form.

It was in the 1960s that the General Post Office, which was

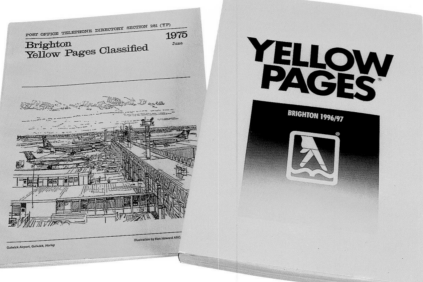

the controller of most of UK telephony at the time, introduced and developed YELLOW PAGES as a national business in the UK. The first such directory was launched in Brighton in June 1966.

In the early years, the YELLOW PAGES directory was bound into the already established telephone directories.

By the mid-70s, YELLOW PAGES had attained almost 100% coverage nationwide and existed as a stand alone product in its own right. YELLOW PAGES became a registered trademark in 1979.

THE PRODUCT

YELLOW PAGES is the UK's most comprehensive information directory. It is designed to give consumers easy access to all the information required to help them find a supplier capable of meeting their needs. There are 74 directories covering virtually every geographical area in Great Britain and Northern Ireland, giving over 1,800,000 businesses access to 29,000,000 homes and commercial premises nationwide.

Advertisers have the option to buy advertising space in any of the YELLOW PAGES directories. Consistent with the advertising message that YELLOW PAGES is "not just for the nasty things in life," only a small proportion of advertisers represent traditional

emergency businesses like plumbers and glaziers. In fact, they have the opportunity to place a wide choice of sizes of adverts in any of the 2,500 classifications available. So from abattoirs to zoos, YELLOW PAGES have the capability to meet most advertisers' needs, no matter how unusual.

In most cases, these advertisements are designed in the print studios of YELLOW PAGES.

As well as the classification section, each YELLOW PAGES also contains locally useful information such as town centre maps and national helpline numbers. Product innovation of this type will continue to play a major part in the future development of the directories. The "Inside Guides," which can now be found in a number of the London YELLOW PAGES and which provide pages of ideas for things to do in the capital, are evidence of a move to make YELLOW PAGES more than just a directory.

Central to the success of YELLOW PAGES is the virtuous circle resulting from building usage. Put simply, the more people who use YELLOW PAGES, the more calls shops and businesses receive in response to their advertising. The increased payback on advertising encourages more shops and businesses to buy more space to tell consumers about what they have to offer. This in turn increases the value of the directory to users, who use it even more as a result.

RECENT DEVELOPMENTS

By being sensitive to technological developments and changing customer needs, YELLOW PAGES has continued to refine and improve its core directory product and extend into new areas of information dissemination. More recent brand extensions include Business Pages, a specialist directory covering businesses that supply goods and services to other businesses, Talking Pages - a 24 hour freephone line providing up to date details on businesses, shops and services throughout the UK, Electronic YELLOW PAGES for Windows, producing a comprehensive online information service for computer users, and Yell, the YELLOW PAGES Web site comprising 3 key services - the UK Yellow Web which summarises nearly 3,000 UK Web sites, Film Finder detailing what's on and when, at over 400 major UK cinemas and Electronic YELLOW PAGES.

All of these developments mean that YELLOW PAGES is well placed to maintain its status as a leading information provider well into the next century.

PROMOTION

YELLOW PAGES have always recognised the importance of building and maintaining a strong brand via advertising. The success of YELLOW PAGES advertising is testimony to a belief in the power of long term campaigns.

Running for 13 years through the 1970s and

HAPPY CHRISTMAS.

Running for 13 years through the 1970s and early 1980s, the "Let Your Fingers Do The Walking" campaign put YELLOW PAGES on the map. The rapid growth of the telephone provided the basis for building this campaign - with YELLOW PAGES and a telephone, people could find the right supplier fast without having to leave their home.

By 1983, YELLOW PAGES had reached a crucial stage in its development. A review of the brand highlighted that though everyone had heard of YELLOW PAGES, consumers had very limited views about it. It was seen as a product largely associated with less pleasant tasks like finding a plumber or electrician in an emergency. As a result, consumers found it difficult to attach many positive brand values to YELLOW PAGES. Instead it was seen as a product 'best forgotten' rather than a brand 'best remembered'.

The opportunity for usage growth lay in positioning YELLOW PAGES as the place people would think to turn for all their information needs - not just nasty ones. YELLOW PAGES needed to mean something more in people's lives than just a yellow book full of company names and addresses.

A fundamental redesign of the YELLOW PAGES product was undertaken in 1983. This involved a total revamp of the core product design, giving the directory a more consistent and striking cover design, a design which still exists today.

The "not just for the nasty things in life" campaign began with a simple TV execution. A man uses YELLOW PAGES to find a book that he had written in his younger days. The man's name was JR Hartley. This advertising signalled the starting point for one of the UK's longest running and most famous advertising

campaigns. Since 1983, a whole plethora of commercials have been developed around this simple, yet powerful idea - the boy needing a French polisher to mend his parent's coffee table after a riotous party, the gardener who was bought a motorised lawn mower by his employers, the ex-England football managers buying Terry Venables a cake to wish him good luck in his new job. All have helped catapult YELLOW PAGES into the hearts of the nation.

A good indicator of the fame and popularity of the campaign is the number of comedy spin-offs it has spawned. There is a long list of comedians who have produced spoofs of YELLOW PAGES commercials. Jasper Carrot, Hale & Pace, Fry & Laurie, Spitting Image are just some of the artists who have helped shape popular perceptions of YELLOW PAGES with the hilarious send-ups they have written for their TV programmes.

The results speak for themselves. Since 1983, YELLOW PAGES usage has increased by two-thirds. But the health and success of the YELLOW PAGES brand is not only reflected in usage growth. In recent tracking research, over 40% of those interviewed considered YELLOW PAGES to be quite a good friend - an incredible achievement for a simple telephone directory which just over a decade ago meant very little to consumers.

BRAND VALUES
As the UK's leading directory, YELLOW PAGES meets information and contact-finding needs of people by bridging the gap between buyers and suppliers. The brand plays a crucial role in people's lives - both at home and in the workplace. It is a lifeline to a number of businesses, which can advertise their wares and services to the huge proportion of the

public which use YELLOW PAGES on a regular basis.

Thinking ahead to a digital age, YELLOW PAGES has also positioned itself at the cutting edge of new technology, to take advantage of the new media for dissemination of information.

® Registered trademark of British Telecommunications plc in the U.K.

Things you didn't know about YELLOW PAGES

○ On average, 57 people use YELLOW PAGES every second of every day in the UK.

○ "Fly Fishing" by JR Hartley was not written until 1991 - eight years after the commercial was first aired. Even then it became a Christmas best-seller. "Golf" by JR Hartley has recently been launched to coincide with the follow-up JR Hartley commercial where he uses YELLOW PAGES to find a golf-instructor.

○ YELLOW PAGES is most heavily used during the Christmas period.

○ YELLOW PAGES is most often used to help people find information about the automotive, restaurant and construction sectors.

○ By laying a year's worth of YELLOW PAGES directories end to end, a yellow path could be built stretching from London to Madras.

THE POWER OF SUPERBRANDS
SUMMARY OF RESEARCH FINDINGS CONDUCTED BY INFRATEST BURKE

There has been much debate in recent times about the value of strong branding. The growth of own label and the development of cut price tertiary brands raises the question as to whether the enormous investment put behind power brands really pays off.

Perhaps the ultimate arbiter of such an issue is the consumer. Superbrands commissioned research company Infratest Burke to explore consumer opinion about the relevance of strong branding.

Infratest Burke interviewed a representative sample of 864 adults aged 18+, 80% women and 20% men, in May 1995. Both face-to-face and telephone interviews were conducted. The sample was segmented into 3 groups to consider impact on purchasing, brand personality and brand values.

THE POWER OF BRANDED VS OWN LABEL: SOME CONCLUSIONS

❍ An examination of typical supermarket shopping emphasises the value of powerful branding.

❍ Across a range of six commonly purchased categories, more than three quarters of consumers claim they would be more likely to purchase branded products than own label.

❍ Branded goods benefit strongly from their equity/reputation and perceptions of superior quality. This is evident across all six categories, suggesting that strong branding is a universal benefit for consumer goods.

❍ Consumers will clearly pay a significant premium for branded products. Shoppers claim they will pay a 32% premium, on average, for typical branded goods. Significant cuts in the price of own label are needed to motivate a switch away from brands, yet around 40% claim they wouldn't switch whatever the price.

❍ The most powerful brands have strong awareness to penetration conversion. They are more efficient in converting knowledge of the brand into frequent purchasing. Superbrands such as Coca-Cola, Persil and Perrier outperform their branded competitiors.

LIKELIHOOD TO BUY BRANDED OR OWN LABEL

Base: Total Sample	Average %	Laundry Detergents (120) %	Cola Drinks (101) %	Mineral Water (80) %	Bottled Table Sauces (114) %	Ice Cream (115) %	Margarines (115) %
Much more likely to buy branded	55	67	65	43	57	38	58
A little more likely to buy branded	22	13	24	38	20	23	15
(total more likely to buy branded)	77	80	89	81	77	61	73
A little more likely to buy own label	11	6	6	9	17	14	15
Much more likely to buy own label	12	14	5	9	6	24	12
(total more likely to buy own label)	23	20	11	18	23	38	27

REASONS WHY MORE LIKELY TO BUY BRANDED PRODUCTS

Base: Those who would buy branded	Average %	Laundry Detergents (96) %	Cola Drinks (89) %	Mineral Water (63) %	Bottled Table Sauces (88) %	Ice Cream (70) %	Margarines (84) %
Know the brand/trust it/ always bought it	43	50	27	49	45	47	42
Better product/ Good quality	42	41	44	35	33	47	52
Value for money	5	9	5	6	4	2	3
Alternatives are not good	3	3	5	1	7	-	4
Like the advertising	1	2	2	2	-	-	-
Better Packaging	1	-	-	1	-	2	-
My family/children ask for it	2	-	5	-	5	3	-
Other	23	11	38	20	23	24	24
Don't know/ not stated	3	2	-	8	3	2	2

REASONS WHY MORE LIKELY TO BUY OWN LABEL PRODUCTS

Base: Those who would buy own label	Average %	Laundry Detergents (24) %	Cola Drinks (12) %	Mineral Water (16) %	Bottled Table Sauces (26) %	Ice Cream (44) %	Margarines (31) %
Less expensive	72	70	77	68	91	65	59
Same product inside/ just as good	18	19	13	21	31	16	8
Good quality	6	14	3	13	-	5	2
Like Sainsbury's/Tesco/ Asda etc. products	6	6	10	2	1	12	2
Other	39	28	-	35	-	21	34
Don't know/not stated	1	2	-	-	-	2	2

SUMMARY CHART: BRANDED PRICE PREMIUM

	Laundry Detergents	Cola Drinks	Mineral Water	Bottled Table Sauces	Ice Cream	Margarines
Average price would pay (£)						
Branded	2.60	0.79	0.76	0.91	1.88	0.88
Own label	2.32	0.43	0.74	0.57	1.34	0.93
% Price premium	12	84	3	60	40	-5

HOW MUCH OWN LABEL WOULD HAVE TO REDUCE ITS PRICE BEFORE SWITCH FROM BRANDED

	Laundry Detergents	Cola Drinks	Mineral Water	Bottled Table Sauces	Ice Cream	Margarines
Base: Those buying branded	(100) %	(87) %	(59) %	(89) %	(71) %	(85) %
Less than 10p	3	6	-	-	-	1
10-19p	2	10	19	3	100	6
20-29p	7	16	6	10	7	10
30-39p	4	6	7	4	5	4
40-49p	-	3	7	7	1	5
50-59p	17	5	5	5	11	7
Over 60p	14	-	-	9	7	-
Would not switch to own label	39	42	35	43	30	39
Don't know/not stated	12	13	22	19	30	29
Average price would have to reduce by (£)	0.56	0.22	0.24	0.40	0.51	0.29

Significant reductions in price could persuade respondents to switch to shop's own label. However, an average 35-40% of brand buyers would never consider switching to shop's own label, even if they were offered it for nothing.

SUPERBRAND VALUES
SUMMARY CHART

	The Government	The Royal Family	British Airways	St. Michael	American Express
Base: Total Sample	(144) %	(136) %	(280) %	(280) %	(280) %
Reliable	3.8	6.4	7.5	8.5	7.3
Trustworthy	3.8	6.8	7.2	8.4	7.5
Caring	3.3	6.9	7.2	7.9	6.4
Exciting	2.8	4.8	6.4	6.4	5.4
Modern and up-to-date	6.6	5.3	7.8	7.7	7.5
Irritating	4.3	6.4	4.2	3.7	4.7
Intelligent	5.5	6.7	7.4	7.8	7.4

(Mean scores, where 10 is the highest)

SUPERBRAND VALUES: SOME CONCLUSIONS

○ Clearly, consumers rate their favourite brands much better than the Government. If St. Michael were to run for office, he would surely beat the current Prime Minister.

○ The Royal Family has a much better image than the Government, particularly on the important values of 'caring' and 'trustworthy'. However, despite the best efforts of the younger royals, they are still not perceived as 'modern and up-to-date' or 'exciting'. Are they a true Superbrand?

○ The Superbrands are very successful in projecting their core brand values.